For its third edition this book has been expanded, brought fully up to date, and revised throughout by the author.

Communication in Business is intended for young men and women preparing themselves for entry to the ranks of junior management in commerce and industry; for trainee technicians; for newly appointed local government officers and civil servants. The emphasis is on that aspect of communication most relevant to such readers – effective use of language for conveying factual information; but Part IV of this revision is devoted to non-verbal communication. Illustrative material and examples are drawn from engineering and the construction industry as well as from marketing, public administration, and general office work.

Part I considers basic principles, with special reference to verbal communication, Part II written applications of these principles, Part III oral applications. Part V consists of thirteen extracts in varying registers (with questions) designed both to exercise the skills required in accurately receiving written communication and to encourage (by stimulating discussion) improved oral communication.

Peter Little

*Head of the Department of Office Studies
and General Education,
The College, Swindon*

Communication
in Business

Third Edition

Longman

Longman Group Limited
London
*Associated companies, branches and
representatives throughout the world*

© Peter Little 1965
New Edition © Longman Group Ltd.,
1970, 1977

First published 1965
Second edition 1970
Fifth impression 1975
Third edition 1977

ISBN 0 582 42229 9 cased
ISBN 0 582 42230 2 paper

Set in 9/11 point 'Monophoto' Plantin
and printed in Great Britain by
Richard Clay (The Chaucer Press) Ltd.,
Bungay, Suffolk

Contents

Preface

Communication in Business is intended for young men and girls training to enter junior managerial or technician employment in industry or commerce and for the young local government officer or civil servant. Non-verbal communication is included but the emphasis is on that aspect of communication most relevant to such readers: effective use of language for conveying factual information.

My original object in preparing a third edition was no more than to endeavour to keep the material as up to date as current rapid changes in the business and economic world permitted; but in carrying out this task I began to make an increasing number of other modifications. As a result this edition has ended up considerably different from its two predecessors. Several sections have been rewritten to allow for changes in usage or fashion, or to reflect shifts in my own viewpoint. Some exercises which seemed to be drooping a little have been rooted out and fresh ones substituted. Much additional material has been introduced, including a chapter on non-verbal communication, considerable expansion of the chapters on oral communication, and an appendix on note-making.

That business efficiency depends on good communication is now generally accepted; but more than efficiency is involved. In any firm or organisation the sense of belonging, of unity with a team, also depends on communication; and this is something affecting the happiness of everybody working there. The aspects of communication that affect happiness concern management attitudes – willingness to share knowledge possessed; awareness that subordinates need to know more about the job than just how to do it; recognition that communication is two-way and that it is part of the function of management to listen for and respond to suggestions, doubts, criticisms, coming from lower in the chain of command. These are important matters falling outside the scope of this book; but certainly every aspect of communication demands competence in employing the instruments of communication.

The English language is the principal instrument of communication for the English businessman (or woman), technician, civil servant, local government officer. My aim has been that all who use this book will afterwards be able to speak, write, and read English with sufficient accuracy and ease to ensure that they are reasonably effective communicators (at least in everything to do with their work) while being aware also of the potentialities of non-verbal communication.

Part I of *Communication in Business* considers the basic principles of good communication by means of language. Part II deals with written applications of these principles in commerce, engineering, construction, and government. Part III covers oral applications in similar fields. Part IV introduces non-verbal communication. Part V consists of thirteen extracts (and questions) designed both to exercise the skills required in accurately receiving written communication and to encourage (by stimulating discussion) improved oral communication.

I make two assumptions about those using this book:

1 That they are young adults, either already employed in office or works and seeking qualifications that will lead to promotion and positions where they will be in charge of others, or undertaking a full-time course of instruction at a technical college with a view to ultimate appointment to a post of technician level in industry or commerce.

2 That they have already a reasonable command of the English language (at, as a minimum, approximately the standard of Grade C in GCE 'O' level).

Although my primary intention in preparing this book has been that it should be used in conjunction with an English or Communication course at a college of further education, I have not overlooked the possibility that it may also be used by students working on their own, or even by those already in managerial positions who wish to improve their command of language for communication purposes. All the exposition, and many of the exercises, will prove adaptable to private study.

I have aimed to make this a practical book that will be of daily help to the young man or girl using it whenever his or her work requires the use of language for communication purposes (and that is a very high proportion of the working day for most). At the same time I have not forgotten that the majority of readers will be looking to obtain a specific qualification, probably involving passing an examination in English or Communication. Both in the original planning and in this revision I have accordingly borne in mind existing or proposed relevant syllabuses, and it has been my design that *Communication in Business* should provide a working text and/or examination preparation for all courses involving communication that the target readership is likely to be concerned with.

These could include: BEC courses (above General Certificate level) and (as long as these continue) Ordinary National Certificate and Ordinary National Diploma in Business Studies or Public Administration; Stage III English examinations of the Royal Society of Arts and the regional examination boards; the London Chamber of Commerce Private Secretary's Certificate/Diploma; 'Communication in the Office' in the Royal Society of Arts examinations for the Clerical and Secretarial Diplomas; and General and Communication Studies units in TEC programmes.

The names and addresses of individuals, firms, and organisations used in examples and exercises in this book are fictitious. Any resemblance to the name or address of an existing individual, firm, or organisation is coincidental. Fictitious addresses have been arbitrarily allocated postcodes which may in fact be the postcodes of existing areas of even specific addresses but which for the purpose of this book refer only to the fictitious addresses.

Peter Little

Acknowledgements

We are grateful to the following for permission to reproduce copyright material:
Edward Arnold (Publishers) Ltd. for material from *The Science of Wealth* by C. P.
Carter; *The Association of Teachers in Technical Institutions* for an extract from an
Association Document; Chatto and Windus Ltd. for material from *The Long
Revolution* by Raymond Williams; The author and The Guardian for an article by
Judith Cook published in *The Guardian* 28th October 1963; The Daily Telegraph
for part of an article by Norman Selwyn published in *The Daily Telegraph* 25
October 1968 and an extract from an article by Patrick Davies and a graph
published 26 February 1969; Encounter for an extract from a questionnaire;
Heinemann Educational Books Ltd. for material from *Exploration in Management*
by Wilfred Brown; European Journal of Marketing for an extract from an article by
G. W. Smith from *European Journal of Marketing 1975*, No. 9.2; The Controller of
H.M.S.O. for material from *Monthly Digest of Statistics* and '*15–18*' *Report of the
Central Advisory Council of Education (England)*; Hodder and Stoughton Ltd.
for material from *The Story of My Life* by Helen Keller; The Institution of
Electrical Engineers for Regulations for the Electrical Equipment of Buildings
(c) The Institution of Electrical Engineers 1976; The Institution of Electrical
and Electronics Technicians Engineers for an extract from an article 'Electronic
Techniques in a Ship Model Experiment Tank' by O. Anyaegbu from
Electrotechnology January 1976; *The Journal of the Institute of the Motor Industry*
for an extract from an article by Donald Lockyer form Vol. 5, No. 1, January 1969;
Journal of the Royal Society of Arts for a statistical table, originally derived from
the Bureau Internation d'Education, Geneva; The author and the Society of
Industrial Artists and Designers for an article by L. J. Lickorish published in the
Journal of the Society of Industrial Artists and Designers; The Editor of *The
Manager* for an article published in *The Manager*; John Murray (Publishers) Ltd.
and Houghton Mifflin Company for material from *Inlaws and Outlaws* by C.
Northcote Parkinson; New Science Publications for an extract from an article by
David White from *New Society* 29th January, 1976 and an extract from an article
by John Nicolson from *New Society* 20th May, 1976. Both articles first appeared in
New Society London, the weekly review of the Social Sciences; The author and
Granada TV for material from *Man to Man* by Eric Nixon; The Observer Ltd. for
an extract from an article by Professor Colin Buchanan, published in *The Observer*;
Sir Isaac Pitman & Sons Ltd. for material from *Some Reflections on Genius* by Lord
Russell Brain; Routledge & Kegan Paul Ltd. and McGraw-Hill Book Co. Inc. for
an extract from *Understanding Media* by Marshall McLuhan. Copyright © by
Marshall McLuhan; Unilever Ltd. for figures and diagrams from an advertise-

ment of 22nd April, 1976 covering Unilever's combined figures.
And the following examining bodies for extracts from examination papers:
The Corporation of Secretaries, the London Chamber of Commerce, the Royal
Society of Arts, the Local Government Training Board.
We are also grateful to Oxford University Press for permission to reproduce on the
cover an extract from the *Advanced Learners Dictionary of Current English*.
The author wishes to put on record his gratitude to Mrs. Norma Dobie for being
able to read his writing and to his wife for checking proofs.

Part I

Chapter 1

Introduction

1 THE MEANING OF 'COMMUNICATION'

Communication has become an 'in' word, a vogue word, in recent years and is frequently bandied about with remarkable vagueness of reference. *It's all a matter of communication!* people say wisely – and seem to mean little more than *It's all done by mirrors!*

Communication is a chameleon of a word changing the colour of its meaning with a change of speaker (or listener) more than most. The military historian thinks of an army's lines of communication; the sociologist of newspapers and broadcasting. The civil engineer thinks of roads and railways, the electronic engineer of telephones and teleprinters. For some elderly businessmen it probably still calls to mind such old-world contexts as *Your communication of the 15th inst. to hand and contents duly noted*, where it was Edwardian commercial jargon for a letter.

It is possible to detect a common element in these varied meanings – the idea of connection between people, originally connection for the purpose of passing a message. Subsequently the word's meaning widened to refer to the act of message-passing; to the channel along which the message passed; or to the message itself.

The last quarter century has witnessed a striking revival of the first of these three meanings – a very old meaning, curiously enough – and most young people today if asked what communication meant would probably reply something like: 'It's how we share information, pass on what we know or what we want to know.'

It is this meaning which is relevant to this book.

Before we can attempt a closer definition of this meaning of communication we must allow for the fact that to pass on messages to others we have to use symbols of some kind (words, gestures, drawings etc) that stand for the ideas we are trying to convey. These symbols have to be ones that other people recognise and accept. It is no use using symbols that are private to ourselves and therefore incomprehensible to others.

3

We must also allow for the possibility that communication can take place not only between individuals but also between firms, institutions, shops, central or local government departments etc; or between such organisations and individuals.

Bearing all these points in mind we arrive at the following working definition of the meaning of *communication* as used in this book. Communication is the process by which information is passed between individuals and/or organisations by means of previously agreed symbols.

It should be noted, in passing, that the plural form *communications* is frequently but erroneously used as a substitute for *communication* in the sense defined in the preceding paragraph. It is best to confine *communications* to the area of meaning 'system of channels which permits communication to take place in an institution or geographical area'. *Communications* refers to how the message gets there. It may be a matter of roads, railways, civil air routes; of posts and telegraphs; of internal telephones and messenger service. If an executive receives a memo that he cannot understand a *communication breakdown* has occurred; if he does not receive the memo at all because the messenger has delivered it to the wrong in-tray a *communications breakdown* has occurred.

The ability to communicate with others is an essential attribute of human life and we are all of us grappling with communication tasks most of the time we are awake. Only when we are alone and also not reading or writing (or listening to radio or watching television) do we, briefly, stop receiving messages from the world of people outside ourselves, stop trying to send out messages to the fellow human beings around us. Communication plays, then, a vital part in our personal daily lives; but it is communication at work that is the concern of this book.

In business two key questions that have to be continually asked and answered are: 'What should we communicate?' and 'To whom should we communicate it?' This book offers no answers to these questions. There is, however, a third question, of equal importance: 'How do we communicate it most effectively?' It is to this question that *Communication in Business* aims to supply answers.

The *How?* of communication is a matter of selecting the right system of symbols to convey the information and employing those symbols with maximum efficiency. Many systems are available apart from the one we immediately think of, verbal language (for example mathematics, mime, and a whole range of pictorial devices – graphs, diagrams, photographs, films etc). Nevertheless it is obvious that for most people words, in the form of the mother tongue, constitute by far the most frequently employed system. It is therefore communication by means of language (the English language since it is written for those who will be doing business in English) that this book concentrates on. (An introduction to the potentialities of non-verbal communication is, however, provided by Chapter 15.)

To quote the earliest use of *communication* in this sense that the compilers of the *Oxford English Dictionary* discovered (by Locke in 1690), our principle intention is 'to make words serviceable to the end of good Communication'.

II COMMUNICATION PATTERNS IN FIRMS

Every firm, or similar organisation, depends for its daily functioning on an intricate communication network which has grown up during the years and has proved itself indispensable. The bigger the firm, the more elaborate the system must be, and the greater the likelihood of expensive and time-wasting mistakes caused through misunderstandings. The precise form of the network will vary from firm to firm, but something of its complexity in a fairly large firm can be appreciated from the following diagrams; and it should be remembered that every practical network will be very much more complicated than it appears in a simplified diagram.

A *Internal communication, vertical*

The instructions of management moving downwards through a firm and reports passing upwards to management will both follow the authority line of the firm. Figure 1 shows in broadest outline, a structure applicable to most firms and similar organisations. Only the largest require the intermediate levels of middle management and first line supervision.

It is important to realise that the titles given to employees do not necessarily reveal their level on the line of authority. Some firms may have an Office Manager who is considered equal to other departmental managers but other firms will consider this rank equivalent only to a supervisor's. The Sales Manager may be either equal in level with, or superior to, the Office Manager in the same firm. The Works Manager may be equal to either, or superior to both in the type of firm where this is the title of the principal executive (who is most commonly called Managing Director).

Each department will have an authority and communication chain of its own; as many as a dozen such chains may come together at the departmental manager's level. An Office Manager with departmental manager ranking may have beneath him a chain like that shown in Figure 2.

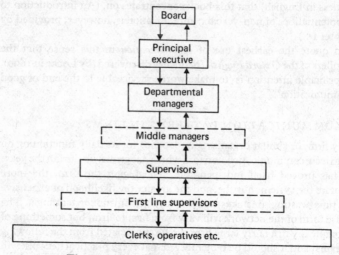

Figure 1 Internal communication, vertical

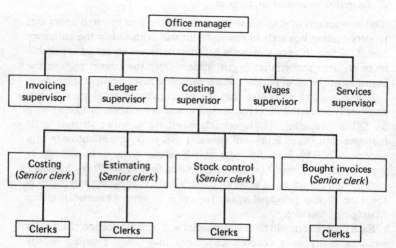

Figure 2 Vertical communication within a department

This is, of course, a simplified diagram – only the costing section's network is shown in any detail – but considered with Figure 1 it provides a basic impression of the vertical communication channels that follow the line of authority.

Running parallel with these channels is another communication line provided by the existence within the firm of a staff association or branches of professional associations and trade unions. The representatives from these usually constitute the only intermediate stage between management and rank-and-file on this line. Part of a firm's total communication will pass up and down this line also. Deciding what communication material is more appropriate to the authority line, what to that of the staff representatives, and what should preferably be passed down both lines, is a major problem for management; but similar decisions have also to be made by a clerk or operative wishing to pass upwards through his firm a comment, a suggestion, a complaint.

B *Internal communication, horizontal*

There must also be communication across the organisation, otherwise each section is operating in isolation; and all departments must have close communication links with the General Office. This will take the form of conversation, both direct and by telephone, internal memos, and reports. Horizontal communication of this kind must be allowed for in considering communication patterns in business. Figure 3 represents the horizontal communication of a manufacturing company that has a general

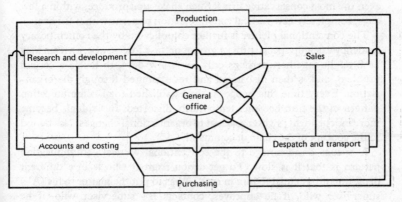

Figure 3 Internal communication, horizontal

administrative office providing centralised services under an office manager with full departmental status.

There is not nearly enough horizontal communication going on in most organisations. In some firms it seems to take place at departmental head level only (and often pretty reluctantly even there; people do like to play a lone hand). In all firms there is a steady fall-off in horizontal communication as you descend the communication ladder. As a result rank-and-file members of one department have little idea of the kind of work being carried out by their opposite numbers in other departments and very little realisation of how what they do in their own department affects what other workers do in their departments.

C *Internal communication, complex*

Figure 1 represents the typical communication pattern of firms organised on conventional hierarchical principles where fixed layers of authority have been established through which all instructions, information, suggestions, complaints etc are expected to move.

Modern developments, however, are rapidly undermining the old power structure of the chain of command. Lively forward-looking firms, quick to react to shifts in the market or the effects of changes in government policy, cultivate a flexible attitude to company organisation, and departments, jobs, people's titles in their jobs, their responsibilities, may be, almost overnight, completely altered. Takeovers and mergers bring sudden reorganisation to the previously settled power structure of even the most conservative firms. Such shake-ups produce, within a few days, completely new vertical communication patterns within the firm.

The conventional picture is further complicated by the contemporary tendency to set up special project groups or 'task forces' where a team may be brought together, perhaps only for a few days, to tackle a certain problem, and is then disbanded and redistributed through the organisation. Every time this happens, the established total communication pattern of the firm becomes temporarily distorted. Individuals become more independent; swifter to adapt to organisational changes; less bound to the concept of the chain of command.

A serious disadvantage to the conventional vertical communication pattern is that it is slow. To get action from B who is in a different department but equal to him in rank, A has to put the matter to his (A's) supervisor who, if he approves, contacts B's supervisor who, if he approves, tells B to do it (see Figure 4a). Of course the strength of the system is that by bringing in the (presumably) superior knowledge and experience of the two supervisors the chance of a bad decision is lessened. If, however, the firm is one that puts a premium on speedy action it may well encourage a short circuit from A to B.

Short circuits of this kind produce the special problem that the supervisors concerned may gradually become less and less aware of what is going on in the sections they are responsible for. This cannot be tolerated. Where horizontal contacts at a fairly low level are encouraged a system has to be established, and enforced, by which the relevant supervisors are notified of what has taken place as soon as possible afterwards. Figure 4b represents this situation diagrammatically, the dotted lines indicating 'information only' communication subsequent to the action-producing communication.

Other factors that make for greater complexity of internal communication pattern than the preceding two sections indicate are:

(a) increased worker participation in managerial decisions;

(b) the tendency among firms that take communication problems seriously to plan for parallel communication down the authority line and through the trade union representatives, timed (in theory at least) to arrive at the rank-and-file worker at the same moment from both channels;

(c) the influx into firms of technical specialists whose expertise (probably understood by very few of the firm's executives) ensures them a position on the communication tree higher than their rank in the chain of command would indicate.

The presence of technical specialists can also have an effect on the horizontal communication pattern. Fruitful communication between men in different departments who have similar specialist knowledge but

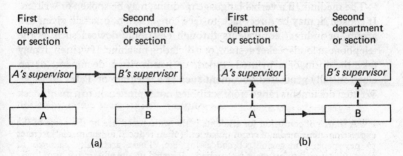

Figure 4 Internal communication, complex

are unequal in rank is now common. Thus a variation in communication patterning is becoming established in some organisations – communication not just at one level, as in Figure 3, but between different levels across the organisation.

D *External communication*

Thus we may picture a firm as, at all times of the working day, pulsing with messages transmitted vertically, both up and down, and horizontally across the organisation. But this is only the internal situation; every firm will also be linked with the outside world: customers, suppliers, government departments, branches, subsidiaries etc. A diagram of this communication pattern would look rather like a child's drawing of the sun, with channels of communication radiating out from, and converging on, the firm like spokes of a wheel.

III THE ACT OF COMMUNICATION

These then are the principal patterns of a firm's communication channels. When a message is sent along the channel there will be somebody to send it and somebody to receive it. It is convenient to borrow from electronics the terms *Tx* (Transmitter) and *Rx* (Receiver) to represent as broadly as possible these two essential components of the act of communication. A *channel* exists when access to the Rx is provided for the Tx. When the channel is used, the message has to be transmitted by some *medium* (for example, words, facial expressions, figures, pictures, graphs). The medium is the system of 'previously agreed symbols' referred to on page 4 (sometimes called a *code*).[1]

The medium, if a verbal language medium, may be spoken or written. If spoken, it may be direct face-to-face conversation, or a talk given to a group, or indirect equivalents through electronic devices such as the telephone, a loudspeaker system, or a dictating machine. If written, it may take the form of a printed, typed, or handwritten document, or an electronically generated document such as a telegram or Telex message. Written documents range from scribbled notes pinned on to a man's desk

[1] A source of confusion for students is the widespread use by the press of the expression 'mass media of communication' (often reduced to 'the media') to refer to newspapers, magazines, broadcasting etc. These are really *channels* of communication; unfortunately somebody dreamed up the alliterative term 'mass media' and it stuck.

in his absence, through internal memos, letters, minutes, abstracts, reports, to printed publicity, user handbooks and technical manuals.

It is important to realise that transmission is not communication. For communication to take place the message has (1) to reach the Rx (2) to produce a response in the Rx. For *successful* communication the response of the Rx must be the one intended by the Tx.

To be fully effective, communication must be two-way. To borrow another term from electronics, *feedback* must be provided from Rx to Tx (i.e. there must be some way in which the response of the Rx can be perceived by the Tx and the latter's message modified to suit this response). It will be seen that one of the principal advantages of spoken communication over written is speed of feedback – the Rx can ask questions of the Tx to clarify the message further and can also often immediately make the response that the Tx requires, when the Tx is asking for information, instead of passing it on.

In such a case the roles of Tx and Rx interchange as the conversation continues. Similarly the roles interchange when a message is passed down or up a vertical internal communication channel. The man who receives a message from above is an Rx then, but becomes a Tx as soon as he passes the information on to his subordinate.

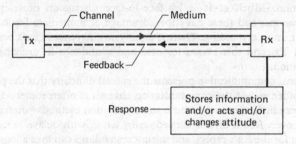

Figure 5 The fundamentals of communication

IV COMMUNICATION DIFFICULTIES IN FIRMS

Undoubtedly the most important distortions and misunderstandings occur in vertical communication, especially where messages shift between the oral and the written. Policy changes arising from a decision of the Board may well be transmitted to his departmental managers by the Managing Director orally. They in turn will probably pass down to their supervisors relevant parts of this information in the form of written instructions. These in turn will be passed on orally to the men actually doing the job. There is very likely to be a distortion of the message at each of these stages unless all concerned are proficient communicators. Middle management and/or first line supervision levels mean additional stages at which distortion may occur.

The man halfway up the ladder of management spends the best part of his working day alternating between Rx and Tx roles, receiving messages from both above and below, and frequently changing these from oral to written and vice versa. He has to be a very good communicator indeed. This man is quite likely in the future to be you.

As has already been indicated, the outstanding criticism that can be directed at the horizontal communication of most firms and organisations is simply that there is not enough of it. Departments tend to work in watertight compartments and do not make sufficient effort to let each other know what they are doing. Even at departmental management level there is often inadequate discussion of common problems and interchange of ideas; at lower levels very little horizontal communication exists at all. Where horizontal communication does take place it is much less liable to distortion and misunderstanding than is vertical communication. Much of it is by face-to-face discussion or telephone conversations, and these have the advantage of immediate feedback if there is misunderstanding. There is usually no difference in rank between Rx and Tx, and this makes for ease and confidence in exchanges of information.

External communication presents the special difficulty that the person at the other end of the communication channel is often somebody you know very little about and whose communication methods you have no control over. Much of it is carried on by letter, with delayed feedback (waiting for the Rx's reply), and misunderstandings can take a long time to clear up. A considerable demand is therefore made on communication skills in external communication; it is more difficult than the average businessman often realises to express yourself clearly and unambiguously to a distant correspondent while at the same time making him feel that you are friendly and cooperative in your attitude (as you must do when your letter is the link between your firm and a customer or supplier, for example). Being at the receiving end of external communication is not easy either; much of the material you will have to read is difficult to understand either by virtue of the complexity of its subject matter or – more often – because of the communication weaknesses of your

'Correctness' has not been mentioned. For communication purposes, formal correctness of grammar is of subordinate importance. Some constructions which have been considered incorrect in the past do not confuse meaning and are so widely established by usage that it is doubtful if they can any longer be classed as incorrect. Nevertheless, many errors of syntax[1] are direct causes of vague or ambiguous meanings. Even where meaning is not affected, faults of this kind may distract, or even antagonise, the Rx who is aware that they are faults. Sound syntax is therefore an important aim of the conscientious communicator, and he will also wish to avoid handling his words in such a way that he offends against educated usage (see Chapter 4).

'Good style' has also not been mentioned. There are few occasions in business where conscious attention to style, in the literary sense, serves any communication purpose. Attention is more advantageously directed to ensuring that the 'register' selected is the right one (i.e. that the kind of language employed is appropriate to the communication situation) and that the tone of what is to be written (or said) is going to encourage, not discourage, the sort of response by the Rx that the Tx is seeking (see Chapter 5).

Nevertheless, the writer who at all times has as his target clarity of expression in the minimum of words will inevitably over the years develop a crisp and economical style, well suited to its purpose, and therefore 'good'.

---

[1] *Syntax*: that part of grammar that deals with the construction of sentences and the arrangement of words within the sentence.

Chapter 2

First Thinking

I FIRST STEPS IN COMMUNICATION

The first step towards clear communication is to have the material to be communicated clear in your own mind; until you are sure that you know what you want to say there is no point in starting to say it. This would seem obvious enough, yet failure to act upon this truism is probably the commonest cause of communication breakdown.

The second step is to find a method of organising your material that will enable you to present it to your Rx in a coherent and logical form, according to a predetermined plan.

In spoken communication we are often called upon to speak in circumstances that do not permit more than the most hasty examination and organisation of our ideas on the subject, but when we write we always have time for *preparation* and *planning*, and this is an advantage that should not be wasted. In the pages that follow, preparation and planning are considered from the point of view of the writing Tx. Similar principles apply, wherever circumstances permit, to the speaking Tx.

II PREPARATION

Preparation may involve the gathering of material from other documents, from personal interviews and telephone conversations, from our own existing knowledge of the subject, and from tests and experiments that we devise, together with the evaluation and interpretation of this material; or it may be merely a matter of sitting for a moment trying to sharpen the focus of what is in one's mind. This sharpening stage must never be omitted because if we start with a woolly idea we shall communicate only a woolly idea. An outstanding aid to clear thinking about your material is awareness of *purpose*. In a work context every document will have a purpose; this may be (1) to supply or request information, (2) to produce action or reaction, or (3) to persuade; or it may be a combination of these.

It is as well to state the purpose to yourself: 'I am writing this letter so that this customer will not develop a lasting grudge against the firm', or 'I am preparing this report so that Mr Thompson can explain exactly what my section has been working on when he attends the Sales Conference next week.' If purpose is brought into the open in this specific way there is much less chance of your producing in the first situation a pompous piece of face-saving that disgusts the customer, or in the second an inflated piece of empire-building that infuriates Thompson by its irrelevancies and unnecessary length.

At the preparation stage you should also try to *know your Rx*. The more you can bring to life the man who is going to read what you write, the better you will communicate. Often you will, of course, already know him quite well, as he is a member of your organisation, or you have had previous dealings with him. Much more frequently you will have to create your knowledge of him by the use of imagination, working upon such clues as a letter he has sent, or how he sounded over the telephone, or your previous experience of the kind of man to whom you have to send this particular type of document. Ideally you will need to know, or estimate, these things about the Rx:

1 His/her sex
2 His/her rank in his/her organisation compared with yours (if relevant)
3 His/her educational standard
4 His/her intelligence level
5 His/her knowledge of the subject you are writing about
6 How your document will affect him/her.

The degree of simplification which you apply to your subject matter, the kind of vocabulary you will employ, even your length of sentence – all will be controlled by the picture you form at this stage.

By combining purpose with your picture of the Rx, you are now in a position to apply to your material the *test for relevance*. This consists in asking, for each piece of your material: 'Is this essential to the document, bearing in mind the document's purpose and the kind of man who is going to read it?' Only where the answer is a confident 'Yes' should the material be included. This is a severe test, but it is easy to lose all sense of what is relevant if you do not apply it strictly. Testing for relevance is not easy and probably you will make errors of judgment from time to time. It is better that these should take the form of omitting subject matter that later turns out to have been relevant after all than that you should give the benefit of the doubt to every borderline piece of material.

The sense of relevance can be developed by practice. You will find précis-writing a valuable aid and you should practise further by checking the relevance of everything you write, and – as often as you can remember to – what you read as well. The smaller news items in newspapers frequently include irrelevant facts; picking these out can be good sport and excellent training.

III PLANNING

Planning is necessary with every piece of communication of any length or complexity, if it is to appear coherent and logical to the Rx. Planning consists of two stages:

1 devising a system of organisation for the material
2 deciding the most effective order of presentation.

The plan is not always written down, but all successful communication of material of any complexity has careful planning behind it. The experienced communicator can often carry the plan in his head, but you are advised to get down on paper at least your principal section divisions and proposed order of presentation.

A *The principle of unity*

Organisation of written communication depends on breaking up the total material into logical divisions so that the material can be supplied to the reader by instalments. These divisions may be indicated by chapters in a book, or section headings in a report, or, in shorter work, by change of paragraph. Clearly in longer work there will be subdivisions as well as the principal divisions.

The reader thus has breathing space between sections, in which to assimilate what he has received and prepare for the next stage. But he will gain full advantage from the breathing space only if he can feel that he has at that point reached the end of something which is complete in itself. Thus every division of a piece of writing, whether as long as a chapter or as short as a paragraph, should possess *unity*. In fact the principle of unity must be observed throughout the document, because on the one hand the entire piece of writing must be felt by the reader as a unity, as one thing not a mixture, and on the other, each sentence must have unity.

The principle of unity is closely connected with testing for relevance, and practice in the latter will make you unlikely to offend against the former. It is not sufficient for two matters to be closely connected for unity to be achieved; they must also be of the same kind. In the sentence frequently used by schoolmasters to demonstrate breach of unity: *Cromwell was a great general and had warts on his nose*, both statements are about Cromwell but they are so dissimilar in kind that we instinctively feel they are ridiculous together.

Breaches of unity in whole sections of a document are not so obvious as those in single sentences. We guard against them most successfully by dividing our work up according to a system, and letting the reader see what our system is. We reveal our system by:

1 an introduction explaining the method to be used; or
2 headings to the sections; or
3 topic sentences to the paragraphs; or
4 a combination of these methods.

The most useful basis for such a system of division, for factual material of the kind that is most frequently handled in business communication, is derived from either *classification* or *analysis*, or a combination of these.

B *Classification and analysis*

When we classify material we organise it into groups according to a governing principle, or criterion. Thus a book on wild flowers may classify the flowers by colour and have one section on yellow flowers, another on white flowers, and so on. Or the flowers may be classified as perennials, annuals, biennials, etc, the criterion here being the plant's life-cycle. Or they may be classified according to their method of reproduction. More scientifically, they could be classified according to their botanical families – compositae, rosaceae, leguminosae, umbelliferae, cruciferae, etc.

Again, various criteria could be applied in classifying the students of a technical college – sex, department, nationality, etc – but only one criterion can be applied at one time. A valid classification of these students could be based on whether they are full-time or part-time students in which case a subdivision of the latter group between day and evening would probably also be made. Written out in the form most useful when planning a document this would appear as:

College students
   1 Full-time
   2 Part-time : (a) day; (b) evening.

An alternative organisation of the same material, equally sound, would be:

College students
   1 Full-time
   2 Part-time day
   3 Part-time evening.

When material is divided into classes all the material should be used up. Similarly when a class is subdivided, the subsection should use up all the material in the class.

If A is divided into B, C, D and E, then $B + C + D + E$ must equal A. Thus the arrangement:

College students
   1 Full-time
   2 Evening

is unsound because it overlooks part-time day students and the parts do not add up to the whole.

The opposite fault occurs in the arrangement:

College students
   1 Full-time
   2 Part-time
   3 Overseas

where the introduction of a second criterion of classification (i.e. whether British or overseas in origin) results in the parts adding up to more than the whole since overseas students will already have been included in the previous two categories.

The value of classification to the communicator is that it enables him to make logical divisions of his material by the application of criteria relevant to his purpose. The resultant groupings become chapters, sections, or paragraphs, according to the scale of the piece of communication. Subdivisions of the main groups are made, and further subdivisions as necessary, so that the same technique of organisation is applied to smaller and smaller units of the final work.

Although only one basis of classification can be employed at a time, there are occasions when it is desirable to classify material according to a succession of criteria. Thus at the beginning of Chapter 9 of this book reports are classified first by content, then as routine or special, then by length, and finally by form.

The method can be applied only to material which is multiple by nature (wild flowers, students, reports). Material which is single by nature (the smaller-flowered goat's-beard, J. J. Smith's academic ability, a report on the new copier) must be divided by analysis, i.e. splitting it up into those parts that together make up the whole.

Thus in the description of an appliance we divide it into component parts; in writing the account of a transaction we divide into stages; in explaining a process we break it down into steps. Again we must take care to check that the total of the parts is equal to the whole and that nothing has been left out inadvertently. Sometimes, for the sake of simplification or for lack of space, some minor parts of the material analysed are deliberately omitted but on such occasions the introductory wording should be modified to include such a phrase as: *The principal component parts are* ..., or *The most important stages of this transaction can be listed as* ...

Having decided on the principal divisions and subdivisions of the material for communication you should make a note of these in the form of headings and subheadings and then apply yourself to deciding the best *order of presentation* both for the main divisions and for the secondary material within those divisions.

C *Order of presentation*

Most business communication material starts with an introduction and ends with a conclusion, though these may be very brief. The main body between presents the greatest difficulty in deciding in what order to present the material now arranged into logical groups.

1 The INTRODUCTION establishes what the Rx is to hear about and provides necessary background information – in short, *what? who? where? when?* In more formal documents, such as reports, it also makes clear the principle upon which the body of the work is arranged. The preface to this book illustrates this use of an introduction.

2 The CONCLUSION sums up what has gone before or makes a final appeal to the reader. In short informal communication some friendly message is sometimes used to round off the note or memo.

A conclusion is not indispensable. The kind of report, for instance, that provides a summary of findings at the beginning needs no conclusion.

3 The MAIN BODY of the material frequently reveals itself wholly or partially as a succession of steps or stages of a kind that inevitably lead to each other: the reader must understand A before he can grasp B, and C

will make no sense unless he knows about B; therefore the order must be: A, B, C. A natural sequence of this kind must take precedence over any other.

However, only a proportion of communication material reveals a natural order of this kind, and it is not common for it to be applicable to every part of our material. In reporting on apprentice unrest in a factory it is natural to detail the extent of the unrest before listing the causes and the causes before the recommendations for their correction. But in what order are the causes to be presented?

Five main methods are used for deciding the order of presentation of material lacking a natural logical sequence:

- (a) Chronological order
- (b) Spatial order
- (c) Descending order of importance
- (d) Ascending order of importance
- (e) Ascending order of complexity

or a combination of these five may be employed.

(a) CHRONOLOGICAL ORDER refers to the order in which events took place or in which they were observed. Its simplicity commends it, but unfortunately only a limited amount of communication material in business has a clear time sequence; even then it is only where the happenings to be narrated or the observations to be recorded are of approximately equal importance also that this is the best order of arrangement. Where there is an element of repetition in the material (e.g. what is observed at 18.00 hours is the same as was previously observed at 16.00 and 14.00), it is an unsatisfactory method.

(b) SPATIAL ORDER refers to the organisation of material on such a basis as north to south, or outside to inside, or front to back, or left to right. Again, where all material is of approximately the same importance (as, for example, a trading report on a company whose area is divided into geographical sectors which have all had very similar results that year) it is a useful method. Repetition material tends to be annoying with this system too.

(c) DESCENDING ORDER OF IMPORTANCE is probably the most useful device, though it will often need to be combined with methods (a) or (b). This would be the method for deciding the order for the causes of apprentice unrest in the report mentioned above; the most important cause would be dealt with first, and the least important last.

(*d*) ASCENDING ORDER OF IMPORTANCE is principally a literary device to build up suspense and a sense of climax. It is valuable in planning essays, but is inappropriate for letters and reports, where the aim is certainly not to create suspense. It is also very important to use this method in presenting a succession of arguments. We expect in argument or oratory to be led up to climax. If our expectation is disappointed we experience anticlimax, and the communicator's efforts have been wasted.

(*e*) ASCENDING ORDER OF COMPLEXITY is a particularly suitable order for explication (i.e. communication where the Tx's principal purpose is to explain something with which the Rx is unfamiliar). It is a method frequently used in this book. It is commonsense to arrange to put the simplest aspect of the subject matter in front of the Rx before proceeding to the more complex. A variant on this method is to proceed from the familiar to the unfamiliar. By starting with what the Rx knows best, you start with what he will find simplest.

The order of presentation will be finally selected on a basis of the considerations enumerated above, but will also be influenced by the purpose of the piece of communication and the qualities of the Rx, especially his previous knowledge of the subject.

Your previous note of the principal divisions and subdivisions of your subject matter should now be written out again in the form of an *outline plan* in the order you have decided on, with indications to yourself of how you intend to start and finish. The following example illustrates how the principles discussed can be employed in the preparation of an office document.

IV AN EXAMPLE

Outline plan for a directive on office reorganisation

A Introduction
```
1  The need to improve organisation of office
2  Subject to be treated under three main
   heads - communications, filing, reprography
```

B Communications
```
1  Letters in
2  Letters out
3  Telephones
4  Messenger service
5  Public address system
```

C Filing
1 Effects of change to centralised filing
2 Redeployment of filing equipment
3 Improvement of classification methods
4 Agreed storage periods
5 Security

D Reprography

1 Ink stencil duplicating
2 Spirit duplicating
3 Dye-line copying
4 Dual-transfer photocopying
5 Offset-litho duplication
6 Electrostatic copying

E Conclusion
1 Appeal to all staff to cooperate in improving office efficiency
2 Stress the importance of the individual in making the reorganisation work

V EXERCISES

Exercise A

You are attempting to explain cricket to an American who has never seen the game played. What would be the best order for the following topics: the object of the batting side; how the result of the match is decided; the toss; how a batsman is out; the pitch; the object of the bowling side; the number of players; equipment required; how runs are scored?

Exercise B

By what criteria can the following be classified? Try to find as many different bases of classification as possible for each: cricketers; photographic films; books; typewriters; newspapers.

Exercise C

Analyse the following, and arrange the parts in logical order : a cricket bat ; a book (physical components); a newspaper (content); driving out of a garage; opening a current account.

Exercise D

The following points were noted when Site 12 on Ridge Trading Estate was inspected with a view to building a new factory there for Adpress Engineering of Bandham.

(a) Rearrange them in sections under section headings.
(b) Indicate the order in which you would put these sections in a report.
(c) Indicate the order in which you would put the points in each section.

As the points are numbered there is no need to write them out.

1 Working population (male), 30 km radius Ridge, 24 600
2 Site 12 well drained, gravel subsoil
3 Ridge Estate 30 km from port of Seamouth
4 Skilled operatives would have to be brought from Bandham
5 Electricity to site
6 A111 passes through Ridge. Bandham 140 km
7 Estate in development area, so government grant possible
8 Site 150 m from A111, cinder road connecting
9 Plentiful supply of unskilled female labour locally
10 Three local building firms of adequate size for factory building, so local tenders possible
11 Housing shortage in area
12 Map reference, Ridge Estate, O.S. 163 : SS 4943
13 Station, Ridge, goods only
14 B road – Ridge/Seamouth
15 Water mains and sewers to site
16 Rail – Ridge/Seamouth
17 Unemployment figure (male) for area 6 per cent, mostly unskilled or semi-skilled
18 Hostel necessary for accommodation of workers from Bandham
19 Site slopes 1 in 14, north to south
20 Railway siding to site, connecting with line, Ridge/Seamouth
21 Site 12 one of three sites still unoccupied on estate, and only one suitable in size for our purposes

22 Suitable site for hostel available 0·8 km north-east of Site 12
23 Ridge Estate 1·2 km south-east of Ridge on A111.

Exercise E

Here is a letter about central heating systems. You will find it difficult to
follow because the writer has no plan; he moves from topic to topic just as
the points come into his head. Read it through several times and then
prepare the outline plan that the author should have used.

Dear Harry,

    You asked me to let you have an outline of
whole-house heating systems currently available; so here goes.

    Gas-fired boilers are still popular,
especially with ducted warm-air systems,
although gas is expensive. Of course, you can
have conventional hot-water radiators from a
gas boiler as well, or a ducted warm-air
system from a solid-fuel boiler or oil-burning
boiler. These oil-fired boilers are popular as
they do not need stoking or raking and the fuel
is easily delivered. The same advantage
applies to the gas-fired boiler. A large
storage tank is required for the oil and this
can be difficult to find room for, or un-
sightly. At the same time it must be
remembered that considerable storage space is
necessary for solid fuels too, if you are not
to be left without fuel during that part of the
winter when demand is very heavy. This is the
advantage of electricity and gas - no storage
problem. However, both these supplies have
been subject to cuts in very severe weather,

and solid fuel has the further advantage of being comparatively cheap.

We have learned over the last few years that oil is a scarce fuel the supply of which can be affected by the international situation and subject to sudden big increases in price. Oil-fired boilers are also dearer than gas or solid-fuel boilers to buy. Total installation costs depend on whether hot-water radiators or warm-air ducting is selected.

Installation costs are avoided altogether by putting oil-filled radiators in every room of the house, but these cannot be centrally controlled. Electricity is an expensive fuel but you have the opportunity to switch the appliance off quickly when not required which is not possible with boilers. However, boilers should not be very wasteful of fuel as they are thermostatically controlled. One method of reducing the running costs of electricity is to employ storage heaters that use off-peak electricity at a lower cost to supply heat when you require it next day. They are much dearer to buy than ordinary electric radiators but do not require piping or air ducts as boiler systems do. Modern small-bore piping systems with a pump to improve circulation are efficient and unobtrusive, but some people prefer warm-air ducting. Such systems tend to be a little noisy as they are fan-forced. Electricity has the advantage of complete silence and cleanliness. Hot-water systems are subject to noise in the piping if not installed with very great care.

Some gas boilers have a very efficient automatic device which prevents use of the boiler at times when heating is not required. Many solid-fuel boilers have automatic hoppers thus reducing their traditional disadvantage while raising the price of the boiler to about the same as a gas boiler. The gas boiler shares with the oil-fired the advantage of cleanliness and freedom from daily maintenance.

A method which has not really caught on fully although it has been around for over twenty years is underfloor electric heating. This is convenient and spacesaving but very expensive to install unless it is incorporated at the time the house is being built.

I think this covers the principal methods. I hope you have sufficient information now to enable you to come to a decision.

Yours sincerely,
Jack

Exercise F

In each of the following rearrange the sentences (or sections of sentences) so that they seem to you to be in logical order and explain your reasons for the order you select. As the sentences are lettered there is no need to write them out.

I

(a) Someone was drawing water and my teacher placed my hand under the spout.

(b) I knew then that 'w-a-t-e-r' meant the wonderful cool something that was flowing over my hand.

(c) There were barriers still, it is true, but barriers that could in time be swept away!

(d) That living word awakened my soul, gave it light, hope, joy, set it free!

(e) Suddenly I felt a misty consciousness as of something forgotten – a thrill of returning thought; and somehow the mystery of language was revealed to me.

(f) We walked down the path to the well-house, attracted by the fragrance of the honeysuckle with which it was covered.

(g) I stood still, my whole attention fixed upon the motions of her fingers.

(h) As the cool stream gushed over one hand she spelled into the other the word *water*, first slowly, then rapidly.

2

(a) The community needed (and, of course, still needs) men who could read and write, conduct complicated business, sing elaborate music, build cathedrals, lead armies, frame and administer laws.

(b) – to provide for the children of the poor something of what the benefactor acknowledged to be his duty to supply for his own children.

(c) The visitor to an old parish church will often see on the walls a list of parish charities and among them, often enough, gifts for the education of the poor

(d) To meet this need there were founded schools so that 'there may never be wanting a succession of persons duly qualified to serve God in church and state'.

(e) Entangled here, as always, are the twin conceptions of education.

(f) – his gift was a form of capital investment.

(g) And so, today, as the methods by which wealth is produced become ever more complicated, new colleges are founded that the supply of men trained in their operation and development may not fail.

(h) Look at it one way and the gifts are designed as a form of social service

(i) But from another point of view, he was indirectly providing for a supply of craftsmen to maintain the wealth of the community

(j) or for enabling orphans or poor boys to be apprenticed to a good trade.

3

(a) No young novelist should ever dare to imitate the style of Dickens.

(b) Of Dickens's style it is impossible to speak in praise.

(c) But the critic is driven to feel the weakness of his criticism, when he acknowledges to himself – as he is compelled in all honesty to do – that with the language, such as it is, the writer has satisfied the great mass of readers of his country.

(d) If such a one wants a model for his language, let him take Thackeray.

(e) Both these great writers have satisfied the readers of their own pages; but both have done infinite harm by creating a school of imitators.

(f) To readers who have taught themselves to regard language, it must therefore be unpleasant.

(g) It is jerky, ungrammatical, and created by himself in defiance of rules – almost as completely as that created by Carlyle.

Exercise G

Prepare an outline plan on the work of *(a)* the BBC or *(b)* the Post Office or *(c)* your local technical college.

Chapter 3

Clear Wording 1
(Problems of Semantics)

I THE VERBAL COMMUNICATION PROCESS

A perfect act of communication takes place when the idea in the mind of the Tx is transferred, unchanged, into the mind of the Rx. *Idea* is here used very broadly, to include a piece of information, a question, an appeal, an order etc as well as the more usual meaning of 'a notion or concept'.

To communicate by means of words the Tx codes his idea into words (or, frequently, recodes it, as it is in words of some kind already) and transmits these words by speech or writing. The act of communication has not taken place, however, until the Rx has received and decoded these words to establish the 'idea' in his own mind.

As the message passes from Tx to Rx it is subject to distracting and distorting factors which (borrowing again from the vocabulary of the electronic engineer) may be called '*noise*'. 'Noise' is, in fact, frequently ordinary physical noise which, in a factory for example, substantially reduces the efficiency of spoken communication, or it may be electronic noise which interferes with communication by telephone or loudspeaker system. But it is used here to refer also to such things as illegible handwriting or smudged copies of duplicated typescript and all distractions(whether toothache or a pretty girl passing your desk) which reduce the concentration of either Rx or Tx.

For perfect communication (a) and (d) must be identical. This is something extremely difficult to achieve because of the combined effect of noise, and distortion at (b) and (c).

We have all had experience of the strain of communicating when attention at either end is distracted or when the medium itself is in some way defective, and we must in fact recognise that conditions will sometimes exist where noise causes complete communication breakdown. Such conditions are unusual, however, and the effect of noise can generally be overcome by will-power, by increasing the effort put into concentration. Noise too is most often encountered in spoken communication, where there is usually the possibility of asking immediately

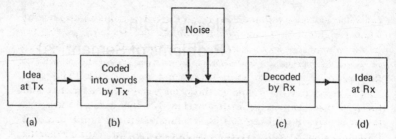

Figure 6 The verbal communication process

for a repetition of that part of the message that was interfered with.

The distortions at (b) and (c) are less simply overcome – at those points we confront the fundamental difficulty of communication by means of words. The key questions are:

1　How accurately do the words used at (b) express the idea (a)?

2　How can we be sure that the Rx will at stage (c) assign the same value to those words as the Tx did at (b)?

This chapter considers some of the problems inherent in our use of words to convey meaning (*semantics*) and attempts to show how the Tx should choose his words so that his meaning is conveyed to the Rx with minimum distortion, maximum clarity.

II WORDS AS SYMBOLS

When we use words, we are using symbols. As the Union Jack can be said to stand for our country, so a certain sound made by our breath passing over our vocal chords while tongue and lips move into various positions stands for the male parent. When we write the word down, *father*, we employ a double symbolism, since the letters that represent this sound are themselves symbols.

We are free to assign whatever value we choose to our symbols; but we shall not get very far in communicating with others unless our symbols are recognised by them. Thus if I choose to symbolise Great Britain by means of a yellow flag with purple stripes and the male parent by the word *ogboo*, I shall meet continual incomprehension when I attempt to use my symbols.

When we are speaking to fellow Englishmen we do not have to worry when we use the word *father* that the Frenchman uses *père* and the German *Vater* as their symbols for the male parent. We know that our particular audience will understand. Similarly it is not necessary for the whole community to recognise our symbols. An economist writing for fellow economists uses a vocabulary of symbols, many of which (such as *value*, *wealth*, *margin*) have a rather different meaning for the majority of the community from that which they have for his readers. There is no confusion, because the economist knows his readers will be familiar with his use of these symbols before they start to read. If he does not know this, he must make his special use clear immediately. A prime cause of communication breakdown is the unsound assumption by the Tx that the Rx knows already the special interpretation to be given to his symbols (the economist lecturing to a general audience who forgets that they will interpret *value*, *wealth*, *margin* in their way, not his).

The Tx should endeavour, as far as possible, to confine himself to symbols which he believes to be familiar to the Rx in the interpretation that he (the Tx) is putting upon them. It is, however, sometimes necessary to introduce unfamiliar symbols (which may be new words or old words with a slightly changed meaning). A number of symbols probably unfamiliar to the reader are employed in this book. In this chapter, so far, *semantics* is an example of an unfamiliar word and *idea* and *noise* are used in unfamiliar interpretations. The interpretation of these special symbols was made clear as soon as they were used – essential if misunderstanding is not to result.

All this may be formulated as rules:

1 Prefer words that are familiar to the Rx in the interpretation you wish him to give to them.

2 If you want the Rx to give an unfamiliar meaning to a familiar word within the context of your communication, make this clear the first time you use this word.

3 If you use a word likely to be unfamiliar to the Rx, make its meaning clear the first time you use it.

You will realise that for you to be able to apply these rules efficiently you will need to have:

1 a fairly accurate impression of the vocabulary of the Rx

2 an extremely accurate knowledge of the accepted meanings of words (with particular realisation of which words your own trade or profession uses with meanings differing from the generally accepted ones).

When we are communicating with men and women of more limited vocabulary than our own, breakdown may occur when we use what seem to us familiar words in their most everyday senses – simply because these words are not known by, or are only distortedly known by, the Rx.

Judging what will, or will not, be familiar vocabulary for the Rx demands imagination, continual alertness to the other man's point of view, and a good knowledge of the Rx.

When you yourself are the Rx you too may make errors of interpretation because the words you hear or read are unfamiliar. You can reduce the number of occasions on which you make such errors by improving your vocabulary. The more words you are familiar with, and the more accurate your interpretation of those words, the better you are as an Rx. You improve your vocabulary by reading and listening, with reference to a dictionary when you come across a word you are not certain about. The more demanding the material you read and listen to, the faster your vocabulary will develop; do not be satisfied with material already well within your range. Continued subjection to communication material intended for a Tx of smaller vocabulary than your own (and this will include much popular newspaper, magazine, and television material) cripples development.

III AREAS OF MEANING

You will already be realising that it is a fallacy to believe that there is one 'correct' meaning for every word. The decoding process at (c) is never as simple as $15x + 27y$ where $x = 8$ and $y = 6$, because the symbols of language can stand for more than one idea each.

Radium is a metal of great value. What does this mean? That radium costs a great deal of money or that it does a great deal of good? Or both? Consider these sentences:

What is the value of this ring?
What is the value of learning about communication?
I value my good name.
I got good value for my money.
There is something wrong with the tone values in all his paintings.
A crotchet has twice the value of a quaver.

What is the meaning of *value*? Even without bringing in the economist, *value* is seen to have a series of meanings or, more accurately, a series of *areas of meaning* (since each sentence illustrates a group of meanings). Notice too that it is only when we meet *value* in context that we know how to interpret it. We can often form only an approximate idea of the meaning of a word out of context, since we cannot tell which area of meaning to assign to it.

IV THE USE OF DICTIONARIES

The feeling that somewhere there must be a final court of appeal where 'correct' meanings are laid down dies hard. 'Look it up in a dictionary', people say. But the dictionary, if it is a good one, will not attempt an $x = 8$ type of answer but will show as many areas of meaning as there is space for within the limits of the cost of the dictionary.

Furthermore the dictionary is not a legislator telling you what you are to do; it tells you only what other people are already doing. A dictionary is compiled by a large number of scholars each of whom is assigned a small part of the dictionary alphabetically (say FEA to FEV). Each notes examples of written uses of the words in his section, especially unusual uses, as he reads an immense number of previously selected books. From the large number of contexts for each word supplied him by his assistants the editor subsequently deduces the areas of meanings which are (1) current (2) have been accepted in the past but are no longer live. Thus a dictionary provides a systematic record of usage, not a series of rules for linguistic behaviour. But this is exactly what we want. If you as a Tx are in any doubt about a word you propose to use, you can – and should – check it in a dictionary – not to find out its 'correct' meaning but to find out, approximately, what meaning or meanings the Rx is likely to assign to it. The authority of the dictionary arises partly from this, but also from the fact that the Rx in turn, if he is uncertain of this word, will check it in a dictionary. Thus the dictionary acts as code-book to both Tx and Rx and in the end does influence their view of what the word means. Certain dictionaries (notably the Oxford series in England and Webster's in America) have greater authority than others, partly because they are those that have been compiled on sound research lines and are not simply taken from other dictionaries, but partly because they are known to be those most frequently consulted. If you use a cheap dictionary there will not be space in it for sufficient areas of meaning to be shown, and if you use a little-known one you may find yourself with a different code-book from the one your opposite number is using.

Buy therefore the largest dictionary you can afford and let it be one of wide repute; it will be the most useful aid to communication you will ever find.

A good dictionary supplies not only definitions of each word's areas of meaning but also illustrative contexts, its grammatical function(s), an indication of its origin (derivation), and a guide to its pronunciation. For some words it will supply still more information – if you look up *penny*, for example, in even the pocket version of the Oxford dictionary you will be amazed at the amount of information crammed into so small a space. It is certainly a pity to use a dictionary just to check spelling, or to buy the kind that has entries so brief that they lead you in a circle (e.g. you look up *value* and find 'worth' – you look up *worth* and find 'value').

An inevitable limitation to the usefulness of a dictionary is that it is always out of date. While the compilers have been busy, the language has changed; by the time the dictionary is printed the language will have changed again. Dictionaries are very expensive to compile so one compilation will have to stand for many years; though from time to time additions to, and revisions of, the original edition will be made by a conscientious publisher, these will never keep us with the continual vocabulary changes of a living language – new words entering the language, old words shifting their meaning. This is not quite such a serious limitation as it would at first seem, as changes in the use of existing words establish themselves fairly slowly and new words are often generally familiar words that do not need to be checked in a dictionary. However, it is something that should be borne in mind by those who tend to look to the dictionary as the final authority on meaning.

V MAKING MEANING CLEAR

We saw in Section II that we are often in the position of having to make clear the interpretation we expect the Rx to give to a word we are going to use. Three devices are particularly useful in making meaning clear – *illustrative contexts*, *glossing*, and *definition*.

A *Illustrative contexts*

We have learned the meanings of nearly all the words we know from the contexts in which we have heard or seen them; from childhood on, we all carry out a similar process to that which is the task of the dictionary editor. As an Rx reads what we have written he will start to assign a meaning to a new word from the contexts in which it appears. This is the natural way for him to learn our meaning.

This process can sometimes be speeded up and made more accurate by supplying illustrative contexts as soon as the word is first used – this method is used at the beginning of Chapter 1 of this book in an attempt to establish the critical word *communication* quickly for the reader.

As we need one context for each area of meaning it can, however, be a cumbersome device and is in fact little used outside dictionaries and examination answers.

'Write sentences to bring out clearly the meaning of ...' or 'Illustrate the use of the following by means of sentences ...' are common questions in English papers. Two points should be noted about answering such questions:

1 only one area of meaning is required

2 the sentence used must, as far as possible, 'fix' the meaning of the word – a good test of this is to see if you can substitute a word of opposite meaning. Thus to illustrate *courageous* the sentence *The soldier was very courageous* is valueless as we could in fact substitute *cowardly*. We need something like *The soldier was courageous for he stood his ground although attacked by three of the enemy*.

It is not easy to fix the meaning of a word by means of a single sentence. The fixes we obtain in the normal communication situation are the result of comparing a number of contexts each one of which helps to limit the field of meaning of the word and sharpen our interpretation of it.

It should be noted, by the way, that an attempt has been made to indicate the author's use of *fix* in this section by illustrative context only.

B *Glossing*

A *gloss* was originally a note inserted in the margin to explain a word in the text. Today we use footnotes or put the gloss in parenthesis. Sometimes the word glossed comes after the gloss itself, as in example 4 below.

1 *In general they are extremely ductile – that is they pull out very easily.*

2 *The outer parts of the atom are occupied by electrons – that is by particles of pure negative electricity.*

3 *Work hardening (toughening under strain) is a common behaviour of metals.*

4 *If any polished metal is lightly attacked with acid – 'etched' as it is called ...*

The essence of the method is that a simple equivalent of the word glossed is put beside it; it is a form of paraphrase. It is a very useful device as it gives the Rx a rapid indication of how he is to interpret a word, without holding up the communication for a full explanation. It is particularly suitable where the Tx is not sure whether the Rx will know the word or not, or where he thinks the Rx will need only a reminder. Because it uses few words it is frequently employed in business communication, especially firm-to-customer communication where technical language appropriate to the firm must be briefly explained for the non-technical Rx.

C *Definition*

When we define a thing we separate it from every other thing in the universe. We do this by first classifying the thing and then subclassifying for as long as possible. Finally the smallest amount of additional information is added that will separate the thing defined from all other things in the last subdivided class. Things outside that subdivided class are ignored. Thus a violin falls into the general class 'musical instruments' and can be subdivided first as 'stringed' and subsequently as 'four-stringed' and 'played with a bow'. *A violin is a four-stringed musical instrument played with a bow* puts the violin into the correct subdivided class but is not a definition as it permits the violin to be confused with the viola, the cello, and the double-bass. *A violin is the smallest of the four-stringed musical instruments played with a bow* is a sound definition of a violin although it would give no idea of what a violin was like to a man ignorant of musical instruments and leaves for a second definition the question of what constitutes a bow.

Your Rx would get a very much better idea of a violin if you could take him to a concert and point one out. The fact that you can point out makes a difference between words like *violin, potato, volcano* on the one hand and words like *value, idea, definition* on the other. Words in the first group are said to have 'referents'. There will always be much more doubt as to the meaning of words that have no referent in the physical world about us, and defining such words is a demanding task.

There is a further difficulty about defining words without referents. When we define *violin* we do not readily think about whether we are defining the word or the object that the word stands for; but this does concern us when we have to define *value*. It is perhaps safest when attempting to define words that refer to ideas in our heads rather than to objects in the world appreciated by our senses to use a form of words such as '*value* refers to' rather than '*value* is'. This difficulty becomes more pronounced when we turn to the definition of other parts of speech than nouns. Some modification of the system of definition applicable to things becomes clearly necessary when we start to define *to radiate* or *small*. Since definition is so much associated with nouns it is usual to convert verbs to nouns (i.e. to define *radiation*) and to associate adjectives with the noun they are to be used with (e.g. *For the purpose of this paper, the term 'small boiler'* is taken to mean a boiler with a heating surface not greater than 3 sq m and an output not in excess of 30 kW).

A recent court case[1] illustrates (as legal processes so often do) the need for precise definition of words without referents, particularly when such words are not nouns. The General Rates Act of 1967 made premises rateable if they were 'completed' but left unoccupied. The case turned upon whether a particular unoccupied office block was 'completed' since although the structural work was finished, the floors had not been partitioned and telephones and electrical wiring had not been installed. The ruling at the Court of Appeal was that to be 'completed' in the meaning of the statute a building had to be capable of being occupied for the purpose for which it was intended. As the building could not be occupied as an office in the state in which it had been left the owners were not liable to pay the rates claimed by the local authority. Note how the court was obliged first to interpret this particular use of 'completed' and then to provide a narrowing definition of it so that all concerned could now understand the intention of the Act. It would have been easier for everybody if the framers of the statute had incorporated a definition or gloss in the original wording.

VI DISCRIMINATION BETWEEN SYNONYMS ON A BASIS OF MEANING

The English language is unusually rich in synonyms (words of similar meaning) chiefly because so many languages have contributed to ours. Thus we have *regal* (directly from Latin *regalis*) alongside *royal* (from Old French *roial*). Synonyms, although closely connected in meaning, are rarely fully interchangeable; we cannot talk about 'the Regal Family', and 'he surrounds himself with furnishings of royal magnificence' sounds a little strange. Even where meaning is identical, as in the pair *violin* (from Italian *violino*) and *fiddle* (from Middle English *fithele*) there is usually a difference of register (e.g. *fiddle* is used contemptuously or in rather undignified contexts). We shall consider the effect on communication of these differences of register in Chapter 5; at this stage it is the small differences of *meaning* that exist between so many synonyms that concern us. If we are aware of these differences we can improve our communication by selecting the word which most exactly conveys our meaning. On the other hand, uncertainty as to the precise degree to which two

[1] Ravenseft Properties Ltd *v* Newham LBC (Court of Appeal, 1975).

synonyms are interchangeable can lead to blurred transmission of our ideas.

Many words are treated as synonymous, by those unskilled in language, that are so different in meaning that it is questionable whether they can be called synonyms at all (e.g. *illicit* and *illegal*). It is convenient however to consider such words at the same time as true synonyms and in this book the word *synonym* is therefore used subsequently to include such near-synonyms.

Often the key factor in discriminating between words closely connected in meaning is their *relative narrowness of application*. *Illicit* is more limited in use than *illegal* since it refers only to those actions which offend against the law because they are performed without a licence or permit. *Illegal* refers to the general range of actions contrary to the law. Generally there is a gain in precision of meaning by choosing words of narrow application, but sometimes circumstances require us to prefer the broader word. If in a report we mention the necessity either to *oil* or *grease* a certain appliance when in fact both processes are necessary, either word is too narrow and we should have preferred *lubricate*, broad enough to include both processes. *Maintenance* of an appliance is broader still as it includes lubrication along with, for example, cleaning and checking.

Another type of difference between synonyms is that of *intensity*. *Tired*, *weary*, *exhausted* represent increasingly intense forms of the same state of being. We should choose the one that has just the right degree of intensity for our subject matter and – especially in factual communication of the sort that is the subject of this book – avoid trying to add drama by choosing words that exaggerate the situation.

Some words carry an overtone or suggestion of emotion along with their more factual meaning; this *emotional connotation* is another way by which synonyms can sometimes be differentiated. Thus *lonely* has an emotional connotation absent from *solitary* or *unaccompanied*. (These in turn, by the way, can be distinguished by the fact that *unaccompanied* is limited to those animate objects which can be accompanied; *solitary* is the broader word.) Often the emotional connotation of a word is disapproval. Such words are often said to have a *derogatory* or *pejorative* connotation. Thus *notorious* is distinguished from *famous*; *cunning* from *astute*; *obstinate* from *unwavering*. There are many such pairs and sometimes the one of the pair which is not derogatory carries a connotation of approval. Frequently we have a group of synonyms which represent the range; disapproval, neutrality, approval – as *gross, fat, plump*.

All these factors should be borne in mind when choosing between synonyms, but they will not always be applicable and many synonyms have slight but important differences in their areas of meaning that cannot be fitted into these categories. It is a matter of familiarising yourself with the contexts in which these words appear and deciding for yourself what makes one word fit a context better than another.

Synonyms should not be looked upon as merely a device for avoiding the same word used several times. Too much attention to this (a practice known as 'elegant variation') is a waste of the Tx's time and a source of confusion to the Rx who has to keep on readjusting to new symbols. They should be looked upon primarily as a way of improving the accuracy of our coding. It is not the similarities between synonyms that matter, it is the differences.

VII CAUSES OF CONFUSION

A *Homophones*

Friend, Charles Lamb is reputed to have called to a poacher he passed in the fields, *is that thine own hare or a wig?*

Opinions may differ as to whether puns are all that amusing, but there is no doubt that unconscious puns that arise through confusion between homophones (words spelled differently but sounding alike) harm communication. It cannot be often that genuine misunderstanding arises (*There is a boy adrift in the harbour mouth*) but the attention of the Rx is distracted while he laughs at the mistake, and the Tx loses authority.

We need to be particularly careful in checking dictated material for misspelling of homophones, and it is as well to spell out the word when dictating if the context is likely to cause any doubt in a secretary's mind.

B *Malapropisms*

Malapropisms are words which are used in error for other words somewhat like them in sound or appearance. They are named after Mrs Malaprop, a character in Sheridan's *The Rivals* who describes another character as *the very pineapple of politeness* and hopes that her daughter who has just been told to *illiterate* a young man from her memory will never become a *progeny of learning*.

They are more common in speech than in writing and are very damaging to the Tx. Since the confusions often occur between words which are long and unfamiliar the Tx lays himself open to the accusation of conceitedly attempting a vocabulary beyond what he can master.

A similar error occurs when the Rx misinterprets a somewhat unfamiliar word because he confuses it with one rather like it in appearance or sound.

C *Colloquial meanings*

Some words with well established areas of meaning in writing develop an additional area of meaning (or more than one) in speech. *Catch on, drag, square, fabulous* are examples – many thousands could be listed. Quite apart from the effect on register (separately referred to on page 72) confusion over meaning may result if we employ such words in writing intending them to carry a meaning they have only in speech.

Such colloquial extensions of meaning do gradually become absorbed into the written language, first in such informal contexts as newspaper articles but eventually in even the most formal writing. The complete process takes many years and it is often difficult to decide just how far a colloquial extension of meaning has become acceptable in writing (i.e. with what sort of Rx and in what sort of writing it can be used without misunderstanding). Some of the words in Exercises H and J at the end of this chapter illustrate this. Certainly, local and central government and the world of business will be among the last sectors to recognise such colloquial extensions of meaning, and this is therfore a point of some importance for the readers of this book.

Occasionally the colloquial meaning of a word is so well known (while still considered suitable only for speech) that we are unable to use it in its original sense except with a very conservative Rx and are virtually deprived of the use of the word altogether. An outstanding example of this is the word *nice*. This has acceptable written contexts which include:

This is a matter for nice judgment.
A nice balance is maintained throughout the report.
The factory works to nice tolerances.
Very nice stitching will be necessary.

The area of meaning of all these is 'precise and delicate'.

In colloquial use *nice* is a handy blunderbuss of a word to be aimed vaguely at everything one approves of – *nice weather, nice girl, nice food, nice work, a nice fit, nice stitching*. These familiar speech uses blur the response of the Rx to the written contexts so that he is, for example, quite at a loss to know what the Tx means by *nice stitching* in the last sentence above.

In commerce and local or central government the safest advice for the Tx is:

1 Avoid using words in their colloquial sense in writing.

2 Avoid using in writing, in any sense at all, a word which has a very well established colloquial sense.

VIII EXERCISES

NOTE: The intention of these exercises is not so much to expand your vocabulary as to make you more aware of the kinds of problem involved in selecting words to convey your meaning. Reading, and listening to, material expressed by those whose vocabulary is wider than your own is the natural way to expand your vocabulary. The majority of these exercises will prove most useful if attempted orally in a class so that group discussion can follow; if you are working on your own the best substitute for this is to write down your answers and check them in a good dictionary.

Exercise A

Write sentences (similar to those on page 34 for *value*) to provide contexts for as many separate areas of meaning as you can distinguish, for the following words:

leaf   try   plant   point   heart

Exercise B

Write sentences to bring our clearly the meaning of:

1 alien   impenetrable   individual   deteriorate   emigrant   interim
  irrelevant   pacify   analysis   inconclusive

2 determination   alternate   sinecure   menace   eradicate
  contemporary   predicament   reconnaissance   exonerate

3 temporal   crustacean   phenomenon   machiavellian   polytheism
  jejune   intrinsic   obviate   allegation   eclectic

Exercise C

With the aid of a dictionary compose a logical paragraph to include all the following words, in any order:

  responsibility   stultify   induction   assiduous   conducive
  environment   innate   initiative   crucial   procrastinating

Exercise D

1 Make one-sentence definitions of the following:

  a trombone   a pencil   a table   a canal   an axe

2 Attempt definitions of the following:

  democracy   efficiency   justice   beauty   love

If you try the second part of this exercise in a group, you will almost certainly find important differences between your definitions because your ideas of what you are defining differ. See how many different kinds of definition you can think of (for example how *love* will vary according to the definer's age, sex, nature). You will realise that the man who, in a discussion, says, 'It all depends what you mean by ...' is not splitting hairs; he is trying to make sure you are both talking about the same thing.

Exercise E

In the following groups of sentences the words in italics are synonyms, yet the sentences will not make good sense until these words are redistributed amongst the sentences. Carry out this redistribution and try to decide what has made the change necessary.

A

1 The judge sentenced the prisoner to six months' hard *work*.
2 No sooner had I finished one *toil* than he set me to another.
3 When do you start *labour* again?
4 There is too much *task* in farming for it to be a suitable occupation for one who likes an easy life.

B

1 The speaker had an attentive *crowd*.
2 The *audience* swept the speaker off the platform and trampled him underfoot.

3 A *mob* had by now collected round the speaker and many were listening seriously to his words.

C

1 The solicitor spent an hour advising his *patient*.
2 The butcher was always polite to a new *client*.
3 The doctor's *customer* complained that the waiting-room was uncomfortable.

D

1 She is *liable* to give me a present at Christmas.
2 It is *apt to* sink at any moment now.
3 In all the years I have known him I have found only one fault in him – he is *likely* to tell lies.

E

1 The *antique* woman could walk only with great difficulty.
2 Many people consider an *obsolete* warming-pan a suitable decoration for the wall of a timbered room.
3 The wardrobe mistress had spent weeks making the *old* dresses for the company.
4 As a weapon of war, molten lead is now *old-fashioned*.

F

1 The new secretary appeared to be quite *effective*.
2 His stern reply seemed to be *efficient* for the man immediately returned to his bench.
3 The lighting in the last scene of the play was particularly *effectual*.

Exercise F

Arrange the words in the following groups in ascending order of intensity:

  tepid hot warm
  frighten alarm terrify scare
  momentous significant weighty important
  reprehensible wicked iniquitous improper
  idiotic stupid injudicious foolish
  ugly ill-favoured plain homely hideous
  quickly hurriedly rapidly swiftly precipitately briskly

Exercise G

Distinguish the following on the basis of emotional connotation:

home   residence
childish   childlike
politician   statesman
helpful   officious
pious   sanctimonious

Exercise H

Distinguish between the colloquial and the accepted written meanings of the following words:

decent   hectic   literally   putrid   lovely

Exercise I

1 Distinguish between the following synonyms or near-synonyms.
2 Are there any words that you consider identical in meaning and fully interchangeable?
3 If any are identical in meaning but not fully interchangeable why is this so?

synthetic   artificial   imitation   manmade
expensive   dear   costly
illegible   unreadable   indecipherable
lady   woman
man   gentleman
reticent   secretive   taciturn
short   brief   concise
tall   high   lofty
personnel   staff   employees   workers
presumption   assumption   hypothesis   postulate
massive   huge   vast   colossal   gigantic
merry   gay   happy   jovial   jolly
confirm   verify   endorse   corroborate
constantly   continually   continuously   perpetually   incessantly
make   construct   form   create   build   shape   manufacture
    fabricate   erect   produce   contrive   generate   run up
payment   wage   salary   fee   remuneration   emolument   stipend
    gratuity   honorarium

Exercise J

For each of the following words indicate which of the 'meanings' given is closest to the accepted written meaning:

1 *unique* : unexpected   the only one   very rare
2 *aggravate* : irritate   make worse   become bigger
3 *livid* : lead-coloured   brilliant   red-faced
4 *chronic* : long-lasting   incurable   very bad
5 *anticipate* : do something in advance   wait for something to be done   expect something to be done
6 *transpire* : become known   happen   change into another language
7 *hypercritical* : over-sensitive   over-critical   pretending to be virtuous
8 *rostrum* : list of duties   a platform for public speaking   a patent medicine
9 *disinterested* : bored   not interested   without self-interest
10 *unexceptionable* : ordinary   out of the ordinary   above reproach

Exercise K

Distinguish between the words in the following pairs or groups, which are sometimes confused because of similarity of sound and/or appearance. If any of these words are unfamiliar to you, use a dictionary to discover their areas of meaning but do not attempt the exercise with the groups in which they appeared.

persecute   prosecute
imminent   eminent
draft   draught
observance   observation
ingenious   ingenuous
expedient   expeditious
affect   effect
defective   deficient
flaunt   flout
deprecate   depreciate
credulous   creditable   credible
consul   counsel   council
luxurious   luxuriant
perspicacity   perspicuity
statue   statute   stature   status

resort   resource   recourse
exotic   erotic   esoteric
illusion   allusion   elusion   delusion

Exercise L

1   Write the following words and phrases in a column and, at the side of each, give a word or phrase which expresses the same idea disapprovingly:

astute   generous   famous   esprit de corps   collaborator   new idea
ingenious plan   delicate hint   wide discretion   shrewd thrust

2   Write *brief* explanatory notes on the *difference in meaning and use* between the words or phrases in each of the following pairs:

impassable   dependant   judicious   compare with   truism
impassible   dependent   judicial   compare to   axiom
           [*Royal Society of Arts, English Language Stage III*]

Exercise M

1   Make a numbered list of ten words which could be used to fill the ten numbered spaces in the passage given below. You may use *six only* of the following nine words and must therefore repeat one or more of them.

principles   methods   standards   philosophical   philosophy   science results   scientific   principal

There are two different ways in which a philosophy may seek to base itself upon ... 1 ... It may emphasise the most general ... 2 ... of science, and seek to give even greater generality and unity to these results. Or it may study the ... 3 ... of science, and seek to apply these ... 4 ..., with the necessary adaptations, to its own peculiar province. Much ... 5 ... inspired by science has gone astray through preoccupation with the ... 6 ... momentarily supposed to have been achieved. It is not results, but ... 7 ..., that can be transferred with profit from the sphere of the special sciences to the sphere of ... 8 .... What I wish to bring to your notice is the possibility and importance of applying to ... 9 ... problems certain broad ... 10 ... of method which have been found successful in the study of scientific questions.

2 State the central idea of the passage in one sentence and in your own words.

3 Give other words or phrases, one for each, which could be used to replace the following in the passage without either altering the meaning or disturbing the flow of words:

seek to base itself   emphasise   generality   adaptations   peculiar
inspired   preoccupation   transferred   sphere   possibility
[*Royal Society of Arts, English Language Stage III*]

Chapter 4

Clear Wording 2
(Problems of Handling)

I WORDS IN SENTENCES

The responsibility of the Tx to ensure that his wording does not obscure or distort his meaning does not end with his choice of words. When he begins to build his sentences new problems arise from interaction between words. Words (especially those next to each other in the sentence) influence each other in a way perhaps not expected, producing a surprising second meaning (ambiguity); the order in which the words are set down has more effect on the total meaning than he realised; the construction of the sentences becomes muddled, causing a blur in transmission – these are the kinds of problem of syntax which confront the Tx every time he speaks or writes.

Besides determining the best order for his words – and this has a direct effect on the quality of the transmission of his meaning – the Tx will also have to decide a number of more purely grammatical points (do the subject and verb agree in number? Is that the right case for the relative pronoun? can I use that word as a preposition?). These matters are of subordinate importance, but they are not without effect on the clarity of his wording; and he will certainly want (especially when writing or talking in a business context) to appear 'correct', as he will feel that if he does not conform to educated usage he will be putting himself in a position of inferiority to his Rx.

Faults of handling may produce four types of unsatisfactory sentence: (1) the unintelligible sentence (2) the sentence which conveys two or more meanings at once (3) the sentence which by faulty syntax or failure to conform to accepted usage makes the task of the Rx harder than it need be (4) the sentence which conveys its meaning, but ineptly or in a manner which reveals its author's unfamiliarity with educated usage.

II AMBIGUITY

A *Types of ambiguity*

To produce a sentence capable of one meaning only every time you write (or speak) a sentence must be your aim as a communicator. Second meanings have a way of appearing in what we write without our being aware of them. We know what we want to say and we are amazed when the Rx sees something quite different in our words. You will have to be alert to the possibility of ambiguity all the time, but especially when you are reading through, and revising, what you have written.

Some sentences are completely ambiguous – that is to say with the best will in the world the Rx cannot detect which meaning the Tx had in mind. *John told Tom that he had passed the examination* is an example of such a sentence. More often the second meaning is a ridiculous one, obviously not intended by the author, as in the well-known *If the baby does not thrive on fresh milk, boil it*. Although the first type of ambiguity is certainly the more important, it is no defence to say, 'Anybody can see what I meant.' If the Rx is laughing at you he is not concentrating on what you are telling him. Even the most ridiculous second meanings are therefore harmful to communication; and in business nobody wants to be laughed at.

B *Causes of ambiguity*

1 VAGUE REFERENCE OF PRONOUNS. The trouble with both the ambiguous sentences above is that we are not sure of the reference of the pronoun – does *he* mean John or Tom, does *it* refer to the milk or the baby? Notice that it cannot be assumed that the Rx will always associate a pronoun with the last noun mentioned – in the second sentence *milk* is the last noun but almost everybody who hears that sentence thinks of the baby as the antecedent of *it*.

In the following sentence from a national newspaper, context revealed that the first *he* referred to the unit sergeant-major but it remained a mystery whose men were being persuaded by whom to transfer to another unit.

When he returned to the drill ground a week later he was 'ordered off' by Major Starling, who told him he had been trying to persuade his men to transfer to another unit.

Although, for convenience, ambiguity is discussed here in terms of single sentences it may, of course, manifest itself in more than one sentence. A *this* or *these* at the beginning of the sentence leaving the reader uncertain which of two things mentioned in the previous sentence is referred to is a common form of this sort of ambiguity.

2 THE RULE OF PROXIMITY IGNORED. Words to be associated together

by the Rx should be physically together in the sentence; otherwise the Rx, assuming you are observing the rule of proximity, associates the wrong things together.

Writing desk for sale by lady with Queen Anne legs. (A common type – some improvement can be made by commas round *by lady* but fundamentally unsound.)

The meeting will be held in the old Men's Staff Room. (Devastating when spoken, not ambiguous at all when written, because of the use of capitals.)

The man on the horse with the wide-brimmed hat was the one who told me. (Commas after *horse* and *hat* produce very little improvement.)

Less obviously, it was difficulty with the rule of proximity that betrayed the film critic of a great newspaper into writing of *a beautifully observed study of a man who commits suicide in the last days of his life.*

3 INDECISIVE PLACING OF ADVERBS. There is an important difference between *He did not win luckily* and *He did not win, luckily.* Doubt is avoided by rearranging the order of the second sentence as *Luckily, he did not win.*

All adverbs need to be placed where there can be no doubt what word they are modifying, but some adverbs (*hardly, scarcely, almost, even,* and, above all, *only*) need special care.

Her mother only guessed the cause of her tears. (Does this mean only her mother guessed, or the mother guessed only, i.e. she was not certain?) Note the differences between:

That student passed only in Economics (he had only one success)

Only that student passed in Economics (only one candidate was successful)

That student only passed in Economics (he did not get a very high mark).

4 FAULTY PUNCTUATION (see also Appendix I). Although punctuation is a poor aid for a sentence ambiguous through neglect of the rule of proximity, some sentences are ambiguous purely because a comma has been omitted or, sometimes, wrongly introduced.

She likes coffee and rolls in bed has quite a different sense with a comma after *coffee.*

5 AMBIGUOUS WORDS. Words which have two or more areas of meaning can cause ambiguity if care is not taken to ensure that context makes it clear which area is required, e.g.

If you wish to retain the book after fourteen days you must ask for a renewal or telephone.

There was an unfortunate pharmaceutical chemist who took as his slogan: WE DISPENSE WITH ACCURACY. In 1976 the *Daily Telegraph* drew attention to a notice in a Dublin laundrette that read: PLEASE REMOVE YOUR CLOTHES AS SOON AS ALL THE LIGHTS ARE OUT.

Occasionally two areas of meanings of the one word are used in close proximity, with baffling effect:

The two little girls took nearly twenty minutes to reach the pillar-box only to find they could not reach it.

In reviewing a film about archery, a magazine devoted to that sport referred to *the unselfconscious shooting of children* leaving the reader in doubt whether the children were shooting arrows, being shot by cameras, or being shot by archers.

A motorist writing to a Wiltshire newspaper to draw attention to a dangerous exit into a main road combined this type of ambiguity with the falsely related participle (see page 57) to produce *Being on a bend one has to drive through 'blind' hoping no one is coming from the other direction* – thus apparently publicly confessing to drunken driving.

Probably the most serious ambiguities are of this kind, where the Rx is uncertain which of several possible meanings to assign to a word used by the Tx or the Tx uses the one word in more than one sense. Often such ambiguities are not just the results of carelessness in choice of word but reveal a basic uncertainty in the Tx's original ideas. Persistent ambiguity is a sign of woolly thinking and cannot be put right by mechanical means or the application of rules.

III COMMON FAULTS OF SYNTAX AND USAGE

A *Faulty agreement*

1 The verb agrees in number with its subject – this is familiar enough but there are many points of difficulty.

A man is walking down the street
A man and his wife are walking down the street
BUT
A man with his wife is *walking down the street.*

The multiple subject is here joined together by a form of words that makes one part of the subject so much subordinate to the other, that we have to treat the subject as singular. *With, together with, as well as* are the principal links that produce this effect:

Mr Tomkin, as well as his secretary, is to be present at this meeting.

Sometimes even multiple subjects joined by *and* are treated as singular if they are felt to combine together to form a unity:

Fish and chips is a nourishing food.

On the other hand, items consisting of two parts invariably used together (e.g. *pyjamas, scissors, pliers*) are always treated as plurals and can cause awkward sounding constructions:

Pliers are a useful tool.

The neatest solution here is to add *a pair of* and treat as a singular:

A pair of pliers is a useful tool.

There are a few words which are plural in form but singular in agreement (e.g. *news, measles, mathematics, economics*). *Means* can be either singular or plural.

2 Collective nouns can also be troublesome.

The congregation is bigger this week, we say, but not *The male congregation on entering the church takes off its hats*. The second context forces us to think of the individual heads belonging to the individual members of the group and as soon as we do that we find the singular unsatisfactory.

Alternatively, if we were to say *The congregation are bigger this week* it would suggest that the individual members had become larger since the previous week (as they well may have done). We prefer the collective, then, as a singular – unless something in the context forces us into thinking of the individual units of the whole, when we treat it as a plural:

The fleet is in port again
BUT
The crew of one ship are quarrelling amongst themselves.

The same noun can hardly be treated as both plural and singular in the same sentence, however:

NOT *As the jury have disagreed it will be dismissed.*

A collective followed by *of* plus a plural noun (*a case of instruments, a team of athletes, a flock of sheep*) is often wrongly treated as a plural subject.

NOT *A collection of valuable paintings are on display.*
BUT *A collection of valuable paintings is on display.*

3 *Each, every, everyone, everybody, anyone, anybody* are all singulars.

THUS *All of the workmen are to get a rise*
BUT   *Each of the workmen is to get a rise.*

4 Most people are uncertain whether to treat *none* as a plural or a singular. For a long time it was always considered singular (*None of these items is indispensible*). Gradually the plural version (*None of these items are indispensible*) became more and more accepted until, by about 1970, the singular version was looking distinctly old-fashioned. Recently, supported by the BBC, it has returned to favour, especially in situations where the highest degree of 'correctness' is aimed at. Thus usage seems, at the present time, to support both versions. It is difficult to see how what is less than one can be thought of as plural; to any reader of this book who is looking for guidance on this point the author would suggest treating *none* as a singular when writing, or speaking, formally.

5 *Kind, sort, type* are all singular nouns.

NOT *I do not care for those kind of people*
BUT *I do not care for that kind of people*
OR   (better, because it avoids the clash of singular and plural that worries some readers)

    I do not care for that kind of person.

6 *Either, neither* are also singular:

    Neither of the gardeners knows much about gardening.

For *either ... or, neither ... nor* constructions, the grammatical rule is that the verb agrees with the nearer of the subjects.
THUS *Neither my brother nor I am very interested in gardening* is sound grammar but reads a little strangely and would seem distinctly affected if spoken. In writing, the solution is not to substitute unsound grammar (*are*) but to rephrase the whole sentence to avoid the construction:

    My brother and I take no interest in gardening.

In speech the informal *are* is usual.
NOTE: This is one of many constructions where the dictum of the grammarian clashes with what the ear is used to. The grammarian's role

should really be, like the dictionary compiler's, that of recording usage, not laying down rules; but over the years he has become an accepted legislator in matters of doubt. In the business world where so much stress is laid on 'correctness' you will be ill-advised to stray far from orthodox grammar in your formal writing. Speech is much freer, and it is in fact our greater familiarity with colloquial forms that makes us sometimes unprepared for the grammatically 'correct' forms.

B *Faults connected with verbs*

1 The tenses of a passage should not be changed unnecessarily between past and present. If the main verb is in the past, all subordinate verbs must usually be in the past too:

NOT *He told me he will carry out the work immediately*
BUT *He told me he would carry out the work immediately*.

2 The perfect infinitive (*to have spoken*) is often used unnecessarily:

NOT *I should have liked to have spoken to him*
BUT *I should have liked to speak to him*.

There is no difference in meaning between these sentences and the clumsy perfect infinitive has been used in the first only as a result of a quite unnecessary attempt to treat the infinitive as a subordinate verb and turn it into the past tense after a past tense main verb.

He was believed to have visited their office in Milan

does not mean the same as

He was believed to visit their office in Milan

and the perfect infinitive serves a purpose in the first of these two sentences.

3 Verbal nouns (gerunds) and present participles are often confused.

The mother was watching the child dancing
The mother was watching the child's dancing.

A valuable distinction is made here. In the first sentence *dancing* is a present participle having an adjectival function with *child*. The mother is interested in her child who is clearly the direct object of *was watching*.
In the second sentence it is the dancing which is the direct object of *was*

watching; it is what the child dances that interests the mother. *Child* is reduced in strength to its adjectival equivalent *child's* so that the noun function of *dancing* comes to the fore (i.e. *dancing* is a verbal noun in the second sentence). Similarly,

NOT *Do you mind Brenda coming with me*
BUT *Do you mind Brenda's coming with me.*

Nobody is minding Brenda. The object of *Do you mind* is *coming*, the verbal noun.

4 Participles, both present and past, are often used without the noun, or pronoun, they are intended to serve as adjectives to. These 'unrelated participles' frequently then appear to the Rx to attach themselves to other nouns with which they either make sense not intended, or no sense at all:

NOT *Standing on the bridge the river flows away to the south* (the river is not standing on the bridge)
BUT *Standing on the bridge you can see the river flowing away to the south.*
NOT *Being summer I spent most of my time at the seaside*
BUT *As it was summer, I spent most of my time at the seaside.*
NOT *When detonated at the ground, the surrounding air is heated to a very high temperature*
BUT *When the bomb is detonated at the ground ...*

The noun or pronoun that the participle is to be associated with by the reader must be expressed, not understood. Even if there is no noun for the participle to relate itself to falsely, a participle left hanging gives an impression of slack slovenly writing.

Where *regarding*, *considering*, *concerning*, and *failing* are used IN THEIR PREPOSITIONAL FUNCTIONS the question of false relation does not arise.

Thus *Considering the improvement in output, the capital expenditure involved does not appear excessive* is a sound sentence, while *Considering the improvement in output justified the expenditure, his vote was in favour* is unsound, *considering* being unrelated.

5 Perhaps the best known fault of syntax amongst those ignorant of English grammar, the 'split infinitive', is often not a fault at all. It consists in placing a word or words between the *to* and the word that with *to* forms the infinitive (e.g. *to finally correct*). The objection to doing this seems no more than a meaningless taboo having no connection with clear writing. In fact the determination to avoid splitting the infinitive sometimes leads to ambiguity, as in *He failed completely to understand what I was telling*

him. If the writer meant that the failure to understand was only partial he might have done better to put *He failed to completely understand what I was telling him*.

C   *Difficulties with relative pronouns*

1 Relative pronouns have a dual function. They stand for a noun already used (the *antecedent*). They also serve as a linking device.

Consider the sentence:

He completed the report that had been asked for by the manager.

This can be looked upon as a linked version of:

He completed the report. This report had been asked for by the manager.

The relative pronoun *that* (1) stands for the noun *report*, (2) links the two sentences into one by making the second into a clause.

The principal relative pronouns are: *who, whom, whose* (for persons); *which* (for things); *that* (for either). *That* is in fact not very often used as a substitute for *who*. As a substitute for *which* it should be used only when the clause it introduces is 'defining'. (Defining clauses identify the antecedent for the Rx by answering such questions as *Which one?*)

THUS *The river that flows through London is the Thames* (defining)
BUT   *The River Thames, which is usually mud-coloured, flows through London* (non-defining).

We can use *which* instead of *that* in the first of these sentences – although *that* is preferable – but not *that* instead of *which* in the second.

For the effect of commas in distinguishing non-defining from defining clauses see page 333.

2 Separation of the pronoun from its antecedent sometimes causes it to appear to refer to the wrong noun:

He left the message on the table that he intended for the manager.

Still worse, the antecedent sometimes does not appear in the sentence at all:

He decided to ignore the advice of his committee which was extremely foolish.

What is foolish? The committee? The advice? Most probably his decision – but a pronoun can hardly refer to a noun which is not there.

3 The relative pronoun takes its case from its own clause but its number from its antecedent:

There is the man who is going to win the race
There is the man whom I saw yesterday.

When words in parenthesis such as *I think, We believe* are introduced, confusion sometimes occurs between these two basic sentences:

NOT *There is the man whom I think is going to win the race*
BUT *There is the man who, I think, is going to win the race.*

Where the antecedent is expressed, little difficulty is experienced in making the relative pronoun agree in number with it (this agreement being revealed only by the subsequent verb, as relative pronouns are alike in form for plural and singular):

These are a few of the films that are to be shown next year.

But where the antecedent is 'understood' there is sometimes confusion:

NOT *This film is one of the best that has been shown this year*
BUT *This film is one of the best that have been shown this year.*

4 A relative pronoun preceded by *and* or *but* should be used only with a clause which both (1) follows an earlier clause introduced by the same relative pronoun and (2) refers to the same antecedent as the earlier clause does. Furthermore, both clauses should be defining, or both non-defining. Thus:

He completed his report, which occupied fifteen sheets of typescript and which, incidentally, was most unlikely ever to be read

NOT *He completed a report occupying fifteen sheets of typescript and which, incidentally, was most unlikely ever to be read*
(no earlier clause introduced by same relative pronoun)

NOT *The river which flows through London is the Thames and which is usually mud-coloured* (first clause defining, second non-defining).

D *False ellipsis*

Ellipsis is a process, of leaving some words to be 'understood' in a sentence, whereby we avoid using the same word twice in a sentence to do the one job.

Thus

He had worked for and he had waited for this post many years
by ellipsis becomes:

He had worked and waited for this post many years.

False ellipsis occurs when we attempt to make a word do the work of a completely different word as well as its own:

NOT *I should be grateful if you would send me further details and application form for this post*

BUT *I should be grateful if you would send me further details of, and application form for, this post.*

NOT *Goldcrest cigarettes are as good, if not better than, full-priced cigarettes*

BUT *Goldcrest cigarettes are as good as, if not better than, full-priced cigarettes.*

NOT *At Southampton one can see liners coming and going from many different parts of the world*

BUT *At Southampton one can see liners coming from and going to many different parts of the world.*

E *Confused construction*

Sometimes two legitimate constructions are in the mind of the writer at once and he produces an inadmissible mixture of the two:

NOT *No sooner had she reached the church door when the organ began to play*

BUT *No sooner had she reached the church door than the organ began to play*

OR *Scarcely had she reached the church door when the organ began to play.*

The man who wrote *On some of these islands the population has more than halved in the last thirty years* was trying to apply the *has more than doubled* construction to *has fallen to less than half*.

F *Faulty constructions with correlative conjunctions*

The correlative conjunctions are:

   not only   but (also)
   neither   nor
   either   or
   both   and
   rather   than

   The construction following the second half of the correlative should balance that following the first. The easiest way to ensure this is to check that the same part of speech follows both halves:

NOT *We were not only interested in his achievements but by his potential*

BUT *We were interested not only in his achievements but by his potential* (both followed by preposition)

OR *We were not only interested in his achievement but impressed by his potential* (both followed by finite verb).

G *Difficulties with negative sentences*

1 In English two negatives equal a positive as they do in mathematics. This is not true of all languages – in Italian for example a sentence which literally translates as '*I did not never send you a letter*' is just a more emphatic negative. Theoretically this means that if you want a positive in an English sentence you can put in two negatives and if you put in three negatives you are back to a negative again; but multiple negatives are best avoided. At best they give the Rx unnecessary trouble in sorting them out, and at worst an extra negative creeps in, as in

It must not be assumed that there are no circumstances in which a profit might not be made.

In speech, double negatives are surprisingly common as

I shouldn't wonder if he didn't do it

where the speaker means

I think he did it.

2 *Nor* and *or* following a negative can be confused easily. After *neither* it must be *nor* and after *either* it must be *or*. If the negative is merely a *not* or *no* it is not quite so easy to decide. If the effect of the negative in the first part of the sentence continues into the second part *or* is used, but if the negative is confined to its own part *nor* is used.

NOT *The blame for this rests not with the pupils or with the teachers but with the parents*

BUT *The blame for this rests not with the pupils nor with the teachers but with the parents*

OR *The blame for this does not rest with the pupils or the teachers but with the parents.*

H *Words of limited function*

A small number of words are at the stage of having their grammatical functions extended in colloquial usage (i.e. they are being used as parts of speech that they were not used as previously). Those that follow – although appearing in written contexts in these extended functions more and more frequently – cannot yet be said to be sufficiently established to justify their employment in formal business writing.

1 Grammatically, 'due' is an adjective. It is becoming quite common to see 'due to' used as a prepositional phrase:

We were unable to keep to schedule due to fog.

It is better to substitute one of the accepted prepositional phrases *owing to, because of* or *as a result of*:

We were unable to keep to schedule owing to fog.

Due to is best confined to constructions such as noun + *due to* or noun + verb *to be + due to,* where it has its true adjectival function:

Fog due to industrial smoke is widespread
Fog is due to industrial smoke.

Notice that *Fog, owing to industrial smoke, is widespread* has quite a different meaning from the first of these two sentences.

2 *Quite* is best confined to an adverbial function in writing (as *It is quite likely that Mr Brown will return in time for the conference*). Constructions employing *quite* as an adjective (*quite a crowd, quite an ovation*), are becoming widely accepted but have a makeshift look to them that precludes their use in formal contexts. They have the further disadvantage of vagueness of meaning – what is *quite a crowd*? a considerable number? more people than expected? very many people? In practice it often means 'a small crowd' i.e. not a crowd at all.

3 *Like* is not acceptable as a conjunction in formal English (though it is in formal American English), and its colloquial use in this function should be replaced by *as*:

NOT *I prune my roses in February like the gardening expert on television does*
BUT *I prune my roses in February as the gardening expert on television does*
OR *I prune my roses in February like the gardening expert on television*
  (where *like* is employed legitimately as a preposition).

A typical American usage (increasingly heard in Britain) is *He acted like he had no further interest in the matter*, where the formal English equivalent is *He acted as though he had no further interest in the matter*.

4 *Than* is not accepted by conventional grammarians as a preposition. This colloquial use (as in *I think I know better than him what to say*) is, however, well established and the 'correct' form (*I think I know better than he what to say*) is beginning to seem a little pedantic to many people. Perhaps the way to satisfy everybody is to add the verb (*I think I know better than he does what to say*).

IV EXERCISES

Exercise A

How many separate meanings can be given to the words *In Palladonia the burganders bud only on the chalk hills* by changing the position of the *only*?

Exercise B

A town council put up the notice ONLY DOGS ON LEADS ALLOWED IN THIS PARK but the objection was raised that there was little point in having a dog on a lead unless someone was holding it and in any case it was unreasonable to reserve the park for dogs. It is clear enough what the council intended to say – rephrase the notice so that it is completely free of ambiguity.

Exercise C

Correct the ambiguities of the following letter by a golfer:

I must write to tell you how sorry I am my golf ball narrowly missed you yesterday. I certainly thought for a moment I had hit you behind the bunker. When I got there you had already passed on so I decided to waste no time in writing.

What happened was that as I was about to stroke the ball my eye was caught by a passing squirrel which deflected the ball to the right where you were standing. I have said for years that somebody would get hit there and something needed doing badly about it, so I am particularly distressed at coming so near to offending myself.

Exercise D

Point out and correct the ambiguities in the following:

1 After Jackson was out, Tomkins appeared to play probably the best innings of the season.

2 When did you arrange to meet him?

3 I am not going out because it is cold.

4 During the winter the 15.20 train (which during the summer runs on weekdays but not on Sundays) will not run on Saturdays.

5 Nobody has been in this room for more than an hour.

6 I shall hope to see you some time next week.

7 You will not catch many germs walking in the open air.

8 Despite the traffic that kept her awake for hours she slept some time during the night.

9 Jack and Brenda met Tom and Sheila at their usual restaurant by chance. This was fortunate as they had been wanting to meet her, but Brenda had felt sure she would not come if invited as they had never got on well together. In the event she asked them both to come round to their place for a second meeting, so she felt the whole thing had gone off very well.

10 All men are animals and you're a man; so you must be an animal. I don't care to go out with an animal.

Exercise E

Each of the following sentences contains one fault of the type discussed in this chapter. For each sentence, point out the fault and rewrite the sentence with the minimum rewording.

1 Due to the trading losses we have suffered we are unable to maintain our annual profit-sharing bonus.

2 George Thompson even knows the combination of the office safe.

3 This is a reform overdue for years and which will immediately improve the position of clerical officers.

4 At the end of the year we found that our trading in this country had not only increased beyond expectations but also our overseas sales.

5 The herbaceous border has been replanted and most of the shrubs died since you were last here.

6 I am unable to find proof that either of the accounts have been paid.

7 There is no reason to doubt that what he said in his second statement is not true.

8 It is my considered opinion that he never has, and never will, behave in such a manner.

9 Equipped with several years' legal training, the demands made on him in his new post proved well within his powers.

10 Candidates are recommended to divide their time equally between each question.

Exercise F

Criticise the following sentences carefully, and improve them:

A

1 The solution to the problem, and which should have been obvious from the first, was to alter the filing system, so the new manager ordered this to be effected forthwith.

2 When it was announced that the biggest majority of the electors vote for the Progressive Party, the listeners were so disinterested that they turned off their wireless sets.

3 We intended to have gone to the festival, but Arthur and I was prevented due to a very foggy morning.

B

1 It seems as if you and me are likely to be unlucky in getting a raise in salary from what the secretary let fall about the company's position yesterday.

2 Not having heard from you to date you will not be surprised at me supposing the answer is in the negative to my request to you to kindly support my application for the post in London.

3 Who do you propose as the new Manager? Above all tact and evenness of temper is what is needed and I would not hesitate to say Smith was the man if you ask me.

[*Corporation of Secretaries*]

Exercise G

Criticise the following sentences from students' work and rewrite them making no unnecessary changes.

1 Youth today is fashion-conscious and nearly all young people follow fashion trends, especially girls.

2 In that year membership was 547 000 with the total retail sales being £15 million.

3 Many of these sort of teenagers result from homes where parents either are unable to control them properly or the mother is at work and has no time for her children.

4 The amount of people devoting their lives to youth work and the work and skill that is put in is amazing.

5 The most effective of the main effects is the concluding rocket display.

6 It is impossible to predict the path of clouds of radioactive dust due to variation of local wind direction.

7 These kind of developments were not encouraged in the nineteenth century.

8 Because sea voyages were so long and dangerous there was very little sea travel where unnecessary.

9 Most decisions are only taken by the Council of Ministers as a last resort.

10 The Transport Commission aim to produce a railway system of which the nation will be proud to use.

11 Although traffic is dense in these regions it occurs only at peak periods.

12 British Rail derive the greater part of their revenue from freight than from passenger traffic.

13 Charles Howarth together with William Cooper were constitution makers which still is used today.

14 In the early days of the cooperative movement buying a share not only entitled the customer to dividend on purchases but also to a vote in management.

15 On returning the drawer to its position the next article drops into place.

16 All conditions can be created in the tanks under which the ship models can be tested.

17 At an early stage each cell looks alike.

18 Having ascertained the minimum resistance hull shape, the shipbuilders are given the relevant information and build accordingly.

19 Relatively few families in the whole world have record players and cannot therefore buy and appreciate records.

20 After feeding the plant with liquor containing very slight traces of ammonia it is concentrated into pure ammonia.

21 There was a period of expansion in new areas and then more slowly until it reached a peak in 1903.

22 Very little or even no changes occurred in the next few years.

23 Trade fairs are a commercial feature today many being in new exporting markets.

24 When removing the carburetter the float chamber unfortunately broke in two.

25 It is designed so that the cement being mixed can be emptied into a wheelbarrow which can be placed under the drum when it is upside down.

Exercise H

Comment on the wording of the following sentences from students' work:

1 The court of justice has several judges appointed mutually amongst the member countries.
2 Many ministers were completely disinterested in the maritime aspects of their country's affairs.
3 We have, during the last few weeks, been inundated with forms that have not been returned to us.
4 The surplus between cost and selling price steadily arose.
5 The trading methods of the different cooperative societies are not necessarily the same.
6 The import of foodstuffs into this country is particularly important.
7 The idea of this machine is to test materials before they are used in the factory.
8 This is a small but sturdily built grinder and has a wide range of uses, the maximum height of the wheel being 300 mm.
9 Such a man is still sometimes seen cycling down a country lane, with a large suitcase strapped to the carrier, peddling his goods.
10 Older children take up smoking because they think it makes them look older.

Chapter 5

Appropriate Wording

I REGISTER

Register refers to the total characteristics of any sample of language in relation to the particular purpose for which it is intended. The term is thus merely a convenient name for something we are all familiar with. An account of a football match is not written in the same sort of language as the report of a council meeting. A group of young men discussing a point over a few beers use different language from that which they would employ to discuss the same point in a committee.

Most people find the way a policeman gives evidence faintly comic (unless he is giving evidence against them). This is because his vocabulary often seems a little too dignified for what he has to say, especially considering he is speaking, not writing: *Acting on information received I was proceeding in the direction of Ayrton Park when I observed the accused behaving in a suspicious manner.*

It does sound a little unnatural; but the policeman is in the same difficulty that a manager is in when dictating letters – he is speaking, but what he speaks is going to be read. Policemen are trained to speak like that so that what they say will be uniform and dignified in register and will not offend against the accepted conventions of written English when it appears in a transcript of evidence. We would all recognise that the register was wrong if instead he said something like: *We'd had a tip off so I hot-footed it down to Ayrton Park where who should I see but Jimmy the Creep here up to something fishy by the look of him.* This, however, might be something like the appropriate register for telling his mates about it – if he used court-of-law register in the canteen somebody would soon point out his mistake.

The register changes then not only to suit the subject matter but also to suit the communication situation. It also changes to adjust to the Rx. We use different language in our family circle from that which we use at work; different language with our workmates from that which we use to the boss.

To a friend we may write: *Let me know what I owe you*; but to a firm: *Kindly render your account*; and these are not interchangeable. A firm will write to a customer not: *If you can't get our make in the shops round your way drop us a line* but: *If you are unable to obtain our product locally write to us direct*. The Post Office may properly make the proviso: *Payment will be made subject to the possession by the Postmaster of sufficient funds*; but you could hardly write to a friend who had lent you a fiver: *Repayment will be subject to my possession of sufficient funds next month*.

Register is largely a matter of the degree of formality felt to be required. There is a formality range which has been expressed as; *intimate*; *casual*; *consultative*; *formal*; *frozen* – but there are many intermediate stages. Deciding precisely what degree of formality is appropriate – to the subject matter, to the communication situation, and to the Rx – is an important part of the communicator's skill.

If, in speech or writing, we use extremely formal language in an informal situation or seek to gain effect by using long or unfamiliar words where simpler words would do equally well, we are being pretentious. The opposite fault is, in writing, to employ too informal a register, perhaps by writing in the way we speak; in speech, to make excessive use of colloquial and slang expressions in a fairly formal situation.

The worst fault of all is to keep shifting register when we talk or write. We must aim at a consistent register appropriate to the circumstances.

In written business and technical communication we are usually expected to employ a rather dignified and formal register. Along with all the other factors to consider in choosing our words, we must give some weight to this aspect, eradicating words and expressions that seem beneath the dignity of what we are writing but at the same time avoiding the pretentious and trying to write as simply as possible.

II TONE

Closely linked with register is the question of appropriateness of tone. We are all familiar with the way the tone of voice in which somebody speaks to us affects us, quite apart from what he has to tell us. We may feel the speaker dislikes us, or is friendly towards us; is bullying us, or seeking our help; despises us, or respects us – just because of the way he speaks. When we are ourselves the Tx it pays us to remember how we felt about certain tones of voice when we were the Rx.

Similarly in writing, an attitude towards the Rx, or the subject matter, can be conveyed by the wording and the sentence structure. It is useful to employ the word 'tone' for this also. Many advertisers, for instance, adopt a bullying tone: *Try some today! Act now; don't delay! Buy it now!* With so many people shouting imperatives at him the consumer begins to develop a self-protective deafness. The older tone for this sort of thing was ingratiating, even obsequious: *May we venture to intrude upon your valuable time in order to bring to your attention the advantages to be obtained from the use of our duplicating machines.*

Impersonal constructions and a stilted vocabulary produce a cold tone: *Your request has been received and the matter is under consideration. As soon as a decision has been reached notification of this will be sent.*

Emphasis on 'I' and 'you' and a less formal vocabulary produce a warm friendly tone much more conducive to good communication: *I have received your request and am looking into the matter now. As soon as I have made up my mind I shall let you know.*

But this degree of informality, although certainly on the increase between equals in internal memos and letters, may be felt by some to be inappropriate to many business situations. Finding the appropriate wording for business and technical communication is often a matter of balancing considerations of tone against considerations of register.

With the aid of facial expression, gestures, and above all inflection of the voice, we are able to produce just the tone we want quite easily in speech. In fact, those inexperienced in the art of communication, often inadvertently reveal to the Rx more than they intend about their attitude to him because they forget that these additional media of communication are operating in parallel with the words they use.

Catching the tone we think appropriate is much harder in writing, but a skilled writer can command a considerable range. He can, by subtle choice of words and sentence structure, seem affectionate; humorous; bantering; ironical; disapproving; determined; stern; angry. For the majority of communication situations in business, fortunately, all that is usually required is a calm, unemotional but friendly, tone that will encourage a similar attitude in the Rx.

III INFORMAL LANGUAGE

A *Dialect*

A dialect is the minority language of a region or class. It may vary from the form most widely accepted amongst educated people (rather oddly called 'Received English') not only in pronunciation but also in syntax and vocabulary. The old Devon woman calling down from her window *Oi be up 'ere eatin' winkles* is employing a different conjugation of the verb 'to be' that runs *I be, thou beest, he be*. North of Trent the local ruling for the distinction between *shall* and *will* is opposite from that of Received English. Most areas have their special words (e.g. *griskins* in Wiltshire, *pikelets* in the north Midlands) not widely understood outside, or special uses of words (in the area north of Trent *to mash the tea* is not the same sort of process as *to mash the potatoes* and *mending the fire* has nothing to do with repairing it). A University of Leeds survey team visited eight Wiltshire villages and found six words for 'left-handed': *wotty-'anded* (Ashton Keynes), *kek-'anded* (Burbage), *gammy-'anded* (Steeple Ashton and Whiteparish), *skwippy* (Sutton Veny), *skwiffy* (Fovant), and *Marlborough-'anded* (Avebury and Netheravon, which are near Marlborough, of course).

Class dialects are mostly a matter of pronunciation. In London (as in most great cities) 'low' areas and areas considered of good class frequently abut on each other. There is an old anecdote of the two churches, one each side of a road which was the boundary between two such contrasting districts. On the one side of the road the congregation is singing *Prize 'im fer iz grice and fiver* and on the other side, *Preeze Him for His grease and fever*. The point of the anecdote is that both versions are variants from Received English; both are class dialect forms. From this point of view one is not 'better' than the other.

An ambitious youngster who has dialect elements in his speech is at an advantage when dealing with people of his own region or class; the familiar dialect inclines them to be friendly towards him, prepared to trust him. It is a very different story once he moves outside his own region or class. Regional elements will make him at best the odd man out, something of a figure of fun; at worst, incomprehensible. Class difference shown in his voice will antagonise his Rx; whether the latter feels that the Tx is revealed as either superior or inferior to him in social class he will tend to be suspicious of him just for being different.

The newly appointed local government officer or civil servant, the technician, the girl or young man striving to rise in the business world – all it would seem need to cultivate a rather colourless neutral voice devoid of all but the merest trace of dialect background. Many – to retain the advantages which the dialect offers on home territory – have in practice become virtually bilingual.

Since dialect is a minority language it is automatically ruled out from formal written communication, the aim of which is to be as widely understood as possible. If therefore you come from an area where dialect is strong it is important to be sure that you know which words and constructions are for local use only, so that these do not become unconsciously absorbed into your formal writing.

B *Colloquialisms*

Colloquialisms are expressions properly employed only in speech (and writing imitating speech) or which can have a certain meaning only in speech (see page 42). Such expressions are suitable to all spoken communication and add flavour to private correspondence (after all in a private letter we do want to sound as if we are talking to the person we are writing to) and other kinds of informal written communication. Their use in formal written communication, however, results in an immediate loss of the dignified register required, though there may be occasions in business correspondence where this is worth while for the sake of the improved friendliness of tone.

C *Slang*

Slang consists in the intentional substitution of an undignified equivalent for the received English expression. Its origin would seem to lie in a combination of dissatisfaction with, or embarrassment over, the standard expression when speaking and a need for novelty. The genius who invents the slang expression is seldom recorded in history. Nobody knows who first substituted *browned-off* for *melancholy* or *disillusioned* in such a sentence as *I'm feeling properly browned-off today*, but it was certainly a *squaddy* (soldier) in World War II; nor who later decided that *browned-off* was losing its novelty and substituted *cheesed-off*.

In moderation, such expressions are a valuable addition to our spoken communication but we have to be careful to use them with the right Rx. It must be remembered too that the conscientious use of up-to-date slang by the kind of Tx who would not normally use such expressions is a kind of inverted pretentiousness and is frequently (and rightly) seen by the Rx as condescension. The use of out-of-date slang has nothing to be said in its favour.

Since slang is, by definition, undignified it is ill suited to formal writing. It becomes no more acceptable by enclosure between inverted commas. *All students are requested to refrain from 'kicking up a row' while in the library* is no improvement on the same words without the inverted commas.

IV PRETENTIOUS LANGUAGE

Pretentious language arises when too much attention is paid to dignity of register. If an over-colloquial style can be described as writing in your shirt sleeves, a pretentious style is writing in medieval armour, so weighed down with words that you can hardly communicate at all. It is the fault of inability to call a spade a spade, so that it becomes *a horticultural implement for the excavation of terrestrial matter*. An obsession with long and unfamiliar words at best is time- and space-wasting, and irritates the Rx with its conceit; at worst it substantially reduces the number of people who can understand what is meant.

The practice of substituting the unfamiliar (but more dignified) for the familiar is on the increase. Barbers long ago became hairdressers (and some hairdressers, friseurs) but undertakers are scarce too today and funeral directors and morticians are to the fore; rat-catchers are more socially acceptable as rodent operators and the London County Council found some years ago that it could improve recruitment of road-sweepers by advertising for street orderlies.

One can hardly object to these little concessions to human vanity; but what is one to make of the doctor, quoted in *The Lancet*, who converted what in colloquial language would be *feeling full* into *sensations interpreted as a satiety associated with ingestion of food*; or the report on the suspected use of poison gas bombs in the Yemen which referred to these as *munitions used to disseminate chemical warfare agents*? What of the teacher who in an article on team teaching produced this impressive-sounding piece of non-communication: *The large group element provides good communication across all small group and individual activities but it also provides a gravitational counter to the centrifugal effect of so much satellite activity*?

In 1976, as a result of an outbreak of stealing in army barracks at Aldershot, the following notice was posted throughout the garrison area:

UNUSUAL PREVALENCE IN THE GARRISON OF THE FOLLOWING OFFENCES – THEFT. THE UNIFICATION OF THIS PREVALENT OFFENCE IS TO BE BORNE IN MIND BY ALL PROPER MILITARY DISCIPLINARY AUTHORITIES, INCLUDING DISTRICT COURTS MARTIAL.

That must have given the troops something to think about.

Some years ago the government of the time interested itself in what was to prove a costly failure, a scheme to import on a large scale from West Africa what were then commonly called 'monkey-nuts'. It was understandable that when referring to these the more dignified term *ground-nuts* was preferred, somewhat surprising that when they were shelled to take up less space on a ship they became *decorticated ground-nuts*, but downright amazing that once this term was established the nuts with the shells still on became *undecorticated ground-nuts*.

Politicians seem to excel at this sort of thing. A recent Commonwealth Relations Secretary made this pronouncement to the House: *We have proposed that while maintaining the objective of comparative outlet, the arrangements for the initial period should be reviewed from time to time and, where necessary, amended to take account of changes in the situation or of world-wide commodity agreements which might have been concluded in the meantime.* But businessmen do not lag far behind. An impresario seeking to interest an actor in an open-air theatre project wrote: *The ultimate success of our venture will be completely dependent on the climatic conditions.* The actor is reported as replying: *I suppose you mean, you hope it won't rain.*

There is nothing wrong with using a long or unfamiliar word if it does a job no other word will do (and provided the Tx satisfies himself the Rx will know how to decode it). There is certainly something wrong with the deliberate use of unfamiliar vocabulary in an attempt to impress the Rx ('blinding with science', as the Services call it).

Even where the word preferred is not long enough or unfamiliar enough to cause any decoding problem for the Rx it is a little odd that so many business men seem automatically to select the longer of a pair of synonyms: *inform, tell; commence, begin* or *start; assist, help; purchase, buy; locate, find; proceed, go.* In certain contexts the longer and very slightly more formal word probably has its justification. *A course of lectures on Cybernetics will commence on January 16th* – it could be argued that here *commence* has a little more authority than *begin* and that the context supports this. But *The new clerk will commence work on January 16th* borders on the pretentious.

It is possible that some English teaching in schools inculcates attitudes towards language that are not helpful in business communication. In essay writing at school the pupil is frequently exhorted to display his width of vocabulary; and an ostentatious display of vocabulary is exactly what pretentious writing is.

V JARGON

The word *jargon* is most useful if reserved for derogatory reference to the special language of a trade, profession, or field of study. We may apply it when we consider a Tx is using a specialised vocabulary, or complicated sentence structures, to impress, or in such a way as to isolate himself from his Rx. Jargon is thus in some ways analogous to both dialect and pretentious writing.

The architect talks of *fenestration* when he means the number of windows in a building; the hospital almoner uses *domiciliary patients* to refer to patients in their own homes and *ambulants* to refer to those that can walk. This is the jargon of vocabulary. Sir Ernest Gower quotes in *The Complete Plain Words* this piece of legal jargon, the jargon of sentence structure: *Separate departments in the same premises are treated as separate premises for this purpose when separate branches of work which are commonly carried on as separate businesses in separate premises are carried on in separate departments in the same premises.*

Two forms of jargon are specially noticeable in business and local or central government communication:

1 use of the specialised vocabulary of a trade, industry, government department etc without explanation even though the Rx is from outside that trade, industry, or department.
2 commercial jargon – fragments of that curious style of writing once called 'business English' that was at its heyday before the 1914–18 war.

If you are forced to use a word from the jargon of your job or technology (because no other word exists) you should enclose it between inverted commas and – if the Rx is unlikely to have met this use of the word before – supply a gloss. Such inverted commas mean 'as we call it' and are not to be confused with those that some people put round slang or colloquial expressions, which seem to mean, 'I cannot be bothered to think of the formal equivalent for this'.

Commercial jargon makes a letter or report seem stilted and old-fashioned. Here are a few examples of the kind of commercial jargon still occasionally encountered, with modern equivalents:

under separate cover	*separately*
we are able to quote you ...	*our quotation is* ...
on Friday next	*next Friday* (but date better)
your valued esteemed order	*your order*
we shall have pleasure in arranging for ...	*we shall arrange for* ...
inst., ult. and *prox.*	give the date

we beg to	meaningless – omit
and oblige	omit
re (or, worse, *in re*)	*about*
per (per goods train)	*by*
as per (as per my)	*as (stated) in*
advise	*inform, tell*
same (return same immediately)	*this, it*
enclosed please find	I enclose
We acknowledge receipt of ... *I have to acknowledge receipt of ...*	} *Thank you for ...*

VI OBJECTIVE AND SUBJECTIVE LANGUAGE

An objective statement tells us about the object that the statement is about. A subjective statement tells us about the reaction of the Tx to the object; i.e. it really tells us about the Tx. Thus if John says: *Mary is pretty* he only appears to be telling us something about Mary. What he is really telling us is something about what he considers prettiness. Harry may say: *Mary is not very pretty*, and George: *Mary is plain*. Mary remains the same – what is emphasised is the differences in the three men's ideas of prettiness. Thus *Mary is pretty* is a subjective statement, and *pretty* in this context a subjective word. *Mary's height is 167 cm* on the other hand is an objective statement; it is not dependent on who says it and is capable of external checking (Mary can be measured). If we substitute for this: *Mary is tall*, we have a statement still objective but considerably less objective than the previous one. Interpretation of this statement depends partly on the Tx's opinion of what constitutes 'tallness' for a girl. A Swede and a Japanese would probably have differing views on this. We may feel therefore that it is the impression of tallness made upon the speaker that is being referred to and that the statement is to this extent subjective. Nevertheless we know that there is substantial agreement about what is meant by 'tall' for a girl, especially within members of the same racial group, and we are prepared to accept 'tall' as a predominantly objective word in this context. For the statement to be completely objective we would have to associate it with a definition of 'tall' girls in terms of measurement (cf. the definition of 'small' boilers on pages 38–9).

It is important then to be aware, both as an Rx and as a Tx, whether the words we are using are subjective, objective, or predominantly objective. There is a place for subjective wording in business, when we are seeking persuasion and to communicate attitudes (in advertising, for example), but the bulk of business communication is factual and demands objective or predominantly objective writing. This is not to say that even in reports (one of the most objective forms of business communication) the occasional subjective word which serves a special purpose may not be employed. For example, in a report, *During this stage of the operation the mixture reaches a temperature of 180°C* is completely objective; but *During this stage of the operation the mixture reaches the dangerously high temperature of 180°C* may be much more helpful to the Rx. The great weakness of subjective wording in business communication is that it intrudes the Tx's opinions and viewpoints into what should be factual matters and the Rx may be betrayed into accepting as a fact what is only an opinion. When you are the Rx you should check carefully to make sure you are not making this mistake yourself.

VII CLICHÉS AND VOGUE WORDS

Vigorous lively language leaps from Tx to Rx demanding his attention. Tired overworked expressions (and that is what clichés are) have little impact on the Rx – he has met them so often before. It is part of the craft of communication to avoid slipping into the use of clichés.

Today imitation of the inventiveness of others is so rapid and so widespread that within a few months what was a new and perhaps effective use of language becomes a cliché, obsessionally used by everybody. Here are a few examples of fairly recent clichés of this kind (some people call contemporary clichés 'vogue words'): the student will probably be able to add his own up-to-date examples without great difficulty.

affluent permissive society
(major) breakthrough
(in) depth
dichotomy
to escalate
expertise
factor (as *consideration of the price factor*)
guidelines
hassle
image (as *company image*)
massive (*build-up* etc.)
to mastermind

meaningful (dialogue)
mystique
ongoing (situation)
parameters
to phase out
rationalisation
(broad) spectrum
spin-off
(to go) upmarket
viable

A vogue word speech usage which the author finds particularly irritating is the obsessional employment of *hopefully* to mean not 'full of hope' but 'it is to be hoped that'.

Vogue words are by their nature infectious and it is difficult to avoid picking them up. It is worth while making the effort to avoid them. Those who freely sprinkle their speech (and writing) with vogue words always show a lack of individuality and often give the impression that they are employing a fashionable vocabulary to cover up a lack of substance in what they have to say.

Older clichés are still popular with senior staff and it is necessary for new entrants to the business and government worlds to familiarise themselves with expressions such as *Hobson's choice* or *He'll not set the Thames on fire* – not so that they can use them themselves but so that they will understand their meaning when employed by others (see Exercise G).

VIII SUMMARY OF RECOMMENDATIONS

It will be seen that in choosing his words the conscientious communicator has to give consideration to a large number of criteria, some of them possibly contradictory. His first consideration must always be to ensure that meaning is conveyed as exactly as possible by the words selected; the points raised in this chapter are therefore of secondary importance. These points may be summarised as the attempt to choose words appropriate to

1 the type of subject matter
2 the circumstances in which communication is taking place
3 the Rx – his educational background, previous knowledge of the subject, likely width of vocabulary etc.

The communicator should:

1 decide whether objective or subjective language is called for and select his words according to his decision
2 decide the degree of formality or informality required and select words of suitable register to achieve this
3 decide the tone he wishes his communication to have and select words that maintain this
4 endeavour to use words freshly and vigorously, avoiding clichés
5 at all times keep his Rx in mind and seek the words that will best suit that particular Rx
6 prefer the simplest words that will achieve all these aims.

IX EXERCISES

Exercise A

The following is adapted from a letter in a Malayan newspaper. Rephrase the young man's letter for him so that it is consistently dignified, but not pretentious, in register.

I am handsome Sikh teenager whose betrothed is beseeching him to purchase motor vehicle. At last at great expense I am proud possessor of 100 per cent car but my driving lacks proficiency. Sometimes I am exchanging brake for exhilerator and other times I am passing wrong side oncoming traffic at great rapidity.

My beloved covers eyes with hands and moans softly and now declares she will be accompanying me only by public transport or Shanker's pony. Shall I bow to feminine whim or seek Another to occupy hot seat?

Exercise B

Rewrite the following in a more consistent register.

Whatever may have been true of the early prospectors who began to poke about in the earth for oil in a slap-happy fashion nearly a century ago, nowadays we try to hunt it out scientifically. Often the oil is hidden quite a way down and before drilling is done we have to make scientific observations and measurements on the earth's surface to try to spot where the oil is. First the geologist gets going and tries to put his finger on those regions where he reckons oil is likely to have piled up in underground beds of rock or sand. But often the geologist cannot get enough 'gen' to go on because the rock formations are completely covered up. Then the geophysicist comes in on it. His first ploy is to measure the force of gravity as accurately as possible over the whole area where the presence of oil seems 'on'. This is because oil-bearing rock is usually denser and therefore has a bit more gravitational pull than the rocks lying above it. He cannot as yet pin-point the oil itself but he can get a hazy idea of which rocks might contain oil.

Oil fields have an awkward habit of turning up in tricky places, rendering field operations frequently hazardous. Much prospecting is done in the 'back of beyond' where jungle and swamp make the going pretty slow. It says a lot for the gravity meters employed that they stand up to the belting they get on the job and yet are capable of such delicate measurement.

Exercise C

Consider the following pairs of words. Indicate for each a context in which you would prefer the first to the second, and one in which you would prefer the second to the first. Are there any pairs where you would prefer one word to the other in all contexts? Justify your answers.

think	give	show	start	make
consider	donate	evince	initiate	render

end	try	watch	necessary	get
terminate	attempt	observe	requisite	obtain

Exercise D

1 Which words in the following passage do you consider subjective?
2 List the *facts* you know about the COPY-BOX 5 after reading the passage.

The widely-acclaimed COPY-BOX 5 produces perfect copies in up to five colours, more cheaply than any other duplicator. Operation is extremely simple and wonderfully clear copies result. Paper pressure can be manually adjusted and it copies on all thicknesses of paper in sizes up to 20 × 30 cm. The duplicator is supplied with foolproof automatic paper feed and an easily removable damping pad. The large-capacity fluid tank is pump-fed, exactly the right degree of damping being achieved by regulation of the accurate control disc.

The COPY-BOX 5 is clean, fast, and remarkably versatile. Elegantly styled and finished in corrosion-resistant enamel (black or cream) this precision-built appliance will form a handsome and valuable addition to your office equipment.

Exercise E

Write an *objective* description of one of the following in about 150 words:

1 a relative or friend
2 your home town or village
3 your vehicle
4 your usual classroom.

Exercise F

Write a short speech (about 200 words) for one of the following occasions, *to include the maximum number of clichés*:

1 A distinguished Old Boy presenting the prizes at his old school
2 A senior executive urging harder work and higher production from his factory
3 A shop steward on 'Management and the Workers'
4 A politician on 'The Future of England'.

Exercise G

What is the meaning of the following figurative expressions, now clichés? Do you know the origin of any of them?

A Parthian shot
To cross the Rubicon
A nest-egg
On the knees of the gods
A flash in the pan
A bone of contention
The fourth estate
The thin end of the wedge
Caviare to the general
Pearls before swine
An Achilles' heel
A square peg in a round hole
An olive branch
The devil's advocate

To view the world through rose-tinted spectacles
A red herring
To take the bull by the horns
To change horses in mid-stream
Between Scylla and Charybdis
To go cap in hand
Making bricks without straw
Under the aegis of
To have too many irons in the fire
To rob Peter to pay Paul
A sop to Cerberus

Exercise H

Comment on the following with special reference to the use of inverted commas.

1 This is a useful 'gadget' that will probably prove to have a considerable sales potential in the home market.
2 The highly polished surface is first lightly 'etched' with acid.
3 I am not entirely satisfied that the method by which we obtained this information was completely 'above-board'; there does seem an element of the 'wangle' in what was done.
4 We send out 'crews', groups of operators specially trained to make geophysical survey in the field, at regular intervals.
5 We should be very grateful if you would give the 'tip-off' when the process is ready for development.
6 A group of parasites of particular interest to this department is that causing 'scours' in sheep. Losses from this disease can be reduced by phenothiazene applied by drenching or, in pellet form, by means of a 'balling gun'.
7 On the fifty-third flight, four more approaches to the stall were made with the aircraft 'clean'.
8 This time the stall, or 'G break', was large and abrupt, causing the aircraft to drop but with its nose still up in the flying position.
9 The word 'stock' is derived from Old English *stocc*. His word stock is less than 3000 words.
10 We signed for the goods 'unexamined'. We signed for the goods unexamined.

Exercise I

Improve the expression of the following sentences giving special attention to (*a*) suitability and consistency of register, (*b*) avoidance of pretentious language, jargon, and clichés.

1 Anthony in the funeral oration tends to down Caesar for his vaulting ambition.

2 In this modern world too many people devote their leisure to things like television, the cinema, and football, where they have everything laid on for them.

3 Re your order *Sexual Customs in Togoland* of 15th ult. we beg to advise this volume out of print.

4 Customers are requested to obtain a check from the waitress and to present same at cash-desk prior to departure.

5 Maximum expedition in plant installation is envisaged subject to early site availability and adequate recruitment of personnel.

6 We thank you for your esteemed order for quality rose trees which will enjoy our most careful attention. Notification will be forwarded a few days prior to dispatch.

7 *Extension to Boxhead Golf Club*

We would be pleased to receive tender from you in respect of the above. Enclosed please find specification, tender form, tender envelope, and Drawing No. S26/1/2 in connection therewith.

8 This agreement is likely to be instrumental in effecting no inconsiderable amelioration of present conditions of employment of company executives not least with reference to the remuneration factor.

9 Although we have left no stone unturned in our investigation into the causes of the delay in forwarding this consignment success has been conspicuous by its absence. We deeply regret the inconvenience inevitably occasioned you by our procrastination.

10 Mr Tompkins has been employed in this department in a subordinate capacity for six months and has done his job pretty well; it would be a good idea to provide him with an opportunity to demonstrate his potential for initiative.

Exercise J

The words *lady dog*, *edifice*, *inquire* may be described as 'genteelisms' for *bitch*, *building*, *ask*. Give genteelisms, one for each, for the following 'normal' words:

read sofa toothpaste servant before underclothing boarder jam go stop

[*Royal Society of Arts, English Language, Stage III*]

Chapter 6

Concise Wording

I THE IMPORTANCE OF CONCISE WRITING IN BUSINESS COMMUNICATIONS

When a young man working in an office is first entrusted with dictating letters on his firm's behalf or is called upon for his first written report, it is natural enough that he tends to spread himself – short letters seem inadequate letters, a short report seems an insignificant report. Nevertheless, this tendency should be resisted from the start; the habit of verbosity, once entered on, is difficult to shake off, and in fact grows more pronounced as the years go by. Verbosity in written business communication has nothing to be said in its favour. Conciseness, on the other hand, offers the following advantages:

1 reduction in typist time
2 saving in paper, and wear and tear of typewriters and ribbons
3 saving in storage space when material has to be filed
4 reduction in printing costs when material has to be printed
5 saving in reading time for the Rx (the most important consideration).

Conciseness must come last of the points to be considered when choosing our words – accuracy, clarity, and appropriateness of language must never be sacrificed to brevity. In practice, however, observation of sound principles in selecting words – particularly discrimination between synonyms and avoidance of pretentious language and jargon – usually takes the writer well on the way to maximum conciseness. After that, it is mostly a matter of substituting for the initial tendency to pad out what one has to say an awareness that words are precious and easily wasted, and the determination not to use any word that is not doing a necessary job.

II THE TRUE MEASURE OF CONCISENESS

We usually judge the length of what we write by the number of words used. This can be deceptive. *The lateral fenestration of domestic accommodation units* is only seven words long while *the number of windows in the sides of houses* is nine words long. These figures are irrelevant when conciseness is thought of in terms of the advantages listed above. The relevant count is that there are fifty-five letters and spaces in the first sentence and forty-four in the second. The pretentious sentence is not shorter than the simple one – it is 25 per cent longer. Except where we are preparing copy for a certain limited space (in an advertising block for example) we shall probably never count letters and spaces; but we should always remember that the more convenient word count is not a reliable measure of conciseness if we are addicted to long words.

III REDUNDANCY

Grammarians distinguish various types of redundancy and give these special names. For communication in business it is sufficient to recognise the types that exist and to avoid them.

1 The simplest form is where a second (and therefore redundant) word is used to give meaning already conveyed by a first word. *He arrived tired and weary. He has returned back to the office. The reason why ... is because ...*

2 A second type occurs when words are used to specify something which can already be understood from the rest of the sentence. *As they strolled back the sun was setting in the west.*

3 A third type consists in the addition of adjectives to nouns that need no adjective – *actual facts*; *definite decisions*; *serious dangers* – and intensifiers added to words that should not be intensified – *very perfect*; *very perceptible*; *extremely dead.*

4 A fourth category is brought about by the meaningless introduction of adverbs or adverbial phrases. *Definitely* and *of course* are widely used in this way.

In the days before the death penalty was discontinued in 1965, Sir Alan Herbert dealt with *definitely* in inimitable fashion: 'I offer a prize to the first foreman of a jury to announce a verdict of *definitely guilty* and another to the judge who informs the prisoner that he will be *definitely hanged by the neck until he is very definitely dead.*'

Of course is often tucked into a sentence with no motive at all except to pad it out, but sometimes produces the irritating effect of making the Rx appear an ignorant fool: *This matter should, of course, have been dealt with at branch office level* (and nobody but you would have thought otherwise).

Relatively, comparatively, unduly, although capable of precise meaning, are frequently used in contexts where they can have no meaning. *The new process is comparatively inexpensive* means nothing unless the cost of the old process has been mentioned. *Delivery of this order has been unduly delayed* is meaningless unless we expected delivery to be delayed but not for so long as it was. In sentences of the type, popular in business and government circles, *Our research department is actively engaged in investigation of the cause of this phenomenon*, *actively* is redundant as it is not possible to be inactively engaged in an activity.

In the sentence *Man's direct influence on geography is really quite negligible*, *quite* is ambiguous. If it is intended to mean 'completely, entirely' it is redundant because *negligible* includes this idea; if it is intended to mean 'tending towards, somewhat' it is redundant because such a qualification of *negligible* is meaningless. Removal of *quite* necessitates removal of *really* (independently redundant, anyhow, because there is no distinction to be made between *quite* and *really quite*). Two words are saved, and the sentence gains in vigour and impact.

5 Finally, there is legal redundancy. Lawyers must be particularly careful to avoid ambiguity; redundancy is a clumsy but automatic check on ambiguity; legal documents are therefore deliberately repetitive, avoiding generalisations and naming each specific instance.

Thus in typical bye-laws controlling behaviour in a public park we are told that we must not *(a) remove, cut, or displace any soil, turf, or plant, (b) pluck any bud, blossom, flower, or leaf of any tree, shrub, or plant.*

This cumbersome kind of writing arises from the attempt by the man drafting the regulations to envisage every possible infringement and to deal with it specifically so that no loophole of escape exists for the offender. It is a style – whatever its merits or demerits for the legal profession – not to be imitated by businessmen. Local and central government officers have frequently to write to members of the public about matters that are the subject of such regulations. There is no need to copy the redundancies of the original, except where interpretation of the legal point involved depends on the exact wording.

IV CIRCUMLOCUTION

Redundancies are easily enough detected in revision and, even if overlooked, will cause only minor inflation of your wording. Circumlocution is altogether more serious. Its essence is an unconscious preference for the longwinded and roundabout over the short and direct. It arises deliberately rather than accidentally and runs right through a man's writing, and often his speech as well. It is closely allied to pretentiousness; the man who employs a pretentious vocabulary will almost always be addicted also to circumlocution. It is important to detect the symptoms early; circumlocution quickly becomes a lifetime habit.

Here are some tendencies which should be looked on as warnings that you are moving that way.

1 Preference for

in this connection	*with regard to*
in connection with	*as regards*
in regard to	*with reference to*
in respect of	*as to*

instead of their simple prepositional equivalents:

> *I am writing to you in connection with your application ...* for
> *I am writing to you about your application ...*
> *Your estimate as to the number to be ordered ...* for
> *Your estimate of the number to be ordered ...*

Use of these expressions, especially as a lead into material, often results in gross inflation of the wording:

> *With reference to your Order 591/A, these goods were despatched on the 15th ult.* for
> *We sent your Order 591/A, on May 15th*

(80 letters and spaces against 37).

2 Compulsive use of *case* and *instance*:

> *A large number of students have left the College this year, in many cases before taking their examinations* – for
> *A large number of students have left the College this year, many before taking their examinations.*

The substitution of *instance* for *case* does not improve such sentences.

Particularly absurd are unnecessary uses of *case* where its meaning as 'a container' is brought to mind by the context:

> *These were very large ships for the period carrying twenty or more rowers and cargoes of cattle in many cases.*

3 Preference for

> *as/so far as ... is concerned*

from ... viewpoint/angle/standpoint/point of view
in view of/owing to/in spite of/the fact that ...

Thus *This post is not so well paid* can become
  This post is not so attractive so far as salary is concerned or
  This post is not so attractive from the remuneration viewpoint.
  As your application was not received before the closing date ... becomes
  In view of the fact that your application was not received before the closing date ...

Although becomes *in spite of the fact that*; *because* is replaced by *owing to the fact that* or – often and ungrammatically – *due to the fact that.*

4 Love of abstract nouns. It is difficult enough to be sure that the Rx decodes as the Tx wants him to even when they are dealing in concrete nouns. When the Tx writes *table* he has a certain picture of a table in his mind unlikely to be identical with the table that comes into the Rx's mind when he reads the word, since no two tables are absolutely alike. The semantic problem becomes much greater as soon as the communicators start using abstract words. It is curious, then, that a certain type of Tx will deliberately force abstract nouns into what he writes, even if it means a longer sentence, e.g.

  This material is of a resilient character for
  This material is resilient or, better,
  This resilient material ...
  Owing to the expensive nature of this operation ... for
  As this operation is expensive ...
  Completion of this contract should be delayed until the position in regard to availability of raw materials has been clarified (Note: *completion, position, availability, in regard to*) for
  This contract should not be completed until we are sure that the raw materials will be available
  Admission must be made of a certain lack of due carefulness on the part of our staff in this connection (Note: *admission, lack, part, in this connection*) for
  We must admit our staff were rather careless about this.

5 Excessive use of the passive voice. The verb is the mainspring of the sentence. As its name implies (from Latin *verbum*, a word) it is *the* word. As we have just seen, emphasis on nouns, especially abstract nouns, at the expense of verbs weakens our sentences. Adjectives in turn weaken nouns

(they have been called 'the enemy of the noun'). The verb is weakened if it is put into the passive voice. The passive is favoured for reports because it is impersonal. Just because it is impersonal it is unsuitable for much business communication. It puts a distance between Tx and Rx (see also page 70).

The passive is usually at least one word longer than the active equivalent, and can, especially when associated with abstract nouns, produce considerable circumlocution.

ACTIVE *Mr Jones will pay this account next month*. (8 words)

PASSIVE *This account will be paid next month by Mr Jones*. (10 words)

PASSIVE WITH CIRCUMLOCUTION *Payment of this account will be made by Mr Jones next month*. (12 words)

ACTIVE *In cricket, the batsman sometimes hits a six*. (8 words)

PASSIVE *In cricket, a six is sometimes hit by the batsman*. (10 words)

PASSIVE WITH CIRCUMLOCUTION *The hitting of sixes is an activity occasionally engaged in by cricketers when acting in the capacity of batsman*. (19 words)

Technicians, with their long experience of having to write laboratory reports in the impersonal passive (*The crucible was weighed* rather than *I weighed the crucible*), are particularly inclined to make too much use of this construction in situations where it has no advantages.

V VERBIAGE

Verbiage is a convenient term for reference to a particularly cumbersome accumulation of words in an attempt to communicate. Verbiage will include redundancies and circumlocution but its characteristic is a sustained disproportion between the number of words used and the amount of information conveyed. It most commonly results from a combination of the desire to pad out material to make it seem more important, or to impress the Rx with a grand manner, and sheer linguistic ineptitude (see Example 1 below). Occasionally, as in Example 2, it appears to be employed consciously, with the aim of disguising from the Rx how little is really being said.

Whatever its source, verbiage is a use of words that is diametrically opposed to communication principles.

EXAMPLE 1 – an extract from a schools circular issued by a local education authority:

GAMES. *In view of present pitch conditions attributable to the long spell of dry weather, staff responsible for games (particularly competitive matches) may find it advisable to pay particular attention to this aspect with a view to deciding in connection with any particular activity whether it can be proceeded with with safety to the pupils or should be changed to a practice or should be postponed.*

Rephrasing to remove the verbiage reduces this to less than half the length (30 words against 66) and greatly increases the readability:

During the present dry spell, staff responsible for games should assure themselves before starting any game that the pitch can be used with safety. This applies particularly to competitive matches.

EXAMPLE 2 – an announcement by an estate agent:

The property is joined on to one other similar character property on one side, but otherwise is equivalent to being detached.

In other words, the property is semidetached.

VI CONDENSATION

So far we have considered conciseness only as a matter of not putting in unnecessary words. For most communication purposes this is all we have to worry about. When we are making a précis, or reducing advertising material to fit into a limited space, we may have to adopt more positive measures to condense our wording. Condensation consists in a combination of three principal devices:

1 substitution of single words for phrases
2 substitution of phrases for clauses
3 elimination of adjectives and adverbs (and adjectival and adverbial phrases and clauses) not essential to meaning.

1 WORDS FOR PHRASES. Substitution of single words for phrases is usually only possible if the initial selection of words has been a little clumsy. As we saw in Chapter 3 one of the principal advantages of choosing the right word for the job is that it saves using a phrase. Thus *The alterations were carried out with the least possible degree of interruption of normal business* can be more concisely expressed as *The alterations were carried out with minimum interruption of normal business.* This in turn can be expressed still more concisely as *The alterations were effected with*

minimum interruption of normal business provided it is felt that *effected* is an appropriate word for the subject matter and type of Rx.

2 PHRASES FOR CLAUSES. *This employee, who has now passed his qualifying examinations, should be considered for a Grade III appointment* can be slightly shortened by substituting a participial phrase for the adjectival clause – *This employee, having passed his qualifying examinations, should be considered for a Grade III appointment* – and considerably shortened, at the expense of an insignificant loss of detail, as *This employee, now qualified, should be considered for a Grade III appointment.*

3 ELIMINATION OF NON-ESSENTIAL ADJECTIVES AND ADVERBS. We have seen (pages 86–7) that adjectives, adverbs, and adverbial phrases are frequently redundant as used in business communication. Where they (and adjectival phrases and clauses and adverbial clauses) although not redundant do no more than add descriptive detail, they may be omitted to condense a piece of writing. Thus in the first example above, *normal* can be omitted; and in the second example, *now qualified.*

Somerset Maugham is reported as having advised a young writer to go through what he had written striking out every adjective. Reduction in the number of adjectives, and adverbs, probably improves any piece of writing; all that can be left out without loss of essential meaning should be left out. Factual communication particularly gains by this treatment as the objectivity of a passage rises with the elimination of qualifying words, which are those where subjective elements are most to the fore.

VII EXERCISES

Exercise A

Comment on the following expressions:

    foot-pedal   assembled together   renovated as new   sole monopoly
    timeclock   facilitates easier assembly   leading protagonist
    the larger majority   as from   as and from.

Exercise B

Today is 1 March. Approximately when will it be:

   1 soon

2 in the future
3 in the near future
4 in the very near future
5 in the foreseeable future?

If you find difficulty answering this question, what have you learned?

Exercise C

Shorten the following passages by removal of redundancies. The first is another extract from park bye-laws; the second is from a committee report on a proposed NATO nuclear fleet.

1 A person shall not affix any bill, placard, or notice to or upon any wall or fence in or enclosing the park, or to or upon any tree, or plant, or to or upon any part of any building, barrier, or railing, or any seat, or of any other erection or ornament in the park.

2 The size of the nuclear resources at the disposal of the NATO Allies is so considerable in quantity that any increase in it is superfluous. This would only increase the existing 'overkill' for which from a military point of view there is no need whatsoever.

Exercise D

Shorten, and increase the vigour of, the following sentences.

1 A relatively sharp increase in prices has been apparent during the week.
2 A marked improvement in quality has been effected since the introduction of quality control was brought about.
3 Destruction of the entire central section of the building took place as a result of the conflagration.
4 Refusal by management to consider an outlined scheme for staggered working hours which had been put forward by the works committee was a cause of grave dissatisfaction on the part of the latter.
5 The application of time and motion study to this section will, of course, result in appreciable improvement from the production standpoint.

Exercise E

Rephrase the following sentences to remove redundancies and circumlocutions.

1 Diesel and electric engines were substituted in place of steam-

powered engines on the railways during the period of the late 1950s.

2 Malnutrition is widespread in China and many thousands of children die at a young age.

3 The need for consumer protection organisations has become very necessary over the last few years.

4 The other methods of financing available are too innumerable to mention.

5 In some societies a share must be first obtained by accumulating dividends before the customer can become a voting member.

6 It is fact that at this time of year there are more deaths on the road caused by drunken driving than at any other time of the year.

7 Finally, to conclude my remarks, I want to pay tribute to all those who, unnoticed and unrewarded, have unobtrusively helped throughout the year with nobody until this moment to draw attention to the support and assistance they have rendered the organisation at all times.

8 The subject of our lecture tonight will be about cybernetics.

9 We must apologise for the delay in delivering your order the cause of which was due to staff absences in the packing department as a result of the present epidemic of influenza, which is as you know extremely widespread, and has forced several of our men to take time off from work.

10 The situation of these exporting countries is in a most advantageous position in so far as foreign trade is concerned as they are so placed as to have easy access to other countries.

Exercise F

Reduce the following passage of 290 words by at least 100 words by removal of redundancies, circumlocutions, and other unnecessary wording only.

Many stories and tales of a most exciting kind are told of how in the old days of the past men used to adopt all sorts of various disguises in order to penetrate, without being recognised, into the factories of their competitors to try to steal their competitors' secrets that were jealously guarded. Even in the nineteenth century this was not by any manner of means entirely unknown as a method of procedure, and it is said that not more than five people only were ever allowed into one of Bessemer's early factories. Nowadays, information about new processes and products is usually widely published to all concerned or interested and we do not have to adopt measures of such a desperate nature to be in a position to obtain it.

On the other hand, there is a great deal more of it to be had. Thousands of widely scattered firms and institutes all over the world are carrying out research into finding out about the applications of science in industry and it is vitally essential that results are made known to the right people relatively quickly. More and more scientists with their long tradition, stretching back for so many years, of prompt and speedy publication are coming increasingly into industry. Industrial processes are developing all the time a more and more complex character as the years go by. In fact we have actually reached a stage when a great deal of knowledge is required to be in the possession of the makers of our presentday high quality products. It is a sobering thought, one which is bound to make us seriously consider the present situation, that any electrician of today now knows more about electricity than Faraday did in his time.

Exercise G

This passage of 130 words can be halved by condensation, and removal of redundancies. How near can you get to 65 words?

Prices which can be maintained at a constant and unchanging level are the essential prerequisite to peace in the industrial world. Increases in the workers' pay-packets which coincide with upward trends in prices provide no solution at all. The question we have to ask ourselves is, 'Can we have, at one and the same time, simultaneously full employment, prices held at a steady level, and negotiations freely entered upon for increases in the workers' wages?' In my opinion, I think that the aim of seeing that each and every member of the community has employment should be removed from the sphere of party politics. If we are unable to achieve all three of these very desirable goals that we are all aiming at, let us at least achieve that one.

Part II

Chapter 7

Summaries

I PRACTICAL APPLICATIONS

The most obvious occasion when concise writing is necessary is the preparation of a summary.

The student tends to think of summarising exclusively in terms of the form he knows best – précis for examinations; but he will probably later on meet many practical applications in his work. It is true that précis for examinations is governed by certain conventions – notably that it is written in continuous prose, not note form, and that it avoids the words of the original – which are not obligatory when preparing summaries in the course of business; but all types of summary are likely to be better executed as a result of training in précis.

Précis for examinations is almost invariably set in the form of the reduction of a short continuous passage to a third or a quarter of its length (occasionally, a fifth). Précis in business is more likely to be of correspondence, of a report, of evidence – material not already in continuous prose form. Illustration of the kinds of minor differences of technique necessary for handling this sort of material is provided in Chapter 8 under the heading: 'Précis of correspondence' (pp. 138–143). Where material already in continuous prose has to be changed to a more concentrated form to save reading time for a senior executive, this is likely to be lengthy material (e.g. papers read before learned societies, articles in magazines, or even whole books, or sections of them, relevant to a firm's products), and the reduction required much greater than for précis, perhaps to one-tenth or even less. Reductions of this order are usually referred to as *abstracts*. Where material is concentrated still further (as would normally be necessary with a book) the term *digest* is often used. The particular type of highly concentrated summary which is prepared by a solicitor to put the facts of a case before a barrister is called a *brief*. This word is also used with extended meaning; for example, the notes prepared by a secretary for the chairman of a committee so that the latter will have an adequate grasp of the main facts about an item for discussion may also be referred to, at least colloquially, as a 'brief'

As the kind of summary required in business is usually much more concentrated than the examination précis it is useful to practise reducing some passages to a ninth or a tenth of the original. A strongly recommended exercise is to reduce a passage first to a third, then to a third again – thus producing a reduction to a ninth in two stages. The passage can then be further reduced to a single sentence of, say, twenty-five words (see A Worked Example, p. 103, and Exercises).

The situation also often arises where material has to be reworded so that it takes up slightly less room with no loss of content (to fit space left for copy in an advertising block, or to avoid extending a pamphlet by another four pages for the sake of an extra couple of hundred words, for example). Such tasks are very like the final stages of précis-writing and are the easier for previous précis practice.

Thus it can be seen that the examination type précis is not just an end in itself, but provides valuable training for various types of practical summary. It also encourages the utmost economy in the use of words, and that is a valuable attitude to acquire for anybody who expects to make much use of words in his business career.

11 PRÉCIS IN EXAMINATIONS

The essence of précis in examinations is the seizing of the original author's principal facts and arguments and their reproduction in the student's own words (except where use of the original wording is specifically permitted) as sound continuous prose of a length prescribed by the examiner. To achieve this successfully the student must be competent in three aspects of communication.

1 He must be able to understand the original passage in detail and also to form an overall view of its principal purpose. His ability as an Rx is under review.

2 He must be able to divide the author's points into the relevant (which must be included) and the irrelevant (which must be excluded). The relevant he must further divide into the essential and those which are relevant but not essential; and balance the proportions of his version according to the priorities he allocates to these points. His powers of logic and organisation are under review.

3 He must reduce the material to the requisite word limit. His facility with words and especially his capacity to write concisely are under review.

When we remember that the resultant summary must also satisfy the examiner as a piece of well-written prose of a high standard of 'correctness', we can see that précis in examinations represents a very demanding test of a student's linguistic ability.

III A STEP-BY-STEP METHOD

1 Check the instructions given. Is reported speech compulsory? Is a title asked for? *In not more than 150 words* means just what it says. *In approximately 150 words* may be taken as meaning in 140–160 words. If no word limit is mentioned it is usual to assume that reduction to one-third of the original length is required.

2 Read the passage through quickly to grasp the general sense. Reread if necessary.

3 Read through slowly, noting the divisions of subject matter in the passage and trying to give meaning to every word. Some students prefer to write down headings for the principal divisions; others can get the outline clear in their heads without writing anything down (see page 105). Whichever method is used, this stage must not be shirked.

4 Give a title to the passage. This should be specific, not vague, and should cover all the subject matter. It is not likely to be a one-word title, but rather a phrase that expresses the whole passage in miniature. Even if a title is not asked for, you should still try to form one, if only for your own benefit to ensure that you understand what is the essence of the passage.

5 Some examining bodies expect the source of the original to be incorporated in the précis. (It may be assumed that this is required if the examiner himself shows the source of the passage he sets.)

There are two ways of doing this:

(a) by starting with a form of words such as: *James Dogsbody in an article in 'The Times' of 4th May 19.. writes that ...*

(b) by a title such as: *Précis of an extract from an article by James Dogsbody in 'The Times' of 4th May 19...*

With the second method, if a title has been asked for by the examiner a descriptive title will have to be linked on as well by a connective such as 'concerning' or 'referring to'. Thus the final title may become (cumbersome but impeccable):

Précis of an extract from an article by James Dogsbody in 'The Times' of 4th May 19.. concerning the high incidence of shoplifting in self-service grocery stores.

The second method *(b)* has the advantage of not consuming any of the permitted words (titles are not included in the total of words); the first *(a)* has the special disadvantage that unless a present tense verb is used, as in the example, the writer is committed to past tense reported speech.

6 It is usual to summarise spoken material (e.g. an extract from a speech) in past tense reported speech, i.e. as if introduced by a clause such as *The speaker said that*, though these words need not be actually included unless to show source by method *(a)* above. A few examining bodies expect this for written material too. (It may be assumed that this is what is required when 'reported speech' is specified in the instructions.)

Otherwise, for written material there is no reason why present tense reported speech should not be used, i.e. as if introduced by a clause such as *The writer says that*.

For further distinction between past tense and present tense reported speech see Appendix II.

7 Write out a rough draft. Except for the few examinations where use of the original wording is permitted, this should be in your own words, substituting simpler words for unusual ones in the original. Material should be selected on the basis of the categories: essential; relevant but not essential; irrelevant. Endeavour to make some reference to all material that is not irrelevant to the main theme. A good rough draft is always rather longer than is required.

8 Avoid questions, and convert rhetorical questions into statements.

9 Change the order of the material if it is to your advantage to do so.

10 Briefly, everything to do with expression is your responsibility; everything to do with subject matter, the original author's. Thus you must not change his 'facts' even if you know them to be wrong, or indicate your disagreement with his viewpoint or arguments.

11 Illustrations, examples, analogies, must be omitted except where they take up a very large part of the original or are essential to the argument. Particularised statements should be replaced by generalisations, specific examples by a statement of the tendency that the example illustrates.

12 Omit all figurative language.

13 It is useful to write the rough draft on alternate lines to leave room for revisions.

14 Check the number of words in the rough draft and reduce to the required limit. Every effort should be made to achieve this by rewording, not by removal of material. The ways of achieving conciseness discussed in Chapter 6 will be useful at this stage. Rewriting of complete sentences is usually more effective than the removal of a word here and a word there. A running score of words saved should be kept in the margin and the

process continued until this equals the number of words your draft was above the limit.

15 Reread your revised draft. Check that it still makes sense, is grammatically sound, in full sentence form, properly punctuated, and is not too jerky. With a considerable reduction there is bound to be some loss of smoothness, as the passage is now overpacked with facts. This effect can be minimised by the use of connectives, avoiding very short sentences, and keeping the paragraphs of normal length. Avoid the common mistake of converting each paragraph of the original into a separate little paragraph in your shortened version. Short passages can be summarised as one paragraph and no examination is likely to produce a passage long enough to require more than three paragraphs for its summary.

16 Write out a fair version of your précis, making further improvements in the expression if this can be achieved without adding words.

17 Check the number of words in the final version and write this at the end of the précis.

18 In examinations, the timing of the précis is important; if more time is spent on it than was allowed for by the examiner, insufficient time will be left for completing the rest of the paper. A useful formula to give an approximate idea of the time that should be spent is 15 minutes for each 50 words of completed précis. Thus a reduction to approximately 150 words should be completed in 45 minutes.

IV A WORKED EXAMPLE

NOTE: The student working on his own is strongly recommended to attempt the following exercise for himself before reading the notes and model answers that follow. The complete exercise should take not more than 1¼ hours.

A The Exercise

Make a précis of the following passage

    (a) in not more than 150 words
    (b) in not more than 60 words
    (c) in one sentence not exceeding 25 words:

Whatever may be its wider implications, the explosion of a hydrogen bomb is, for the meteorologist, simply another atmospheric disturbance and therefore to be classed with certain rare natural occurrences, such as a volcanic eruption. But there are certain features of a manmade disturbance that require special examination.

As with all events on this scale, it is impossible to describe what happens in detail, but we can be reasonably sure of the main effects, and the most impressive of these arise from pressure waves.

The immediate result of the detonation is that the air surrounding the bomb is raised very rapidly to an enormously high temperature. The hot gases expand violently as a great fireball, compressing the air around them into what is called a shock wave, or 'blast wave', that is responsible for much of the terrible destructive power of the weapon.

Another kind of wave arises because of the weight of the air. The force of the explosion lifts the atmosphere around the bomb and causes what are known as 'gravity waves', resembling ordinary ocean waves. Waves of this type are not normally felt by human beings, and they have no effect on weather.

The most significant feature of a nuclear weapon is the production of radioactivity. When the weapon is detonated near the ground a vast mass of highly radioactive matter, solid and gaseous, is thrown upwards. Because of the high temperature, the gigantic 'bubble' ascends to very great heights, possibly 35 000 metres or more.

The heavy debris soon falls to earth again, but the fine dust settles very slowly and drifts for many miles with the wind. The result is that a large oval area, equal in size to the whole of Wales, is contaminated by radioactive debris. The gases and the smallest particles remain high in the atmosphere.

Changes of speed and direction of wind mean that clouds of radioactive dust and gases are broken up and drift in different directions at different heights. If the main mass continued to move, say, westwards in a wind of 80 km/h it would, in theory, travel round the world in about three weeks, but in reality it is far more likely that it would be caught up in local wind systems, and it is almost impossible to predict its path.

Some of the radioactivity decays rapidly, but much is long-lived and remains potentially dangerous for considerable periods.

The Daily Telegraph

B *Notes on passage*

1 This passage falls into three principal divisions – a short introduction establishing the topic (i.e. the atmospheric effects of a hydrogen bomb

explosion); the pressure waves; the production of radioactivity. The second division is subdivided into 'blast' waves and 'gravity' waves, and the third has three subsections – heavy debris; fine dust; gases and smallest particles. About this last subsection further information is supplied, concerning its unpredictability of movement, which is important since we are also told that some of the radioactivity remains active for a long time. This is the kind of grasp of the subject matter and its divisions that should be achieved in the first reading.

The structure and content of the passage could be represented by the following outline:

1 Introduction

Meteorologist, to introduce topic of special atmospheric effects of a hydrogen bomb explosion.

2 Pressure Waves

  (a) Blast waves – how caused – principal destructive force

  (b) Gravity waves – how caused – harmless.

3 Radioactivity

  (a) Heavy debris – soon falls (i.e. vertically)

  (b) Fine dust – contaminates large oval area

  (c) Gases and smallest particles – drift unpredictably with wind – radioactivity remains dangerous.

2 It is now easy to formulate a title for the passage – 'The Atmospheric Effects of a Hydrogen Bomb Explosion'. A typically unsatisfactory title (because not sufficiently specific) would be 'The Hydrogen Bomb'.

C *Model answers*

The Atmospheric Effects of a Hydrogen Bomb Explosion

1 To the meteorologist a hydrogen bomb explosion is just another atmospheric disturbance, comparable with a volcano erupting, though it does produce certain special effects.

Two types of pressure wave result, a 'blast' wave occasioned by the rapid expansion of hot gases round the bomb, and a 'gravity' wave caused by the raising of the atmosphere over the bomb. The second is harmless but the first is the chief destructive force of the explosion.

The most important effect is the throwing up – often to great heights – of radioactive matter. Although heavy particles settle again quickly, smaller ones spread over a large oval area, while the finest remains in the

atmosphere indefinitely together with radioactive gases. It is not practicable to estimate the direction such radioactive clouds will move in,
as they shift with the wind. Some of the radioactivity remains dangerous
for a long time. (144 words)

2 The atmospheric disturbances caused by a hydrogen bomb
explosion included harmless 'gravity' waves and highly destructive blast
waves. Most important was the production of radioactivity. Although the
fallout of larger particles could be predicted, gases and the smallest
particles formed radioactive clouds that would shift with the wind and
could remain dangerous for a long time. (56 words)

3 Hydrogen bomb explosions produce destructive pressure waves and
also radioactive debris some of which remains dangerous a long time and
may fall anywhere. (23 words)

D Notes on model answers

1 Answers 1 and 3 are in the original tense, but 2 is in past tense
reported speech to demonstrate the difference.

2 Note the attempt to avoid the language of the original (*important
effect* for *significant feature* for example – *significant feature* is exactly the
kind of phrase that students tend to 'lift' unconsciously). *Meteorologist* is
retained as a technical word difficult to replace and one which you may be
assumed to know the meaning of by the post 'O' level stage.

3 In answer 2 a simpler subdivision of the third section of the passage is
used – predictable and nonpredictable fall-out. The causes of the types of
pressure wave are judged the least important material and are excluded, as
is the introduction.

4 In answer 3 destructive pressure waves are mentioned but harmless
ones ignored. Similarly, predictable fall-out is ignored.

5 To show the source, the title could be amended to something of this
kind: *Précis of an extract from a 'Daily Telegraph' article referring to the
atmospheric effects of a hydrogen bomb explosion.*

V EXERCISES

NOTES: 1 The following passages are of the length and difficulty to be
expected in post 'O' level examinations, except Exercise A which is of
bridging standard.

The word limits are those most commonly prescribed – a third or a
quarter. You are strongly recommended to experiment with further

reductions, for example to 60 words or to a 25-word sentence, as in the example above.

2 No special instructions as to title, use of reported speech etc are given; you should conform to the requirements of the examination for which you are preparing.

3 More varied summary practice, with longer passages, may be obtained by use of the *Passages for Comprehension and Discussion* (pp. 301–30).

Exercise A

Reduce the following passage to not more than 130 words (one-third):

Britain's industrial and commercial management is a key factor in the solution of our foremost economic problem – how to restore national solvency and earn the standard of living which science and technology have made possible to first-class industrial nations. True, there are other important influences, such as the political and economic actions of governments, some of which are beyond our control; but the one big factor which is thoroughly within our control and which would really boost our country's fortunes is a massive increase in our overall industrial and commercial efficiency.

Better product design, better cost-competitiveness, better marketing and after-sales services, can win new export customers and retrieve sections of the home market which have been captured by other countries. Yet our overall productivity still lags sadly behind that of the United States, alarming advances are being made in Japan, and other countries are rising fast in the international league table. Much of the blame for the plight of the British economy has been placed on the attitude and performance of British managements. Is it, in fact, all their fault? Probably not; but a good deal of it must be – and what is more important, managements are the only people who are likely to be able to put it right.

Many years ago, my first 'chief' in the consulting business taught me a golden rule: 'Get managements to manage, and you won't have too much difficulty getting the workers to work.' There are few things, if any, which British managements could not do just as well as American, German, or Japanese if they would only equip themselves with the necessary knowledge and then make up their minds to manage! The difference between the 'thrusters' and the 'sleepers' of the world's industries is not in the workers, the salesmen, the clerks, the typists; it is in the ability, education, and above all the 'will to manage' of the managers.

The ultimate responsibility of management is, of course, to the shareholders who own the business, to secure the best return it can – in the long term rather than the purely short term – on the assets or resources which it employs and which are entrusted to its care. But this is too narrow a view; in an enlightened society most people believe that managements also have responsibilities to the community which embraces suppliers, customers, and employees, and obligations to recognise national policies.

Donald J. Lockyer in *Journal of the Institute of the Motor Industry*, January 1969

Exercise B

Reduce the following passage to not more than 130 words (one-quarter):

The single discipline of 'engineering' has long since split itself up, amoeba-like. Perhaps it began when Smeaton added 'civil' to the military art of fortification, bridge, and canal building in the mid-eighteenth century. Or when the 'civils' refused Stephenson membership of their institution (they thought him illiterate) and so begat the 'mechanicals' in 1847, the presentday builders of cars, trains and planes. Now, in Britain, no fewer than fifteen chartered institutions represent the interests of engineers.

Is there now any such animal as The British Engineer? Certainly there is a quite distinct *style* of engineer, which can best be seen set against the French style. 'There have only been two sorts of engineer', confirms Alan Harris. 'The French and the British. The French invented engineering – twice – and then, quite independently, the British re-invented it.' With the encouragement of Louis XIV, military/civil engineers like Vauban were given their head. They developed enormous prestige and authority. Then, again, after the Revolution, the new social order encouraged a new professional style in technology. The *ingénieur*, encouraged by the state, began to emulate the achievements of Napoleon's generals.

The British 're-invention' was, by comparison a quaint and homely affair. With no state encouragement, a breed of craftsmen began to fit out the industrial revolution. They were clockmakers, instrument makers. James Watt – of the fictional mother's tea-kettle legend – was 'philosophical instrument maker' (lab technician) to the University of Glasgow.

Since the British makers were often necessarily self-made men, they fitted neatly into Samuel Smiles's philosophy of self-help: men like James Brindley, the canal builder. But perhaps they were fitted too neatly. A notable omission from Smiles's *Lives of the Great Engineers* is Isambard Kingdom Brunel, an omission explicable only because his flying start into an engineering career did not conform to the pattern of pulling yourself up by your bootstraps. Certainly it would be difficult to slot some of the top engineers in the twentieth century into a bootstrap pattern. Looking at the careers of five innovators – Sir Frank Whittle (the jet engine), Sir Barnes Wallis (the bouncing bomb), Alexander Moulton (the small-wheel bike), Alastair Pilkington (float glass) and John Baker (air-raid shelters) – Ronald Whitfield of the Council of Engineering Institutions' Committee on Creativity found that none had in any sense a 'deprived' background. Four went to public school, and the father of the fifth was himself an inventor.

Pragmatic, above all, *practical* men, British engineers contrast strongly today with their French counterparts, the *ingénieurs diplômes*. The French engineer's training is almost exclusively concerned with theory. Four of the six years' study are devoted to mathematics. It produces, as it is intended to produce, an élite. In contrast, the 1976 *Survey of Professional Engineers* shows that in Britain just under half the qualified engineers working in commerce or industry – the biggest single area of employment for engineers – have no university degree.

David White in *New Society*, 29 January 1976

Exercise C

Reduce the following passage to approximately 150 words (one-third):

Language is a tool for the expression and communication of thought. Failure to communicate may be caused either through inadequate knowledge of, or through deficiencies in, the language, such as misleading grammar or the possibility of ambiguity of words. No single language exists, however, which is sufficient both for expressing all thoughts and feelings and for precluding nonsense. Some languages in fact seem to encourage the consideration of meaningless questions and the expressing of nonsense.

However, as language is the use of certain symbols according to certain conventions, it should be possible, by the choice of a suitable symbolism and a suitable set of conventions, to minimise the number of meaningless questions which can be asked and to preclude to a large extent the uttering of nonsense.

An ideal language would obviate both of these difficulties. It would be so clear and precise that it would preclude all nonsense and so rich that it would be sufficient for expressing all possible thoughts and feelings.

The construction of such an ideal language is, of course, an impossibility. But in certain restricted fields, such as mathematics and physics, we are able to construct more exact languages which serve as more efficient tools of expression and communication than the language of everyday speech.

Such specialised languages have certain definite advantages.

For example: they are extremely precise, and therefore economic in use; they are known to people throughout the world, and therefore to a certain extent transcend natural language barriers. (It is possible to translate a Russian scientific text into reasonable scientific English by means of an electronic computer.)

Finally they serve as an aid to thought and therefore help progress. But on the other hand they have their disadvantages: they are harder to learn than the natural language which we learn at our mother's knee; they are known only to specialists in the various fields and, therefore, tend to be 'parochial' preventing the specialist from communicating with other people, and indeed with other specialists; and they tend to degenerate into 'jargon'.

Such languages, which of course are not restricted to the scientific field, tend to be more artificial than our normal speech. Think of some of the examples of legal or religious phraseology that you have met. Even so they spring from the same type of cultural background as does our everyday speech and so they are not so artificial as the experimental 'International Languages'. Thus the specialised languages have survived and grown whereas all such experiments as Esperanto and Interlingua, to name but two, are, I feel, doomed to failure because they ignore the cardinal point that a language arises by necessity out of, and along with, a culture.

Eric Nixon in notes on the Granada
TV programmes Man to Man, 1964

Exercise D

Reduce the following passage to not more than 140 words (one-quarter):

Free holidays, especially holidays in the sun, encourage workers to reach their productivity targets. This seems to be a recent realisation by British employers. Some of the biggest names in British industry now use this form of employee incentive. The reasons are clear. First, the holiday incentive has been shown conclusively to produce results in terms of increased output or sales; secondly, there are bonus returns on the employer's investment in the form of increases in employees' loyalty and productivity.

For some time Americans have been induced to put in 'that little extra effort' by the offer of the big prize – in cash, merchandise or travel – for those who exceed the basic norm. And it seems to work. Big incentives and high performance are part of the American industrial tradition. Very often the incentives take the form of free holiday travel, and it is not unusual for an entire boatload of sales staff or dealers to set forth on a major holiday jamboree earned by achieving set targets.

In providing holiday travel awards – as in many other business practices – the Japanese have followed the Americans, and with remarkable success. When Honda moved into Europe one of their first operations was to set up a holiday award scheme for UK motor cycle dealers. The fifty dealers who achieved top sales performance were flown for a two-week holiday in Japan. Honda quickly achieved dealer – and thereby market – domination, and the holiday award scheme has operated nearly every year since.

The Russians, too, seem to acknowledge the value of holidays as incentives, and there are many 'workers' holiday camps' on the balmy Black Sea coast for workers who reach and exceed their targets.

Thirdly, the holiday award is sometimes tax-free, an element of special attraction to boss and worker alike.

The provision of holiday award schemes will not bring automatic increases in output and sales. The holiday incentive, like other kinds of sales promotion, is a highly specialised business, and is becoming increasingly sophisticated. What is extremely important is to set targets which are not only attainable but which, when reached, give the company an adequate return on the investment. Moreover, the type of holiday provided must act as a real incentive. Recent market research shows a strong preference for incentives in the form of holidays, particularly in higher socio-economic groupings, where presumably taxation bites deepest. But in the lower groupings there is some preference for cash. The holiday award must be an 'additional' holiday. Otherwise employees feel cheated, thinking that they are receiving no more than their rightful dues.

The features constituting the main attractions of an incentive holiday are sun, comfort and water. Therefore the best places are undoubtedly the Mediterranean and the tropical and subtropical islands, the Canaries and

Bahamas rating highly in the eyes of wouldbe award-winners. But the United States and cruises are also clearly popular. The facility must include wives, and indeed they often have a considerable part to play in motivation and the drive to increased achievement.

Travel is now increasingly recognised as an effective work-incentive; and it can undoubtedly boost sales. But the travel award must be used as a weapon, not a bouquet. The subject of the incentive – whether production worker, salesman or dealer – should be closely inspected; great care should be taken with the choice of holiday and careful consideration given to the setting of targets. In this way the employer is sure of receiving a fair return on his enlightened investment.

Patrick Davies in *The Daily Telegraph*,
26 February 1969 (*adapted*)

Exercise E

Reduce the following passage to not more than 160 words (one third).
NOTE : This passage is included to give practice in summarising material written in the register usually employed for scientific or technical articles and papers. Those without an engineering background are recommended to check after the first quick reading (by class discussion or reference to a good dictionary) that they understand the use made in the passage of the following words : *parameters ; moment ; dynamometer ; function ; cavitation ; torque ; interface*.

The primary function of ship model experiment tanks is to determine, by means of measurements, all the parameters that are of interest to ship designers and builders. Among the parameters that affect the performance of the ship, the ones of special interest are those which cannot be completely estimated or calculated reliably, such as the bending moment on hulls, the quantity of water shipped on deck in waves, and the speed loss in varying sea conditions.

The rate of consumption of fuel affects the cost of running the ship : in terms of easily measurable parameters, the important factors are the efficiency of the propeller and the variation of hull resistance with ship speed.

The efficiency of the propeller is defined in terms of the thrust power delivered by the propeller against the power impressed on the shaft. As a measurement exercise, therefore, the model of the ship is run in still water at a succession of speeds, over the designed speed range, and the resistance at each speed measured using a force dynamometer. If the resistance test shows a poor hull form, modifications can be made to the hull until a satisfactory form is achieved.

The performance of a propeller is a function of its shape, the pitch and diameter of the blades, and the velocities of the water flow around the propeller. These parameters may be determined most easily by carrying out a wake survey, to find the pattern of water flow in the vicinity of the propeller. A wrong choice of propeller can lead to vibrations occurring (leading to damage of the hull and propeller in service), or cavitation effects (which can also lead to propeller damage, and inefficiency). These undesirable effects can be designed-out, provided that the flow pattern around the propeller is known. A wake survey involves measuring water pressures at different radii in the vicinity of the propeller.

Once a suitable design of propeller has been established for a particular model, that propeller is run in open water to determine its performance characteristics in unrestricted uniform flow: the propeller is fitted ahead of a special model and run at various loadings and rotational speeds, and the corresponding torque and thrust measured. Hence the variation of propeller efficiency with rotational speed and ship speed can be determined.

A good hull form and an efficient propeller are not, by themselves, sufficient to determine whether or not a ship is good overall: the efficiency of the propeller is determined for a uniform flow, whereas the flow in the vicinity of a ship's propeller is far from uniform. This is primarily an interface problem: units can work well separately, but not together. Thus it is necessary to determine the propulsion efficiency of the complete model: it is caused to propel itself at various speeds, and the corresponding torque, thrust and rotational speed of the propeller measured. From these measurements it is possible to determine the propulsion efficiencies at various speeds.

O. Anyaegbu in *Electrotechnology*,
January 1976 (*adapted*)

Exercise F

Reduce the following passage to approximately 150 words (one-quarter):

It is said of the Emperor Caligula that he used to write his laws in very small characters and post them on the top of the highest pillar in Rome, 'the more effectively to ensnare the people'. In a different way, it seems that we are heading for a somewhat similar state of affairs.

It is not just the sheer volume and complexity of new laws passed by Parliament, or the subtle nuances of judicial decisions, which add to our daily burdens – though admittedly these do not exactly help. Nor does the incomprehensible jargon of legal terminology make life any easier.

Basically, the problem is largely one of communication. The non-specialist non-lawyer is left in a state of utter ignorance about the mass of legal rules and, without knowledge, there can be no understanding.

The maxim that 'ignorance of the law is no excuse' is one of the silliest utterances ever made. Its validity presupposes the existence of several important conditions, among which are:

That there is a limit to the sheer quantity of legal rules which are capable of being known;

That ordinary people can readily understand those laws which do exist;

That there is no room for variation of legal rules by the techniques of judicial interpretation;

That everybody has his own tame lawyer who can advise him of the legal consequences of his actions.

In our present society, none of these factors exist. The result is that the overwhelming majority of the population are totally uninformed about provisions of English law which affect their vital interests. It is true that there are various organisations which assist in preventing this ignorance. Newspapers and journals provide articles and features, specialist organisations and societies give advice and help to their members, and so forth. But such a service is not comprehensive and, however valuable it may be, it only skims the surface of the problem.

The remedy seems to be either fewer legal provisions, or more publicity and education. The former situation is unlikely to come about. Each year, the annual output from Parliament increases; each year, more and more judges give an increasing number of judicial decisions, which have to be analysed, digested, compared with and distinguished from previous decisions. Law is becoming so complex that even lawyers are having difficulty in coping with problems which arise. Not many lawyers could explain with complete confidence some of the more abstruse provisions of the Land Commission Act or the Leasehold Reform Act, to name but two recent pieces of legislation.

Clearly, greater publicity and education is the only effective way of drawing the attention of the general public to legislative provisions and judicial decisions. The Ministry of Transport seems to be the only government department which really understands this, for it alone carries on effective campaigns (other ministries have a habit of publishing 'explanatory leaflets', which are more complex than the Acts they are intended to explain!). But something more than this is required. We could expand existing services, like the Citizen's Advice Bureaus, or the Legal Advice scheme, but this too is not likely to be very effective.

A more radical solution was put forward recently by the legal correspondent of *New Society*, who suggested that local Legal Centres should be established throughout the country. Staffed by full-time salaried lawyers, they would be able to deal with queries and legal problems, as well as help to publicise legal rules generally. One can visualise the local Legal Centres operating on lines similar to local Health Clinics, and performing a function no less valuable.

Norman Selwyn in *The Daily Telegraph*, 25 October 1968 (*adapted*)

Exercise G

Reduce the following passage to not more than 150 words (one-quarter):

The most extraordinary feature of life in the next forty years is likely to be the pace of technological change. This, of itself, is something the country has been through before. The original Industrial Revolution brought profound changes in Britain. The population increased rapidly and a vast amount of building development took place.

Millions of people were born into miserable conditions – with bad housing, bad factories, bad or non-existent schools, and sweated labour. But out of their endeavours Britain became a great industrial nation, with a dominant position in the world.

At the root of the Industrial Revolution was steam power based on coal and, although steam was later coupled with electricity and supplemented by petroleum, it can be argued that the curve of technological progress flattened out after the first great surge forward in the application of steam. The two wars, separated by twenty-five years, were not greatly different in their sources of energy.

But right at the end of the Second World War nuclear energy made its first shattering appearance. This and the more subtle development of radar, with all its electronic implications, now seem likely to usher in a second Industrial Revolution as profound in its effects as was the first.

This time, as far as Britain is concerned, there will be two striking differences. Instead of being the sparsely populated country it was when the first Industrial Revolution started, Britain now has a population of 54 million. Many people say the country is full. And instead of having the markets of the world open and waiting, Britain is now fighting for its life against the competition of many other industrial nations.

This is the main prospect – that this milling population of 54 million, which according to official forecasts is expected to increase to 74 million soon after the end of the century, confined within its island home, will be subjected to strains and stresses as violent as any that have occurred during the last two centuries.

Old standards and long-cherished values will tend to be thrown into the melting pot. Society will be turned upside down and inside out as new ideas surge in, as new prospects open out and great wealth – assuming we maintain our position – accrues. It is in this condition of flux and confusion, when old ideals are threatened before new ones have been hammered out, that the danger to the physical environment will be at its greatest.

It can be assumed that in this process of rapid change there will be many individual developments for the better. Slums will be replaced by new dwellings. The factories of the nineteenth century will give way to light, airy, and spacious buildings. The old office blocks will be rebuilt. Schools and hospitals are likely to be incomparably better. Open spaces may be provided where none existed previously.

But the acute risk is that the synthesis will be wholly unsatisfactory, that the new development will be thrown together in a series of hotch-potches, spread and sprawled, wrongly located, inconvenient in use, ugly in appearance, at fault socially, and that in the process of change much that was previously cherished will disappear.

This process, with its paradoxical contrast between the improvement of the environment in microcosm and the utter failure to create the macrocosm, can be seen happening all over the country even now, in spite of the controls exercised under the Planning Acts. There are some things we can be proud to take a foreigner to see; but much of it – starting perhaps with the journey in from London Airport – must make us want to hang our heads in shame.

Professor Colin Buchanan in *The
Observer*, 19 January 1964

Exercise H

1 Reduce the following passage to not more than 160 words (one-quarter):

There have been fundamental changes in the pattern of holiday-taking since Victorian times, when many of our large resorts first came into existence. The approach of the Victorians to travel was essentially a passive one – they preferred 'seeing' to 'doing'. They would generally arrive at a resort by train and stay in the one place throughout their holiday. The hotels of the day were designed to provide comfort, while reflecting in the lavish decoration and expansive rooms, the extravagance of the times. Holidays followed much the same pattern for all, and therefore a resort was able without much difficulty to cater for all tastes by providing a promenade, a bandstand, a pavilion, and entertainment in the centre of the town.

Today's holidaymaker asks for much more than this. The emphasis has shifted towards more active forms of enjoyment and there is a tremendous variety of pursuits to choose from, ranging from sailing and ski-ing to golf and pony-trekking. So great is the demand for participation that we are witnessing the commercialisation of hobbies.

Holiday traffic is no longer homogeneous. There are now many different types of holidaymaker each with an entirely different set of requirements. Some look for solitude while others like plenty of company. Touring has become an important feature of the new pattern of holiday-taking but there are still those who like to stay in one resort throughout their holiday, particularly if they have children.

That 'do it yourself' approach has become increasingly popular and has been marked by a sharp growth in demand for caravans and holiday flatlets in recent years. On the other hand this has been accompanied by an equally rapid rise in the popularity of the holiday camp, which works on the reverse principle, providing everything the visitor could need within the confines of the camp and a high degree of service.

It is clear that the requirements of the different types of holidaymakers are not always compatible and resorts today cannot attempt to cater for all tastes as they did in the past. The answer to this problem of diversification within the industry almost certainly lies in specialisation on a regional scale.

Today reference is made as frequently to a holiday region, e.g. the Lake District, the Costa Brava or the Cornish Riviera, as it is to an individual resort. The growth in the popularity of touring as opposed to static holidays has been largely responsible for this. In Britain certain regions are undoubtedly better equipped in terms of amenities to deal with a particular type of holiday traffic than others, and within the region certain resorts and towns stand out as ideal centres for certain types of activity.

It appears likely that in the next decade the trend towards area specialisation will grow. Already some regional organisations have been set up to study present trends in visitor traffic and from there decide which types of traffic the region is best suited to attract and serve. The planned development of tourist facilities within the region can then follow, taking into account the requirements of the particular category of visitor the area will cater for. It will be more important than ever for a holiday area to create a clear-cut image in the minds of prospective holidaymakers.

All branches of the holiday industry face a challenging period of opportunity in the years ahead. Competition from foreign resorts, already considerable, will certainly grow as the level of prosperity increases. The inclusive tour has already brought the cost of a holiday in some continental resorts to a level very little above that of a holiday at home.

L. J. Lickorish, General Manager of
the British Travel and Holidays
Association, in the *SIA Journal*,
January 1964

2 In not more than 60 words indicate how correct you consider the predictions made in the last two paragraphs of this article have proved.

Chapter 8

Business Letters

I BUSINESS LETTERS AND COMMUNICATION PRINCIPLES

It has been said – more than once – that a firm's letters are its ambassadors. Customers (and other firms and organisations too) base their impression of a firm on its letters as much as anything. To many it seems that correspondence reveals what a firm is really like, as distinct from the picture of it projected by its publicity and advertising. Every letter sent out, therefore, to some extent changes the standing and prestige of the firm. This is even more true of public administration. The principal contact that the man in the street has with government departments is through correspondence; at a local level the public impression of 'the Council' is largely created by the letters sent out by its officers.

The standard of business letters generally in this country is not high. Far from achieving such aims as establishing an atmosphere favourable to business and increasing goodwill for the firm, correspondents frequently fail even to make it clear what they are trying to say. While the firm is seeking – by its publicity material and such details as its office furnishing and the quality of its stationery – to give an impression of efficiency, modernity, and style, its letters are often ungrammatical, old-fashioned, and clumsy. Here is an example from a firm of national repute – the only alteration the name of the product:

We are pleased to note your interest in our Tiles and accordingly have pleasure in enclosing herewith literature giving details of these materials. Prices depend to some extent upon the type and conditions of sub-floor, area required to be laid, and in connection with Nutred Decorative Tiles, the colour or colours selected for use.

We should be pleased to provide you with an estimate for any work you may have under consideration if you would kindly let us have the aforementioned details, together if possible with a small drawing or dimensioned sketch of the spaces concerned.

We trust this is in accordance with your requirements and in the meantime await to hear from you further.

It is difficult to imagine many customers receiving this letter as a reply to a first enquiry feeling encouraged to proceed further.

Here is another, again exactly as received, except for the omission of the stockist's name:

We thank you for your enquiry and are pleased to note your interest in our fireplace designs. We have much pleasure in enclosing our brochure incorporating only a small selection from our varied range of fireplaces, however, a comprehensive catalogue also prices are available at our stockists showroom.

We are requesting our nearest stockist, namely, Messrs ... to contact you and doubtless they will be very pleased to render any assistance possible.

If we can be of any further assistance to you in making your selection we hope you will advise us. It would be very much appreciated if, in due course you could let us know if one of our designs has met with your requirements.

What is wrong here goes much deeper than the punctuation errors (which could be blamed on the typist).

A minimum communication standard for the business letter should be that it is expressed in clear and exact English and contains no errors of syntax, spelling, or punctuation. For all but completely routine letters, however, more should be aimed at than the minimum. The following are typical points that require attention:

1 suitability of register to subject matter and circumstances
2 friendliness and warmth of tone
3 selection of material and choice of wording to suit the Rx (his probable vocabulary level, knowledge of the subject and its technical jargon, the type of person he seems to be etc)
4 psychological factors (tact, courtesy, special care when conveying unwelcome information – which is liable to be misunderstood simply because the Rx *wants* to read it in a sense different from that which you intend)
5 freshness of language (freedom from clichés and commercial jargon).

The letter should contain no padding or wasted words, and be as concise as is possible without sacrifice of any of the aims enumerated.

II CONVENTIONS AND LAYOUT

The business letter has developed over the years certain conventions which – however odd or illogical – must be followed or your letter will not be accepted by the Rx as a 'proper' business letter. Layout too is decided rather by what is traditional and accepted than by what will be most effective. Most businessmen, and local and central government officers, rely on secretaries in these matters; the examining bodies in typing and secretarial duties thus indirectly exert a very powerful influence. If a private person is sending a handwritten letter to a firm he is well advised to follow much the same rules that typists obey or his letter may seem amateur, or even bizarre, to the person who receives it. These matters are to some extent subject to fashion and the model layouts and notes that follow represent the conventions accepted at the time of writing.

Business letters may be classified as:

1 private person to firm (or organisation)
2 firm (or organisation) to private person
3 firm (or organisation) to firm (or organisation).

If the conventions and layout for the first two are known, the third, which is a combination of these, can be easily deduced.

A *Private person to firm (or organisation)*

10 Hilltop Road,
 HIGHTOWN, Wiltshire.
 SN26 6KA
 20th November, 19..

The Colton Engineering Co.,
 Tottenham Street, LONDON.
  SE12 4QD

Dear Sirs,

  ....
....
....
    ....
....
....

Yours faithfully,
James Thompson

NOTES

1 It is assumed that this letter is handwritten. In this book italic type is used in all examples of letters to represent handwriting.

2 Both addresses are shown with progressive indentation, the more usual form with handwritten letters. The punctuation shown for the addresses is still the most widely accepted, although 'open style' (see pp. 126–7), has increasing support. A comma after the house number is not recommended.

3 The placing of postcodes is illustrated. Further details are given in Appendix III on p. 342.

4 The date is in the most widely accepted form. Permissible variants are dropping the comma and substituting 20 for 20th. Abbreviated forms are out of fashion.

5 The inside address is a particular characteristic of the business letter, and is employed even when no carbon copy is kept and therefore no practical advantage is being gained.

6 If the appropriate departmental head is known, the letter is better addressed to him, but by his official title not his name. Thus a letter concerning purchasing should be addressed to:

The Sales Manager,
  The Colton Engineering Co.,
    Tottenham Street, LONDON.
      SE12 4QD

Dear Sir,

7 The term *Messrs* is often used incorrectly. Where two men are being written to at once it provides a convenient plural for *Mr* (*Mrs* cannot be used as that has a different meaning). Thus we can correctly address a letter to *Messrs Thackeray and Dickens*, if we are writing one letter to both gentlemen or if they are in partnership and we are writing to their firm.

But simple partnerships are uncommon today (except amongst professional people such as solicitors or accountants). A firm known as 'Thackeray & Dickens' is more likely to be a limited company incorporating the names of the original partners in its trading name, when the use of Messrs is inappropriate. The accepted form then would be:

Thackeray and Dickens Ltd,
[Address]

Dear Sirs,

8 The subscription *Yours faithfully* is always correct in formal business letters, although other subscriptions may be acceptable in certain circumstances. Strictly speaking *Yours sincerely* should be reserved for situations where you know the person you are writing to and the letter is not, therefore, completely formal in register. The praiseworthy attempts by firms over the last few years to make business correspondence seem more friendly have resulted in increased use of *Yours sincerely* by firms but it is not an appropriate subscription for a private person to employ when writing to a firm.

B *Firm (or organisation) to private person – conventional layout*

THE COLTON ENGINEERING COMPANY
Tottenham Street, LONDON.
SE12 4QD

OUR REF: AJH/PFL   22 November 19 ..

J. Thompson Esq.,
10 Hilltop Road,
HIGHTOWN, Wilts.
SN26 6KA

Dear Sir,

                        Yours faithfully,
                        for COLTON ENGINEERING CO.

                        A J Harland.

                        A.J. Harland

NOTES

1 Firms use stationery with a printed head to ensure that – at the minimum – all letters from the firm show its correct trading name and address. Much more information (telephone numbers, telegraphic address, names of directors, even an advertising slogan or picture of the works) may be included. The address is frequently centred under the firm's name. There are many variants and you should collect a number of examples of firms' stationery to compare.

2 A firm will always assign a reference to correspondence, and this is intended for quotation in the reply. This ensures that the reply goes to the right person, or in a large organisation may be the key to a complicated filing system. The simplest reference consists (as here) of the initials of the person sending the letter combined with those of the typist or secretary. When firm writes to firm each will give a reference to the correspondence and to avoid confusion these are marked OUR REF and YOUR REF. References should always be quoted in replying to a firm (the top lefthand

of the first sheet opposite the date is the place for this). It may be impossible to put your second letter on a certain matter alongside your first letter unless you do so.

3 The inside address and *Dear Sir* are 'blocked', but each paragraph starts an arbitrary distance from the lefthand margin (usually five spaces) while the subscription is placed right of centre. This layout, called by typists 'semiblocked', is still the most widely employed.

4 For a formal letter the firm will probably decide to address Mr Thompson as 'Esq.'. This complimentary mode has been applied so freely that there is little compliment left in its use and it is now a mere convention. It cannot be used except with the initials of the addressee, if these are unknown 'Mr' must be employed. There is no equivalent to *Esq.* for women, who must be addressed as *Mrs*, *Miss*, or *Ms*, followed by her address and *Dear Madam* in completely formal letters, *Dear Mrs ...* etc. in letters subscribed *Yours sincerely*.

5 The form as shown with *Dear Sir* and *Yours faithfully* is for strictly formal, or routine, correspondence. If Mr Thompson is known to the firm at all he would probably be addressed as:

J. Thompson Esq.,
[Address]

Dear Mr Thompson,
with the subscription:

                                  Yours sincerely,

Many firms now employ this form even if the correspondent is not known to them, with the commendable motive of making even routine letters seem personal.

6 The firm's letter may be signed in a number of ways, according to the degree of importance given to the correspondence. In ascending order these might be:

   (a) name of firm only
   (b) name of firm plus initials of Tx
   (c) name of firm plus signature (as example on p. 124)
   (d) signature with office held (e.g. *A. J. Harland, Sales Manager*).

Styles *(a)* and *(b)* should not be used for any but the most routine letters. Persons having delegated authority to sign on behalf of their firms sometimes sign 'p.p.' or 'per pro' (*per procurationem*), e.g.

                        p.p. Colton Engineering Co.
                              A. J. Harland

but this custom is steadily being replaced by *(d)* above, where the exact degree of authority is indicated by the name of the office held.

Increased use of audio-typewriting (especially in association with a system for dictating letters via the firm's internal telephones) has resulted in an additional signature style – *Dictated by Mr Harland but signed in his absence* followed by the typist's signature. Mr Harland may be out of the office by the time the letter is ready but it can thus be posted without waiting for his return, this form of signature protecting him from responsibility for errors that are purely the fault of the typist.

C *Firm (or organisation) to private person – a more modern layout*

THE COLTON ENGINEERING COMPANY
TOTTENHAM STREET, LONDON SE12 4QD

OUR REF: AJH/PFL

23 November 19 ..

J Thompson Esq
10 Hilltop Road
HIGHTOWN WILTS
SN26 6KA

Dear Sir

Yours faithfully
for COLTON ENGINEERING CO

A J Harland

A J Harland

NOTES
1 This diagram represents 'fully blocked' style (all material starting on the lefthand margin) combined with 'open' punctuation (no commas or

full stops at ends of lines). The two styles do not necessarily go together and fully blocked style with conventional punctuation is frequently met. The two together do, however, represent a considerable saving in time for a typist and this layout is rapidly gaining support as a result. Some people find the disappearance of the full stops after initials disturbing, but these look a little odd if retained when the other traditional full stops and commas have been removed from address and subscription.

2 Some people find the unbalanced appearance of the fully blocked layout unattractive. A variant ('blocked') keeping the date and complimentary close in the conventional position while starting all other lines on the lefthand margin is therefore popular.

3 Most people using this book will probably not select the layout of the letters they send at work but will accept what their typist or secretary offers (or there may be a prescribed 'house style' for layout in the firm). It is useful, however, to know a little about layout to be able to discuss this with your secretary if you are ever in a position to choose, and for simulations of business letters in examinations some awareness of the principal variants is necessary.

III SOME POINTS OF STYLE

Many firms have an accepted house style which makes at least their run-of-the-mill letters all look and read as part of one family. Where such local rules prevail they must be obeyed, regardless of any clash with the suggestions that follow.

Some firms seek to impose consistency and minimum standards on their letter writers by the use of 'form letters' – stereotypes to suit all routine occasions, which can be copied by the inexperienced. These 'form letters' may be necessary where many routine letters and postcards have to be sent out by very junior members of staff but they are a prime cause of conservatism in a firm's correspondence, perpetuating outmoded expressions, and run counter to communication principles in that they are not designed to suit a specific Rx. They usually result in a lifeless unnatural letter that does not quite fit the circumstances for which it is being forced into service. The best letters are produced, fresh, for the particular occasion and the particular Rx.

Starting the letter off is a matter that should be given some thought. Many correspondents favour a 'subject head' (centred and underlined, immediately below the *Dear Sir,*) instead of a topic sentence. Thus:

Dear Sirs,

Television Repair Job No.553

may conveniently replace

Dear Sirs,

I am writing to you about my television set which you have now had for repair for over six weeks.

The subject head has the advantage of appearing brisk and to the point. Sometimes it seems a little too much so, and the more leisurely topic sentence gains in friendliness and courtesy. Where there are bound to be a number of letters on the same matter it is certainly worth while inventing a subject head for the correspondence that will probably be repeated by the Rx with a subsequent gain in speed of reference.

Replying to a letter, the correspondent must first acknowledge this letter and refer to its date. Old-fashioned expressions such as *I have to acknowledge your letter of 15 ult. in which you refer to* are better replaced by simple direct expressions such as *Thank you for your letter of 15th October, 19...* If the date of the letter and its reference number or subject head (or both) are quoted there is no need to give a précis of the other man's letter in the opening sentence. Such constructions as *referring to, and with reference to* are, as we saw in Chapter 6, better avoided. Thus *With reference to your order of 15th October, 19.., we are pleased to advise you that the Zapp pre-coated panels now await your collection* becomes (modernising the language throughout) *We are glad to tell you that the Zapp pre-coated panels ordered by you on 15th October, 19.., are now ready for you to collect.*

Letters may be written in:

1 the first person singular: *I have received your application and shall be bringing it before the Board for consideration next week*

2 the first person plural: *We have received your application and shall be considering it at a board meeting next week*

3 the impersonal passive: *Your letter has been received and will be considered by the Board next week.*

The first person singular can be used only by somebody of weight and authority in a firm, as he is reporting his personal actions or expressing his personal opinion yet they also represent those of the firm. A junior member of a firm is advised to associate himself with the whole firm by using the plural. The personal element in these two styles is usually their principal advantage but this can be a disadvantage if the letter writer is very junior or if the matter is exceedingly formal, when the impersonal style is to be preferred.

There is, of course, no reason why the styles should not be combined – for example, using the first person singular so long as the writer's personal actions or views are mentioned but shifting to one of the other two styles where a matter concerning the entire firm is involved.

Letters predominantly in the first person singular are signed by the writer; letters in the first person plural or impersonal passive are usually signed with the name of the firm, the writer's name, if shown at all, appearing beneath. Some correspondents insert the line *I am* or *We are* (according to whether the letter is singular or plural in style) before *Yours faithfully*. There is no point in this unless the letter ends with a participial construction, when this addition is needed to complete the sentence:

> *Trusting this action meets with your approval,*
> > *We are,*
> > > *Yours faithfully,*

However, these participial constructions (*Awaiting your further instructions, Anticipating an early reply, Assuring you of our best attention* etc.) are for the most part clichés from Edwardian commercial jargon and best avoided.

I am, We are (and their absurd variants *I remain, We remain*) have therefore little justification in modern correspondence.

IV EXAMPLES

A *Enquiry and reply*

> 46 *Rawdon Road,*
> *BAMBER, Kent.*
> *BR31 7NP*
> *5th April, 19..*

The Solid Fuel Centre,
> *Gloucester Close, LONDON.*
> > *W1 9XL*

Dear Sirs,

    I should be very obliged if you would send me a copy of the booklet 'Warmer Homes with Solid Fuel', currently advertised in the press.

    I should like also to raise a point that is of some concern to me as I am considering buying a new boiler. Considerable publicity has recently been given to the Condor Thermostatic Boiler No. 3 but I notice it is not included in your list of recommended appliances. Is this an oversight or is there in fact some defect in this boiler that has prevented it from passing the Centre's tests?

Yours faithfully,

John Cole

NOTES

1 Two points for action are raised in one letter. The writer prepares the second point carefully and will probably get both his booklet and a reply to his query. With more complex material it would be better to write two letters even if both are enclosed in one envelope. Raising several points, involving more than one department, in one letter is not the best way of making sure that all points are dealt with.

2 Having reached the end of his query at paragraph two, the writer does not waste time on a vague closing paragraph – he has been polite enough all through to have established goodwill without this.

THE SOLID FUEL CENTRE

Gloucester Close

London　　　WI 9XL

WP/VGF　　　　　　　　　　　　　　　　　　　7th April, 19..

J. Cole Esq.,
46 Rawdon Road,
BAMBER, Kent.
BR31 7NP

Dear Sir,

Thank you for your letter of 5th April, 19.. As requested, I am sending a copy of 'Warmer Homes with Solid Fuel', which I hope you will find of interest and use.

The Condor Thermostatic Boiler No. 3 is not yet included in the recommended list, but I have no doubt that it is only a question of time before it is added. With all new appliances a certain amount of time has to elapse before the necessary tests can be carried out, and as this model has been available for only a few weeks it may be several months before information is received that it has become an approved appliance.

Yours faithfully,

W. Perching

Technical Information Officer

NOTES

1 First sentence acknowledges letter received and quotes its date.
2 At paragraph two NOT *With regard to the Condor Thermostatic Boiler No. 3 this boiler is not yet* ...
3 Tone throughout friendly and helpful. Writer is not afraid to use a few extra words to obtain this effect, yet the letter is concise.

B *Complaint and letter of adjustment*

> Grey Walls,
> TENDERHAM, Kent.
> BR33 2JM
> 9th December, 19..

Krispikorn Ltd,
SHAWFORD, Birmingham.
B81 5KJ

Dear Sirs,
    My little boy has been very disappointed on no less than three occasions by finding no British Battleship cards in packets of Krispikorn. All three packets had wording on them which implied that these cards were in the packets.
    I feel that as this has happened more than once it is reasonable to bring the matter to your attention.

> *Yours faithfully,*
> *(Mrs) Muriel Wyman*

NOTES

1 The most important point about a letter of complaint is to avoid rudeness or sarcasm. A good firm will put the matter right if the facts are laid before it fairly. Rudeness only makes the recipient defensive and uncooperative. This is a calm and sensible letter and deserves favourable treatment.

2 Mrs Wyman does not put *Mrs* in front of her name because she is proud of her married status. She is just making it easy for the firm to address her correctly in their reply. However, since 1975 it has been acceptable to address women who do not indicate whether they are married or not as *Ms*.

KRISPIKORN LTD
Shawford   Birmingham   B81 5KJ

OUR REF: SJH/MLG

11 December 19..

Mrs M Wyman
Grey Walls
TENDERHAM Kent
BR33 2JM

Dear Madam

We were sorry to learn from your letter of 9 December 19.., that your little boy had been disappointed in not finding his British Battleship cards in three packets of Krispikorn.

We must apologise for these deficiencies.   It seems that there was a fault on one of the packaging machines at the time these packets were being processed. We are grateful to you for taking the time and trouble to bring this matter to our notice.

We enclose with this letter six replacement British Battleship cards and hope that your son will be just as pleased with them now as he would have been when he opened the packets to look for them.

We are also sending you separately two packets of Krispikorn which we trust you will accept with our compliments.

Yours faithfully
for KRISPIKORN LTD

S J Heward

Consumer Relations Office

NOTES

no commas.

1 This letter illustrates the fully blocked layout with open punctuation (see pp. 126–7).

2 A letter of adjustment always presents considerable difficulty. First it has to be decided whether the complaint is justified. The customer has to have the benefit of the doubt but if the customer is clearly in the wrong a tactful letter must be sent pointing this out (not easy). If the complaint is justified, the adjustments department (or equivalent section) must: (1) find out what went wrong so that an explanation can be sent to the customer (2) decide what action is best to put the matter right and restore the customer's good opinion of the firm (3) write a letter admitting the fault, apologising (but not crawling), and endeavouring to prevent the loss of the customer's future trade (without letting the customer see too obviously that this is the aim).

C *First collection letter, and reply*

H. AND C. CORNCROFT & CO. LTD

Rose Growers

Wallington Essex CO51 7AB

J. Morris Esq.,   30 January, 19..
The Grange,
HILLFORD, Somerset.
BA42 6DE

Dear Sir,

Account 58236

According to our records, you have not yet settled your account with us for rose trees supplied to you on the 10th October of last year. We enclose our detailed statement. You will note that the amount outstanding is £31.68.

We trust the quality of tree supplied was to your satisfaction and would appreciate your early settlement of this account.

       Yours faithfully
       H. and C. Corncroft & Co. Ltd.

Enc.

NOTES

1 Letters seeking payment of money owed (collection letters) must be very carefully written, as it is easy to give offence. Firms will often submit statements several times with perhaps the addition of a phrase such as 'Account overdue; please remit' before writing the first collection letter. In a first letter of this kind a very cautious approach should be adopted; the wording should be of a kind (as here) that allows for the possibility that the firm is itself in error. Just as well that this letter was so carefully worded in view of the reply (below).

2 The *Enc.* at the bottom left of the letter serves as a reminder both to the person who puts the letter in its envelope and to the person who opens the envelope that there is an enclosure (here the detailed statement).

> The Grange,
> HILLFORD, Somerset.
> BA42 6DE
>
> 3rd February, 19..

H. and C. Corncroft & Co. Ltd,
WALLINGTON, Essex.
CO51 7AB

Dear Sirs,

Order 58236

I have received from you a letter dated 30 January 19.., which asserts that I have not settled the above account. In fact this account was paid at the time of ordering by my cheque Barclays SC 305388. As you have apparently mislaid this cheque, which I note has not been cashed, I have instructed my bank to withhold payment on it, and enclose a second cheque for the amount due.

> Yours faithfully,
>
> *J. Morris*

NOTES

A dignified letter in the circumstances. He makes his points firmly, but refrains from pointing out the inconvenience he has been put to by the firm's inefficiency.

Although in this example the customer turns out to be in the right, there will be many occasions when no satisfactory reply is received and the firm will have to send a series of letters, gradually hardening in tone, in its attempt to obtain payment without losing a customer. Threat of legal action is reserved to the third or fourth letter in the series.

D *Second and third collection letters*

(SECOND)

Dear Sir,

Order 58257

On 30th January 19.., we wrote to you drawing your attention to what appeared to be an unpaid account amounting to £62.85 for rose trees supplied to you on the 15th October last year.

We are surprised to have had no reply from you on this matter and would be grateful to receive your cheque at your earliest convenience.

Yours faithfully,

(THIRD)

Dear Sir,

Order 58257

We have now submitted our statement in connection with the above order three times, and written to you on 30th January and 14th February reminding you that the account is still unsettled.

We have received no reply to our letters

and have therefore no alternative but to put
the matter in the hands of our solicitors if
your cheque for £62.85 is not received by
1st March.

Yours faithfully,

E *Third person invitation, and reply*

The Chairman and Directors of James Hargreaves and Sons Ltd request
the pleasure of the company of James Thompson Esq. on this
occasion of the Open Day and Presentation of Apprentice Awards at
15.15 on Tuesday 7th January 19. .

RSVP to Education Officer,
James Hargreaves & Sons Ltd,
Hillborough, Kent BR49 6DM
before Friday, 13th December, 19. .

Mr James Thompson thanks the Chairman and
Directors of James Hargreaves & Sons Ltd for
their invitation to attend the Open Day and
Presentation of Apprentice Awards on 7th
January 19. . (1) at which he will be very happy
to be present or (2) but regrets that owing to
a prior commitment he will not be able to be
present.

NOTES

Form and wording are highly conventional. The invitation usually takes
the form of a printed card with the name of the Rx typed in, or added by
hand. A third person invitation is usually taken as committing the Rx to a
third person reply. This should be unsigned and have no inside address.
It has been customary for the address of the person replying to appear at
the end, bottom left, followed by the date, but if the reply is sent on
headed paper this is not possible.

Except for invitations, third person correspondence is becoming very
rare. Its formality is out of keeping with modern ideas of directness and
simplicity in correspondence.

V PRÉCIS OF CORRESPONDENCE

Circumstances sometimes arise – for example, when making a report, or when seeking legal advice – when it is desirable to reduce a lengthy correspondence to an easily assimilated piece of continuous prose. The final version can easily be made very much shorter than the original as there is inevitably much repetition in a sequence of letters. It is not always necessary to précis every letter of the series, but the dates at which the various stages of the correspondence are reached are sometimes critical and must always be made clear. Some ingenuity is required to avoid a monotonous sequence of sentences starting *On the 15th May the company wrote, saying* ...

A business-like title making clear the exact names and addresses of the correspondents and giving a very brief indication of the subject is useful for reference purposes, and is also advantageous because it permits the correspondents to be referred to in a more cursory manner in the body of the précis.

In the example that follows a correspondence consists of six letters is reduced to 130 words, excluding the title. These letters may also be read as a more extended example of business correspondence than has been provided in the preceding section.

PIDDERMINSTER TECHNICAL COLLEGE
Pidderminster   Somerset   BA25 2PJ

Department of Business Studies

14th May, 19..

The Library Supply Co.,
Paddington Street, LONDON.
W2 9XZ

Dear Sirs,

Our order 5931

I have received the above order from you consisting of two dozen copies of Fraser: <u>Cybernetics in the Office</u> (Holton & Co). Unfortunately three copies were wrongly bound, pages 31-46 being omitted and pages 47-62 inserted twice in each. I am returning these three books, separately packaged, for your replacement.

Yours faithfully,
T. F. Smythe

Head of Department

THE LIBRARY SUPPLY CO.
Paddington Street   London   W2 9XZ

JHL/JFT   17th May, 19..

The Head of Department of Business Studies,
Pidderminster Technical College,
PIDDERMINSTER, Somerset.
BA25 2PJ

Dear Sir,

Your order 5931

We have received your letter of 14th May, 19.. and the three defective books to which you refer. We shall be taking this matter up with the publishers and shall send you the replacement volumes as soon as we receive them. We must apologise for the inconvenience this has caused you but you will understand that we sent the books to you in good faith, not realising that Holton & Co. had supplied us with defective volumes.

Yours faithfully,
for The Library Supply Co.,

J. H. Langton

PIDDERMINSTER TECHNICAL COLLEGE
Pidderminster   Somerset   BA25 2PJ
Department of Business Studies

Your ref: JHL/JFT   18th June, 19..

The Library Supply Co.,
Paddington Street, LONDON.
W2 9XZ

Dear Sirs,

Our order 5931

It is now more than a month since I wrote
requesting replacement of three defective books
supplied on the above order. I hope this matter
has not been overlooked and that I can expect
the books very soon.

Yours faithfully,
T. F. Smythe
Head of Department

THE LIBRARY SUPPLY CO.
Paddington Street   London   W2 9XZ

JHL/JFT   21st June, 19..

The Head of Department of Business Studies,
Pidderminster Technical College,
PIDDERMINSTER, Somerset.
BA25 2PJ

Dear Sir,

Your order 5931

Thank you for your letter of 18th June,

19.. We are very sorry that there is this
delay in replacing the defective copies of
Fraser: <u>Cybernetics in the Office</u>. As you will
perhaps know, Holton & Co. have recently
transferred their business from London to
Brighton; since then it has been very difficult
to obtain books from them. We are, however,
sending them a reminder, and hope that we
shall soon have the replacement volumes ready
for despatch to you.

                         Yours faithfully,
                         for The Library Supply Co.

                         J. H. Langton

PIDDERMINSTER TECHNICAL COLLEGE
Pidderminster   Somerset   BA25 2PJ

Department of Business Studies

Your ref: JHL/JFT   26th June, 19..

The Library Supply Co.,
Paddington Street, LONDON.
W2 9XZ

Dear Sirs,

<u>Our order 5931</u>

We have just received a second statement
from you for the above order, which has been
the subject of some correspondence. I must
make it clear that I do not propose to pass
this account for payment until we have
received the three replacement volumes
referred to in my previous letters. It is now

six weeks since I first wrote to you about
this matter on 14th May, 19..

Yours faithfully,

T. F. Smythe

Head of Department

THE LIBRARY SUPPLY CO.
Paddington Street   London   W2 9XZ

JHL/JFT   29th June, 19..

The Head of Department of Business Studies,
Pidderminster Technical College,
PIDDERMINSTER, Somerset.
BA25 2PJ

Dear Sir,

Your order 5931

Thank you for your letter of 26th June.

We have still not received the replacement
copies of Fraser: <u>Cybernetics in the Office</u>
from Holton & Co. However, we have managed to
obtain three copies from another bookseller and
are sending these to you by today's post, in
order that this matter can be settled without
further delay and inconvenience to you.

Yours faithfully,
for The Library Supply Co

J. H. Langton

In the précis that follows it is assumed (as is usual in exercises) that an outsider is making the précis. In practice this is not usually so and the task is that much easier as, for example, The Library Supply Co. could refer to itself throughout as 'we' and 'us', if it was itself making the précis.

Précis of a correspondence between T. F. Smythe Esq., Head of Department of Business Studies, Pidderminster Technical College, Pidderminster, Somerset, and The Library Supply Co. of Paddington Street, London. Subject : the college's order No. 5931.

On 14th May, 19.. Smythe acknowledged receipt of two dozen copies of Fraser: *Cybernetics in the Office* (Holton) but drew attention to three defective copies returned, separately packaged, for replacement. The Library Supply Co. acknowledged receipt of these on 17th May and undertook to obtain replacements from the publishers. On 18th June a reminder was sent by Smythe which was replied to by the company on 21st June blaming the delay on the publishers. On 26th June Smythe wrote again referring to a second statement sent for this order and stressing that he would not pass the account for payment until the replacement volumes were forthcoming. On 29th June the company wrote that these volumes had been obtained from another bookseller and were being despatched.

VI EXERCISES

In attempting the following exercises you should invent additional details where necessary to give verisimilitude to your letters, which should be properly laid out and complete in all relevant details such as dates, addresses, references.

Exercise A

Write an application for a post of this kind that you would like to hold. This should consist of a brief letter of application together with a schematically presented data sheet indicating under headings your personal details, education, qualifications, and experience, and providing the names and addresses of referees.

Exercise B

1 Imagine you have moved to another area. Write to the local technical

college enquiring about courses similar to the one you are now following.

2　Write to a distinguished sportsman, writer, or television personality, inviting him to address a students' society of which you are secretary.

3　Write to a local coach hire firm seeking a quotation for an outing which you are organising on behalf of a group of students.

Exercise C

Write a typical letter of enquiry of the sort received frequently by your firm and a reply to it, or (if not employed) a letter of complaint about a purchase you have made and the firm's reply.

Exercise D

Jackson, Hobart & Co. Ltd, who have been good customers of your firm for several years, owe £520.65. Write letters for use when payment is *(a)* six weeks overdue *(b)* ten weeks overdue *(c)* three months overdue. You may assume two statements have been sent before your first letter.

Exercise E

Write letters to suit the following situations:

1　Your firm has received an order for goods to the value of £4200 from a new customer, James Blishford & Co., who do not quote credit references.

2　Your firm has received an order from John Jimpson of 19 Holly Park, London SE11 9KB, for a 'Windstop De-Luxe' folding beach shelter and a cheque for £30.55. This is the price quoted in your advertising for the 'Windstop' standard quality folding beach shelter. The 'De-Luxe' is advertised at £33·75.

3　A Mrs J. Hanbury of Orchard Cottage, Temple Ruiston, Gloucestershire GL48 3ML, has asked you to supply and fit a 'Valiant' No. 3 boiler. Your firm will sell only through the trade and does not do any fitting of appliances itself.

Exercise F

Write one of the following pairs of letters:

1　To the Chief Executive of your nearest town protesting at a scheme to cut down trees as part of a road-widening scheme and drawing attention to the ugly lopping of trees throughout the town; and the Chief Executive's reply.

2 To the Director of Arts and Recreation suggesting the provision of better facilities for games, and an increased number of flowerbeds, in the principal park; and his reply.

3 To the editor of a newspaper or magazine drawing attention to an error in an article dealing with a subject of which you have some knowledge; and the editor's reply.

Exercise G

Write a tactful letter of adjustment in reply to the following letter. On investigation you have found (1) that the bath panels order has been overlooked (2) that the foreman slabber had found he had not sufficient 25 mm tiles to provide a border and decided on his own initiative to omit it. The bath panels can be sent immediately, but you want if possible to discourage the customer from demanding the removal of the present tiles and their replacement to his original specification. You are authorised to offer a 5 per cent discount. Make a particular effort to suit your letter to the personality of the Rx as revealed in his letter.

17 Duckham Drove,
GRANGE GREEN,
Herts.
HER42 5MA

17 October 19..

J. Dodge & Co.,
High Street,
ICKFIELD, Herts.
HER44 3JB

Dear Sirs,

I refer to the provision of wall tiling and bath panels at my new house at this address.

Regarding the bath panels, I am at a loss to understand the cause of the delay in delivery. Your representative personally verified with me, on the occasion of my visit to your showroom on July 7th, that they could be supplied in a colour matching the selected tiles. This was later confirmed in a letter from you to myself, dated July 28th, stating that these panels were available for immediate delivery. This is now nine weeks ago; having occupied my house for nearly a month, I am still awaiting them. If you cannot supply them forthwith please cancel the order.

The wall tiling has not been carried out as directed by me and agreed to by you. The decorative 25 mm border has not been inserted, although this was specifically asked for, and later confirmed by telephone. On enquiring, I was told that the reason for not laying this border was that there were not enough of the 25 mm tiles to do the job. You must agree that this is a quite unsatisfactory way of doing business. I should at least have been informed so that a possible alternative arrangement could have been made. By the time I knew what had been done it was too late to make any alteration, short of having the whole wall tiling pulled away. The statement that there were insufficient tiles can only imply inefficiency in view of your earlier assurances.

I regard the whole business as thoroughly unsatisfactory and would be glad to learn what you propose to do about it.

Yours faithfully,
John Duff

Exercise H

You are employed as sales manager for a company manufacturing *Stabrite* liquid polishing wax. This product contains a high proportion of expensive carnauba wax and is therefore about 20 per cent dearer than its competitors. On the other hand it dries, without buffing, to an unusually long-lasting shine which improves on repolishing and with normal use. The finish is completely water-resistant and will not 'spot' when water is spilled on it.

Sales are to date through over 400 retail outlets regularly visited by a small team of salesmen. Your company now proposes a limited national advertising campaign aimed to increase sales by 25 per cent over six months. Write a letter to an advertising agency asking for first suggestions for such a campaign with indications of the cost involved.

Exercise I

A firm of builders whom you have employed to repair a section of the roof of an annexe to your place of business has submitted an estimate of £580 for the work. The structure of the roof is of bitumenised felt laid over slabs of a patent insulating material known as Strawtex, and the builder has stipulated that his estimate shall not take account of replacement of sections of this material, parts of which may have 'exploded' because of ingress of water through faulty waterproofing. The eventual bill comes to £878 and the itemised account includes a substantial amount of heavy timber and £120 for lead flashing (not mentioned on the estimate or used on the original structure). Write a letter to the builder concerned querying the account as presented and requesting a fuller explanation of the 50 per cent addition to the estimate. Draft a reply from the builder justifying all or most of the increase in cost. Use suitable fictional addresses. Pay particular attention to layout and punctuation.

[*Royal Society of Arts and London
Chamber of Commerce*]

Exercise J

Mr and Mrs Beefy of 9 Paddock Close, Plumpminster, Devon, EX51 7BJ, purchased from Rassemblit Ltd of Dreverton, Somerset, BA46 6FA, a three-piece suite of the type that is despatched as packages of component parts that are to be assembled by the purchaser. On unpacking, Mr Beefy was pleased to find that all the necessary parts had been sent and the instructions were clear and easy to carry out. In less than an hour he had completed assembly; the suite looked in every way as good as the one they had seen in the showroom.

Three days later, when Mr and Mrs Beefy had been sitting on the settee for about two hours watching television, the sponge-rubber seat suddenly gave way and they fell through. As soon as he had freed himself from the resulting uncomfortable and ludicrous position, Mr Beefy examined the settee to see if he had made some error of assembly. It was, however, only too clear what had occurred. The seat was supported on eighteen ashwood slats about three inches wide, joined at their ends by strips of webbing so that they formed a ladder shape. On assembly, these were stretched along the settee, the ends of each slat resting on two angle bars which ran the length of the settee, one at the front and one at the back. These slats were now slightly bent and it was apparent that the combined weight of Mr and Mrs Beefy (who were well built but not enormous) had curved the slats so much that their ends could slip off the angle bars. It looked as if the seat would always collapse when they both sat on it for any length of time.

Mr Beefy reasoned that either there was a serious design fault (the settee would take only a limited load) or there was something wrong with the slats supplied. Although he was not unaware of the comic side of his predicament, he decided he must face writing to the firm and explaining what had happened.

(a) Write Mr Beefy's letter

Rassemblit Ltd had in fact begun to suspect that one consignment of ashwood had been below standard and slats made from it were too flexible, because one or two letters of complaint similar to Mr Beefy's had already been received. Unfortunately the firm had no way of finding out which sets of slats had been made from that particular consignment. The firm's view was:

1 Mr Beefy must be sent a replacement set of slats.
2 They would like to examine the original slats supplied to Mr Beefy.
3 Mr Beefy should not be deprived of the use of his settee for any period or put to any expense.

The firm had no delivery service of its own.

(b) Having decided on an appropriate adjustment procedure in accordance with the indications above, write the firm's reply to Mr Beefy's letter.

Exercise K

Study the following, a genuine letter apart from alterations to disguise the identify of the firm concerned, and write notes on the events leading up to it. (You may find reference to Appendix IV on p. 344 helpful before attempting this exercise.)

PIDDERMINSTER TECHNICAL COLLEGE
PIDDERMINSTER SOMERSET BA25 2PJ

Department of Science

14 February 19..

Cammell and Goate Ltd
Elm Tree Road
WORCESTER WR1 7JF

Dear Sirs

On 29 November 19.. we sent you a request to quote for several items of laboratory equipment. This you wrongly interpreted as an order and delivered the goods. To save you time and expense we wrote to you on 17 December 19.. agreeing to accept most of the items and asking you to collect the remainder from our stores, as you did. We sent you our official order (012662) in respect of the goods retained.

We subsequently received an invoice (760156)
for all the goods, including those returned to
you. You then delivered again all the items on
our order (012662) and sent two further
invoices (767101 and 770023). We wrote to you
again on 6 January 19.. pointing out your
error and asking you to collect the duplicated
items from our stores. This you have done but
we have now received a credit note (68363) for
the items you collected. We have had no
replies to any of our letters.

The whole matter can be settled satisfactorily
if you would cancel invoice 767101 and credit
note 68363 (enclosed) and accept payment on
invoice 770023 which is for the actual amount
we owe you. I therefore shall pass 770023
(only) for payment.

Yours faithfully

E R Beak

E R Beak
Head of Department

Enc

Exercise L

Make a précis of the following correspondence in approximately 120 words, excluding title.

THE MARKET PRESERVING CO.
Kingsborough   Lincolnshire   LIN26 5BQ

OUR REF: JD/AH/W.1   12th May 19..

Hollick, Timms, Bradfoot & Co.,
112 Highfields Lane,
WORCESTER.
WR9 3JC

Dear Sirs,

Our company is interested in establishing a cannery in Worcestershire. For this purpose we shall require an area, where we shall be able to obtain permission to build, of approximately 150 hectares of good fertile land, well irrigated, and suitable for growing soft fruits and green peas. We shall want to build the cannery on a small part of this area; the remainder will be kept under cultivation.

If you have knowledge of such a tract of land, with easy access to a main road, for sale or rent, we shall be pleased to hear from you.

Yours faithfully,
Market Preserving Co.

J. Duncannon
Manager

HOLLICK, TIMMS, BRADFOOT & CO.
Estate Agents and Valuers
112 Highfields Lane
Worcester WR9 3JC

YOUR REF: JD/AH/W.1   14 May 19..
OUR REF: T/A HJ

The Manager,
The Market Preserving Co.,
KINGSBOROUGH, Lincolnshire.
LIN26 5BQ

Dear Sir,

Thank you for your letter of 12th May. We think we may be able to offer you just the kind of site you are looking for. A tract of land measuring 158 hectares at Compton Deverill has recently come into the market. Unfortunately 40 hectares are at present on short lease to a market gardener but the site is fertile, well drained, and has a small spring-fed stream running through it. It is situated only 120 metres from the A.38 to which it is connected by a minor road quite suitable for lorries.

We fear you may have some initial difficulty over permission to build in this predominantly agricultural area but since you are intending to keep most of the land for agricultural purposes this should not prove an insurmountable problem.

The vendor is prepared to accept £2950 per hectare for a quick sale. We hope therefore to hear from you further without delay, when we shall be willing to arrange for you to visit the site if you are interested.

Yours faithfully,
for Hollick, Timms, Bradfoot & Co.

James Timms

THE MARKET PRESERVING CO.
Kingsborough Lincolnshire LIN26 5BQ

YOUR REF: T/A HJ   17 May 19..
OUR REF: JD/AH/W.2

Hollick, Timms, Bradfoot & Co.,
112 Highfields Lane,
WORCESTER.
WR9 3JC

Dear Sirs,

Thank you for your letter of 14th May, 19.. We are interested in the tract of land at Compton Deverill you describe but need further information on one or two points.

First we must know how much longer the lease of that part of the property that is out for rent has to run. Second we should like your opinion of our chances of recruiting local labour to the extent of probably 40 male and 150 female workers in this rather remote rural area. Subject to your being able to give satisfactory answers on these points we are interested in this proposition and would appreciate a detailed large-scale plan of the site. There does not seem much point in arranging a visit at this early stage.

Yours faithfully,
Market Preserving Co.

J. Duncannon
Manager

Exercise M

Read through the following correspondence carefully. Then *(a)* write Emmanuel Bodger's reply to Mr Fore's letter of 16th May; *(b)* make a précis of the correspondence, including the letter you have written, in about 130 words.

5 Hallan Way,
GRANGE GREEN, Kent.
BR65 4BE

11 May 19..

Bodger & Bodger Ltd,
Brick Lane,
ICKFIELD, Kent.
BR61 5AC

Dear Sirs,

Plot 10, Mill Pond Estate, Ickfield

Progress on my new house at Ickfield does not appear to be very satisfactory. It is now seven months since I completed the contract. Your building manager gave the figure of 'fifteen weeks' for completing the house but it has only reached the rafter stage by now. How much longer will I have to wait before I can take over the house and live in it?

> Yours faithfully,
> *John Fore*

BODGER AND BODGER
Builders and Decorators

Brick Lane,
ICKFIELD, Kent.
BR61 5AC
13th May, 19..

YOUR REF:
OUR REF: EB/JHF

J. Fore, Esq.,
5 Hallan Way,
GRANGE GREEN, Kent.
BR65 4BE

Dear Sir,

Plot 10, Mill Pond Estate, Ickfield

Thank you for your letter of 11th May. We are aware of slow progress with your house, but would ask you to bear in mind the following points. (1) Our building manager quoted you a figure for completion which is perfectly possible in favourable conditions, but quite impossible in the heavy snows of the past winter. (2) There has been a nation-wide shortage of bricks and bricklayers and this caused further delay, as the outer skin of your proposed house is entirely brick-built.

We are now experiencing a further hold-up, as we are unable to obtain delivery of the special 'Cotswold' tiles you required. Would you consider accepting 'Antique Red' as substitutes as we hold ample stocks of these? It is desirable to complete the tiling as soon as possible as heavy rain would penetrate the felt roofing at present covering the rafters and wet the structural timber of the house.

Yours faithfully,
Emmanuel Bodger

5 Hallan Way,
GRANGE GREEN, Kent.
BR65 4BE

EB/JHF

16th May, 19..

Bodger & Bodger Ltd,
Brick Lane,
ICKFIELD, Kent.
BR61 5AC

Dear Sirs,

Plot 10, Mill Pond Estate, Ickfield

I was very disappointed to be informed, by your letter of 13th May, that you are unable to obtain 'Cotswold' tiles for my house. This seems a very unsatisfactory state of affairs in view of the fact that I specified these tiles more than seven months ago. However, I seem to have no alternative but to accept 'Antique Red'. This will necessitate a complete change of colour scheme for the exterior painting of the house, and I should be grateful for the return of the scheme now lodged with you.

You still do not tell me when I can hope to occupy the house. Will you please repair this omission in your next letter?

Yours faithfully,
John Fore

Chapter 9

Reports

I TYPES OF REPORT CLASSIFIED

A *Definition*

In this chapter the word *report* is used (in accordance with general business usage) to refer to a document providing an account of something witnessed or examined, or of work carried out, or of an investigation together with conclusions arrived at as a result of the investigation.

B *Classification by content*

The most basic classification of reports is according to their subject matter and/or the circumstances in which the report is required. Figure 7 indicates how this works out and the names most commonly given to the categories of report distinguished in this way.

C *Oral reports*

Although this chapter deals only with written reports it must be remembered that ORAL REPORTS (see Chapter 13) are quite common, especially for categories 1 and 2*a* of Figure 7. Reports made at meetings of societies or committees are also usually oral.

D *Routine and special reports*

ROUTINE REPORTS are reports for which there is a precedent; their purpose and form will have been decided when they were first instituted and their presentation therefore offers no problem. Most routine reports (or returns) are in fact submitted on predesigned forms which reduce the use of language to a minimum.

SPECIAL REPORTS in business are once-only reports called for by a superior, a colleague, or a customer, under special circumstances. Special

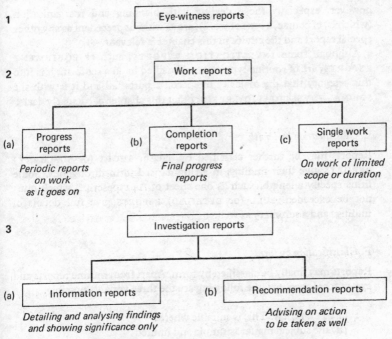

Figure 7 Reports classified by content

reports from individuals may also be called for by an organisation (for example a club that you belong to) and committees are frequently required to produce such reports for the consideration of the organisation that set up the committee. Previous experience in dealing with similar reports may be useful, but each special report poses its own questions; the best pattern for that particular subject will have to be sought from scratch.

It is the special report which is the subject of this chapter.

EYE-WITNESS REPORTS, called for most often in cases of accident, constitute simple narrative writing with a straightforward chronological order. Provided *What? Who? Where? When?* are solidly established in the opening sentences, little difficulty is likely to be met. Diagrams are often useful for clarifying the physical relationships of the people and objects essential to the account. Practice work is provided on page 175.

The majority of WORK REPORTS are routine reports, and even SINGLE WORK REPORTS tend to follow a well established pattern. Some of these, however, especially those dealing with planning and reorganisation (which is, of course, a type of work), are as without precedent as any other special report and the advice in this chapter is relevant.

Although some INVESTIGATION REPORTS, such as EQUIPMENT REPORTS, are of routine type and can be filled in on a set form, it is into this category that the majority of special reports fall and it is with the SPECIAL INVESTIGATION REPORT that this chapter particularly deals.

E Classification by length

Reports may be further classified by length. SHORT (or SUMMARY) REPORTS give their findings in a summarised form throughout. Some firms specify a length (such as one sheet of A4 typescript) which must not be exceeded. FULL (or DETAILED) REPORTS give full details of findings and a summary as well.

F Classification by form

Reports may finally be classified by form. Apart from routine reports and eye-witness accounts, the following are the three variants possible.

1 LETTER FORM. This is suitable where:
   (a) the subject matter is simple and limited
   (b) only one viewpoint is involved
   (c) there is an obvious (probably chronological) order of presentation. It does not differ in layout from any other formal business letter.

2 SCHEMATIC PRESENTATION (see Example B). The great disadvantage of the letter form is that it must all be read, and in the author's order. It is frequently difficult for the reader to see the connection between various parts of the report and he cannot easily select parts only, for close study or to weigh against each other. In short, it is difficult for the reader to find his way through complex material arranged in letter form. A schematic presentation aims to make this easy for him by classifying, analysing, and labelling the material (see Chapter 2). The subject matter is divided into major sections and then subdivided. If the material lends itself to it, further subdivisions are made and suitable headings for the sections devised. The sections are placed in a logical order of maximum convenience for the reader.

Headings of equal importance should be:

1 the same part of speech
2 similarly displayed (this refers to use of capitals; underlining; spacing; and whether centred, at lefthand margin, or indented).

A system of numbering and/or lettering should be employed to show the relative importance of the various sections and to distinguish main headings from subheadings etc. It has been customary to follow such numbers/letters by a full stop; the more modern style illustrated below reduces both typist finger movement and wear and tear on rollers and ribbons as well as looking more attractive.

What follows represents the HEADINGS ONLY of part of a detailed report on the breakdown of office appliances suffered by a company over a certain period.

III   CAUSES OF BREAKDOWN

A   Electrical
   1   Insulation failures
   2   Continuity failures
      (a)   Dry joints
      (b)   Dirty contacts
      (c)   Defective wiring
         (i)   Input leads
         (ii)   Internal circuitry
   3   Component failures
      (a)   Capacitors
      (b)   Resistors

B   Mechanical

Notice how the more subordinate the heading is, the more indented it is. Principal section headings are usually centred in a long report.

The system of numbering used here is useful when five degrees of importance are to be indicated; letters and numerals are alternated, upper case Roman numerals being used for the most important, and lower case Roman for the least important, divisions. For four degrees of importance the lower case Roman numerals are dropped, and for three all Roman numerals. Other similar systems are in use; it does not really matter how you indicate the relative importance of the headings, provided you have a consistent method maintained throughout the report.

Not all material lends itself to this sort of treatment. Sometimes, especially with very long reports, it is better simply to number all the paragraphs of the report and to interpose headings indicating how the subject matter falls into groups of paragraphs.

A refinement of this method is to number the first paragraph of the first section 1.1 and subsequent paragraphs 1.2, 1.3, 1.4, etc., until a change is made to what is considered a new section of the subject matter (whether a heading is used or not) when numbering changes to 2.1, 2.2, 2.3, etc. When the third section is reached the next paragraph will be numbered 3.1. This system is useful when the report is likely to be discussed by a group because reference to a particular section is quick and accurate; but it is not so convenient for the single reader as a system of headings and numbered subsections, which is recommended whenever the material permits.

Detailed reports with schematic presentations are usually accompanied by a *covering letter* (or *letter of transmittal*) but this is unnecessary with a short report (see Example C).

3 MIXED FORM (see Example A). Here the report starts like a letter but changes to a simple schematic presentation when the findings are reached. The scheme will probably involve no more than a numbering of the items, which will be typed on separate lines, with, perhaps, subheadings. The letter style is returned to at the end of the report. This form is suitable where the material is too brief to look well if laid out entirely schematically but is a little too complex to fulfil the conditions for normal letter form.

G *Memoranda*

Reports are *called for*. Sometimes an executive submits an unsolicited work report or investigation report to draw attention to some matter to which he has devoted time. It is more satisfactory to use the word MEMORANDUM (plural MEMORANDA) to refer to such documents. They are usually formal in style, employing schematic presentation and headed:

From: To:
Subject:

A short introductory section should follow this heading, making clear the circumstances under which the memorandum came to be written; this replaces the 'Terms of Reference' section of a report. Apart from these preliminaries, the instructions on report writing that follow will be found to be also appropriate to memoranda of this kind.

II REPORTS IN EXAMINATIONS

These are bound to be of the short or summary kind, although if the report is an alternative to an essay, or a principal question, a length of at least 350 words will be expected, and schematic presentation is essential. In examinations where a much shorter time allocation is made for a report, a very short one is obviously required, and the mixed form may provide the neatest solution.

You will be expected to invent sufficient detail to make the report (1) convincing and (2) long enough to show that you can organise material effectively. The examining bodies requiring fairly long reports supply background material to start you off, but you are still expected to supply additional material from your imagination.

In the sections that follow you will be taken through the various stages of practical report writing, including the preparation of detailed reports. This will not only help you when you come to write your own real reports, but will also assist in stimulating your imagination when it comes to inventing fictitious material for exercises and examination answers in report writing.

III TERMS OF REFERENCE

The first step when you are instructed to prepare a report is to decide exactly what the report is to be about. This is *defining your terms of reference*. If the man instructing you is a good communicator he will take pains to define them for you, but often instructions are vaguely formulated.

The degree of formality in defining the terms of reference is often in direct ratio to the gap in rank between the man issuing the instruction and the man preparing the report. 'I say, Tom, you remember that reorganisation scheme you were talking about last week? Get something down on paper and I'll put it up to the Board next week.' This sort of thing – very friendly and very vague – over the telephone may be the start of an important report where the gap in rank between the two men involved is slight.

At the other extreme, a much more junior manager may receive from the same man who was speaking to Tom a memo like this:

```
Please submit a detailed report on our sales in
the Andover sector over the period 1 April-
1 December 19...  Special attention should be
paid to house-to-house trading compared with our
normal retail outlets in that area, and to
seasonal effects on both.  No recommendations.
Required before 20 December next.
```

Probably the boss here is a good communicator who is aware in the first example that the groundwork has been well covered orally and that Tom knows well enough what he is to include, but in the second that if he is not given tight terms of reference the junior manager will include unwanted material.

The terms of reference should be quoted or otherwise made clear at the start of a well-planned report. For example, the instructions[1] by the Minister of Education in March 1956 that led in 1959 to the very influential report on 15–18 year-old education known as the Crowther Report were 'to consider, in relation to the changing social and industrial needs of our society, and the needs of its individual citizens, the education of boys and girls between 15 and 18, and in particular to consider the balance at various levels of general and specialised studies between these ages and to examine the inter-relationship of the various stages of education'. These terms of reference are quoted in the first paragraph of the preface to the report. Simpler terms of reference can often be incorporated in the title of the report: *'Report on the Breakdown of Five Maddison Electric Typewriters during the week January 10th–January 17th 19..' is self-explanatory*.

With the more important types of report, it is usual to state your authority for preparing it along with the terms of reference. Typical authorisations are: resolutions passed by committees, letters of authoris-ation, and other forms of written instruction, such as internal memos. Frequently the authorisation appears in the report in no more precise

[1] To the Central Advisory Council for Education.

form than *on the instruction of* . . ., the gap being filled by the rank or formal title of the man issuing the instruction.

Often you will need to feed back enquiries, to complete the defining of your terms of reference. You should not proceed until you are clear (1) precisely what is to be included in, and what excluded from, your report, (2) whether it is to be summary or detailed and, approximately, what length is expected if the former, (3) how long you have for preparing it.

IV ASSEMBLING THE DATA

Having made sure exactly what it is you have to report on, you then proceed to assemble your data. You will decide upon certain lines of enquiry, and perhaps action, which will supply information. Your sources of information will be threefold:

1 written (is there a previous report on this; what is there on your files; is there a relevant magazine article or book?)
2 personal (who can you write to, phone, speak to, with first-hand experience?)
3 direct (look, ask, for yourself; conduct experiments, tests).

Thus if you were a personnel officer instructed to report on apprentice unrest in a factory you might:

1 check your files to see if there was any previous history of this sort of dissatisfaction in the firm
2 phone up shop superintendents and foremen to hear their versions of what has been happening
3 go down on the shop floor and question apprentices about their grievances.

At each step you would make notes and try to check the accuracy of the information obtained, taking care to distinguish fact from opinion.

V ORGANISING THE DATA

Having collected what you consider to be sufficient data you then seek to collate it. Which are the significant facts; which bear on each other; do any contradict each other? What is the tendency of the facts; to what conclusions are they leading you? Only when you have answers to these questions can you start testing for relevance. Be careful not to jump to conclusions or to suppress facts which do not fit in with your theory. You may now find some of your data have to be rejected as unnecessary, some reduced in bulk as of limited importance, some perhaps expanded.

The next step is to group your findings into sections under defining headings and decide on the best order of presentation. You will have to decide if your conclusions are going to be given at the end of each section or held back to form a separately headed section near the end of the report. The second method is more frequently used, though with a very long report a combination of the two methods can be effective. You will decide on your recommendations, if these are called for by your terms of reference, and assemble them as a further section.

VI DRAFTING THE REPORT

SHORT REPORTS, whether schematic or in letter form, tend to follow a set order:

1 Terms of reference
2 Procedure, i.e. methods used to collect data, tests carried out etc
3 Findings
4 Conclusions
5 Recommendations (if required).

The report should be dated, and signed by the person who submits it.

THE DETAILED REPORT, by virtue of its length, requires more organisation if the reader is to find his way through it easily. He will want to be able to SKIM quickly through to obtain a general picture of what the report covers but also to DIP to get a detailed view of what particularly interests him (see Figure 8). To facilitate skimming and dipping, your layout of a detailed report should include:

1 A title-page showing about what, by whom (see page 174)
2 A table of contents
3 A synopsis of findings, conclusions, and recommendations (see page 174)
4 Clearly headed subdivisions of the main text with cross-reference to appendices
5 Appendices to which are transferred detailed information which would prevent the reader's quick assimilation of the main facts (e.g. charts, tables of figures, verbatim statements, sub-reports, definitions of terms etc).

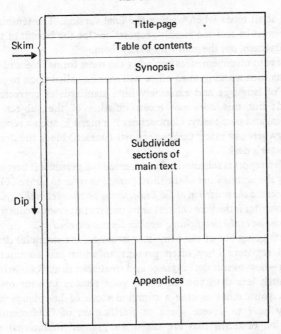

Skim {
Title-page
Table of contents
Synopsis

Subdivided
sections of
main text

Dip ↓

Appendices

Figure 8 Schematic presentation of a detailed report

VII WRITING THE REPORT

The aim of the report writer can thus be seen to be diametrically opposed to the aim of the fiction writer. The latter, by holding back, by the device of suspense, tries to keep his reader reading to the last word; the former brings the gist of his findings forward so that the reader can decide as soon as possible how little he needs to read to find out what he requires.

The emphasis in the report is on the facts, and interpretation of the facts will be logical not emotional. The language throughout will be strictly objective. The author will need to be self-effacing and, apparently at least, neutral.

Except in the more informal reports, this will require impersonal constructions and a loss of that person-to-person contact which is so valuable in other forms of business communication. The other principles of good communication stressed in earlier chapters, however, have in reports one of their most important applications and they should be kept in mind at all times when writing the final version. The temptation to impress must be resisted sternly; reports are for the benefit of the man who reads them, not the man who writes them.

A report to management is probably the most formal piece of writing the young man working in an office will ever be called upon to produce. Dignity of language and extremely high standards of correctness are expected; but this does not mean inflation of the subject matter, wordiness, and pomposity. Conciseness is a merit in such a report more than anywhere; so many verbose reports (unread) block the drawers of the manager's desk.

If such a report is schematically presented the personal is best avoided, either by the author's use of the third person to refer to himself (*The Fire Officer checked the condition of the fire-fighting appliances in the office block*, when the writer *is* the Fire Officer) or by passive impersonal constructions (*The condition of the fire-fighting appliances was checked*).

Reports going out of the firm (to customers, for example) demand a dignified register. They often present an additional communication problem – how to suit the language and treatment to an Rx of whom you know much less than you do about your seniors in your own firm. Further, you cannot assume a common stock of knowledge and will probably have to devote space to clarification of fundamentals and explanation of terms that are taken for granted in internal reports. Broadly speaking it is true to say that you must make a greater effort to simplify your subject matter, to prepare the way for each stage, than you need to with a report inside your own organisation.

Reports across to colleagues need not be so formal in register. In fact, schematic presentation and impersonal constructions may seem humourless or ostentatious in reporting to somebody of the same rank, whom you know quite well. Unless the material is very complex, the mixed form is the most satisfactory, with an informal introduction. The language of such a report, while still maintaining high standards of accuracy and clarity, can to good effect be allowed to become a little more relaxed and unbuttoned.

It is a matter of opinion whether reports should be written in sentence form throughout or whether some sections can be in note form or mere listings of points. The latter method has the attraction of brevity but many departmental heads and senior officers maintain that a report in sentence form is quicker to read although it is longer, because of the gain in smoothness and continuity; this is probably a valid argument. Certainly for examinations it would be safest to keep to sentence form, except for very compelling reasons. You should under no circumstances alternate between sentence form and non-sentence form *within the same section of the report*. For demonstration purposes, both styles are used in *Example B*, sections I and V being in non-sentence form.

VIII EXAMPLES

Example A

MIXED FORM. A maintenance engineer reports to a firm about discoloured tap-water at branch premises.

BARLOW AND BARING LTD
Broadway
Helmstead HEL2 5PB

12th April 19..

The Office Manager
Barlow and Baring Ltd

Dear Sir

Hot water supply, 53 Long Lane

You instructed me, on the 9th April, 19.., to investigate the cause of the discoloured draw-off from the hot water supply at the firm's branch premises at 53 Long Lane, Helmstead. I accordingly visited the property on 11th April and made the following observations:

1 Draw-off from the cold water supply is clear
2 The hot water system is of the direct kind and includes three radiators
3 All piping, together with the hot water cylinder, is of copper
4 The radiators are of pressed steel
5 The Long Lane area of Helmstead is an acid ('soft') water area.

I am of the opinion therefore that the dis-
colouration is caused by reaction between the
acid water supply and the steel radiators and
recommend that these radiators be replaced by
others, of non-ferrous material.

Yours faithfully,

J. F. Jimpson

Maintenance Engineer

NOTE (1) the language, dignified, yet not pretentious (2) the logical
arrangement of the findings (3) the standard order – terms of reference,
proceedings, findings, conclusions, recommendations.

Example B

SUMMARY REPORT (schematic presentation). The personnel officer of a
factory reports on apprentice unrest.

REPORT ON APPRENTICE UNREST AT ADPRESS
ENGINEERING

I   Terms of reference

On the instructions of the Works
Manager (2nd May, 19..) to report on
apprentice unrest and make recommendations.

II   Procedure

A   All supervisory grades concerned
with apprentices were interviewed.
B   Twenty apprentices, selected at
random, were interviewed in the
works.

III Findings

A Extent of unrest

The comments of the Apprentice Supervisor and foremen revealed a wide - spread malaise and resentment amongst apprentices. Although manifestations of this in individual breaches of discipline and a general uncooperative attitude were considered only minor, several foremen expressed the view that the situation was deteriorating and serious outbreaks of misbehaviour might result.

B Causes of unrest

Resentment is felt by apprentices over the following matters:-

1 Training. Complaints were made that:
 (a) supervision was inadequate
 (b) apprentices were kept too long in one section
 (c) apprentices were being used on production lines
 (d) skilled men intent on bonus earnings were unwilling to spend time explaining what they were doing.

2 Conditions. Complaints were made that:
 (a) machines were left dirty by skilled men
 (b) safety precautions were ignored particularly by operation of machines with guards removed.

3 <u>Pay</u>. The belief was widespread that rates paid to apprentices were the lowest in the area.

IV Conclusions

A Extent of unrest

On matters of justified complaint, immediate action must be taken to prevent further disturbances.

B Cause of unrest

1 <u>Training</u>. There is evidence that all complaints were well-founded.
2 <u>Conditions</u>. Complaint 2(a) above is unimportant but removal of safety guards is an offence against the Factories Act and must be stopped.
3 <u>Pay</u>. Our rates compare favourably with those paid to apprentices in other factories of this area, and complaints on this score would cease if apprentices were made aware of this.

V Recommendations

A A Senior Training Officer to be appointed and instructed to draw up a training scheme which will ensure balanced experience in the works and adequate supervision.

B All supervisory grades to be reminded of the importance of keeping machinery guarded when in operation.

C   The Personnel Officer to address a
meeting of apprentices and explain the
favourable rates of pay enjoyed in this
factory.

9th May, 19..

John Smith
Personnel Officer

NOTES
1 The language is formal and impersonal; the author refers to himself in
the third person in the final recommendation.
2 Items similarly numbered and lettered within the one section are
grammatically parallel. Note particularly in this respect the *Recommendations*. These could have been shown in several other ways: (1)
each prefixed by *that*, (2) introduced by a clause (*It is recommended
that :*), (3) *as sentences* (*A training officer should be appointed* etc.). Any of
the four methods is acceptable; but not a mixture.

Example C

SELECTIONS FROM A DETAILED REPORT

(a) The letter of transmittal

BARLOW AND BARING LTD
Broadway
Helmstead   HEL2 5PB

19 December, 19..

The Sales Manager
Barlow and Baring Ltd

Dear Sir

You instructed me on the 10th April, 19.. to
prepare a detailed report on our trading in the

Andover sector over the period 1st April, 19..-
1st December, 19.. and I now have pleasure in
submitting this report.

Yours faithfully
   P. J. Churt

NOTE: Such a letter may well replace the terms of reference section in a
long report.

(b) The title-page

BARLOW AND BARING LTD

Trading, Andover sector,
1 April 19..-1 December 19..

Report to Sales Manager
by P. J. Churt

19 December, 19..

(c) The synopsis

Between 1 April and 1 December 19.. the
overall value of the company's turnover in the
Andover sector rose by 72.2 per cent. Records
of trading with all our normal retail outlets
show a slight rise (4.9 per cent) when compared
with the same period in the preceding year,
negligible seasonal variation, and only minor
differences between branches. Door-to-door
direct trading, however, apart from a sharp
seasonal drop in sales during the months of
October and November, developed rapidly over
the period, and accounted for 80.6 per cent
of the overall sales increase.

IX EXERCISES

Exercise A : Eye-witness reports

1 Write a clear account, in chronological order, of a football or cricket match (or similar event), or of an accident you have witnessed recently. You should keep within the margin 150–180 words.
2 An accident prevention group's survey contained the following story:

A young steelworker risked his life to save a pay packet. He was leaning against a guard rail when his packet slipped on to a conveyor belt. Ignoring shouts from colleagues and a factory inspector, he vaulted the rail, climbed on to ventilation pipes, and leaped 10 feet to another conveyor belt carrying iron ore. He scrabbled 25 yards up the conveyor, grabbed the packet, and jumped on to a gangway just in time to avoid being toppled into a storage tank where he would have been crushed.

Rewrite this, in letter form, as a formal eye-witness account, imagining you were the factory inspector and had been told to report to the works manager. Invent supporting details (including names and dates) necessary for your report.

Exercise B : Summary report with supplied subject matter

As sales manager of British Knitwear Ltd of Beeston Road, Nottingham, you have just returned from a fact-finding tour of West Germany. German wholesalers criticised your firm's products for women on the following grounds: too many pastel shades; conservative styling; poor finishing; lack of *chic*; clumsy turn-out; poor shaping; restricted size range; lack of strong colours.

Organise this material in the form of a summary report approximately 200 words long.

Exercise C : Report practice with known subject matter

Reports 1 and 2 should be about 200 words long and one of these should be attempted first.

1 Compare a ball-point pen with a conventional fountain pen and with a pencil, for convenience, price, efficiency etc. Try to think of as many points of comparison as possible. Write out your findings under headings in schematic presentation form.
2 Make a report on some possession of your own, comparing it with other types on the market and showing where it is better, where inferior.

Reports 3–8 inclusive should be about 350 words long.

3 Prepare a recommendatory report on sports facilities at your technical college. You can assume it has been asked for by the principal.
4 Prepare a short information report on the street you live in that would be helpful to a man of forty and his wife (with two children aged seven and ten, both boys) contemplating moving into the same street.
5 Prepare a short information report on the parks and recreation grounds of the town in which you attend college. Your information is to be the basis of a section in the town guide. Such points as size, situation, buildings, facilities for games, and special amenities should be borne in mind.
6 Prepare a short information report on the library of your college. You can assume your report is for the use of new students.
7 Report on any recent college function, estimating its success and making recommendations for improving similar future functions.

Exercise D : Report practice with fictitious subject matter

In these exercises you will have to invent sufficient imaginary detail to make the report seem convincing. Little points such as dates, times, addresses, names of people and firms, are very important for this. The object is to give you practice in laying out and organising material in report form; it does not matter, therefore, if some of your 'facts' are wrong, or even downright impossible.

You will need a length of at least 350 words if you are going to be able to practise schematic presentation properly; but if you are preparing for an examination where only very short reports are called for you will probably want to try some of these exercises at about 200 words, using the mixed form. Do not forget to define your terms of reference, even though you have made them up yourself.

1 As secretary to a youth club, report on unoccupied premises which have been offered to the club by a local businessman at a very low rental but for three years only. At the end of this period, the premises are to be pulled down to make room for an extension of his offices.
2 Prepare an equipment report on any piece of equipment of which you have some knowledge. You must assume the equipment has been severely damaged – how and to what extent, you can decide.
3 Your firm makes *either* sports equipment *or* cosmetics. Report on the

space available for your company at the Milan trade fair and make recommendations as to the most effective form of display.

4 You have been instructed by your firm to prepare a report on a newly-invented portable appliance for converting salt water to potable water, and its potential uses and commercial possibilities. You can assume technical investigation of this device has been completed already, and a favourable report has been received from the laboratories.

5 You have attended a trade fair on behalf of your firm. Prepare a short report on your visit, drawing attention to new products of importance to your firm.

6 You are the area supervisor for the firm of Hamm and Egg, multiple grocers. Most Hamm and Egg branches have been converted to self-service. Prepare a recommendatory report on the Hamm and Egg shop in Helmstead, which has not been so converted.

7 You are employed in the office of a medium-sized manufacturing firm (product of your choice). Prepare an information report on the effects of unusually severe snow during January.

8 You have been instructed to investigate the possibilities of staggering working hours in the large concern for which you work and to submit a recommendatory report. Write this report.

Exercise E : Practice memoranda

1 As a member of the staff of a small office, prepare a memorandum on office reorganisation (see pages 23–4 for some ideas on how to tackle this).

2 Prepare *one* of the following memoranda :

   (a) To the secretary of your students' association suggesting new directions in which student leisure activity can develop.

   (b) To the college librarian suggesting useful expansion of the services provided.

   (c) To the management of the firm in which you are an apprentice, suggesting improvements in the apprentice training scheme.

Chapter 10

Advertising Writing

1 COMMUNICATION AND ADVERTISING

To be able to sell we have to let the consumer know what goods we are offering. Less commonly, when we wish to buy we may have to make our requirements widely known if we are to obtain exactly what we want. Thus public communication, or advertising, is an inevitable part of the business world.

A useful distinction may be made between advertising that seeks to inform, and advertising that seeks to persuade. Without the former, commerce could not continue; and it is to the consumer's advantage as well as the seller's to know what is available on the market. It is understandable, however, that the seller will not be content merely to announce his goods; he will also want to praise them and to persuade the public to buy from him, not his rival. As soon as persuasion starts it will accelerate steadily, for every seller has the same idea and each finds himself forced to shout louder and louder to draw attention; to make more and more claims for his product; and to seek continuously new ways of influencing the consumer in his choice. During this century advertising has developed from the naïve puffery natural to a manufacturer talking about his product to a highly sophisticated technique of directing the public's spending into accurately preplanned channels. Advertising of this kind is still communication; but it is communication not so much of information about the product as of an attitude towards the product.

This is something very different from factual communication in words, the principal subject of this book, and something which the ordinary business man no longer attempts himself on any scale. For this the specialists exist: the advertising agent and his copywriters. The reader of this book is not likely to be called upon to write copy for his company's national campaigns and major selling drives, and it would be a waste of his time to attempt to learn the specialised skills of persuasion.

There are, however, simpler forms of advertising that may come his way – for example, leaflets publicising small retail businesses; classified advertisements and small display advertisements in the local press and trade journals; public notices; 'handouts' which are to be the basis of a publicity story in the press. The smaller the firm, the more such tasks are left to one of the company's own men, with no specialised training.

With small firms much of the wording of its advertising may still be in the hands of members of its sales staff. Probably the most important kind of advertising still frequently written by a firm's own men is the unsolicited sales letter, or 'circular', distributed either at random from door to door or selectively as, for instance, to previous customers, or to potential customers selected by sex, occupation, geographical location, age, income etc. In the following section, detailed attention is given to the unsolicited sales letter. It is hoped that this will be valuable not only in itself, but also as an illustration of the kind of approach necessary in all simple advertising copy of the kind the reader may be expected to write for a firm.

II THE UNSOLICITED SALES LETTER

A *The eye-catcher*

When the householder opens what appears to be a personal letter (and increasingly firms are using good quality envelopes for their sales letters so that they do not too obviously proclaim what they are) and finds inside a piece of advertising in the form of a letter his natural reaction is one of disappointment, even annoyance. He may very well feel inclined to throw it unread into the wastepaper basket. The reaction of the businessman who finds you are selling, not buying, will be similar. It is necessary, therefore, to provide a striking opening that will catch his eye and start him reading.

A common device is to start with a challenging question:

> *Are you certain your cold water pipes are not going to freeze this winter?*
> *How well did you sleep last night?*

Imperatives are sometimes used:

> *Don't risk your life using worn tyres!*
> *Read this now! It will change your ideas of battery performance.*

Care must be exercised to avoid letting a hectoring note creep into imperatives. Your letter is already forcing its way into the Rx's house or office; do not let it bully him as well. An audacious trick is to make reference to what you most of all wish to avoid:

THROW THIS AWAY UNREAD – if you want to throw away a chance of increasing your business.

Challenging statements of a statistical kind (*It takes 100 bees ONE YEAR to make the wax for ONE TIN of BEEWACK polish*) or quotations from the famous that can subsequently be shown to have a bearing on the goods to be sold are two other useful openers. Most successful of all eye-catchers is something bizarre and unexpected:

HELP ! That is what we are bringing you news of – help in the home !

The language of these eye-catchers must be vigorous and sinewy. The Beewack eye-catcher would have much less effect in the form:

The average beeswax content of a tin of BEEWACK polish may be approximately represented as the annual output of one hundred bees.

Well-tried literary devices help to punch home the message – in the Beewack advertisement, repetition – in the *HELP !* eye-catcher, alliteration – in every example, rhythm.

B *Persuasion*

Having secured your reader, you must now start to sell. The first stage of this is to make him want what you have to offer – you must make it attractive to him by appeal to his desire for pleasure, health, success, love, the high opinion of others, comfort, increased money, or increased leisure. Ask yourself in what way the service or product you are offering can aid your Rx's achievement of any of these aims for himself or his family, and emphasise this.

Having thus given sales appeal to your product you then bring forward those selling points which will carry most conviction. At this stage ask yourself what your product has that its rivals have not got and emphasise this. This may be: its novelty; its high efficiency; its ease of use; its durability; its low price (though increasingly the last is becoming of doubtful value as a selling point as it is often associated with low quality in the mind of the Rx). The best advertising persuades not by unsupported affirmation but by bringing forward evidence – laboratory tests, statistics, specifications, testimonials from users or, better, from acknowledged authorities.

C *The final appeal*

Having put your arguments and persuasions before the reader and, you hope, made his attitude towards your product favourable and receptive, you should at the end of the letter try to provide something which the Rx can do, or offer to do something yourself which will take the Rx a stage nearer to purchasing.

For action, you can provide a tear-off section to be addressed and returned which is either an order form or, with expensive goods, a request for further information or a demonstration. Better still, send a prepaid card. If your product does not lend itself to this method, invite your potential customer to write, phone, or call at your showrooms.

Offers by the firm have been made so often as an additional inducement that something of this kind is virtually expected by the potential customer now. These offers may take many forms. Free samples, goods sent on approval, even a price reduction for a sale within a certain period, are all frequently offered. On a more modest scale, booklets, catalogues, colour guides, patterns, specimens, may be available on return of a card. If you can offer nothing else, at least conclude by expressing your willingness to advise or send further information on request.

D Example

Dear Sir,

Are you judging this letter by the paper
it is written on?

You probably are. Most people do.
Letters on high quality paper gain dignity, are
treated with extra respect - even a sales
letter like this.

This one is on BUSINESS BOND, today's
finest business paper. BUSINESS BOND is snowy
white, smooth-surfaced, and of good opacity.
You can see this for yourself.

What you are not able to see is that
BUSINESS BOND is manufactured in British mills
to very high standards of quality control. It
prints superbly on small offset machines and by

letterpress and die-stamping processes. It can
be supplied by all paper merchants from stock
without delay.

BUSINESS BOND means business. If you want
to try before you buy, fill in the prepaid
card. A trial pad will be on your desk within
forty-eight hours of your posting it.

Yours faithfully,
BUSINESS BOND SALES LTD

III PRESS ADVERTISING

A *Introduction*

Display advertising in the national Press is a very expensive matter. If a
company pays several thousands of pounds for half a page, it will employ
experts to write the copy as well as to prepare the layout. You, as a non-
specialist member of a firm, may, however, be called upon to write copy
for routine newspaper advertisements, especially in local papers. These
will consist principally of classified advertisements, public announcements, and small displays.

B *Classified advertisements*

Classified advertisements have no display (i.e. no special layout, large-
type headings etc). They are printed in columns under headings such as
'Business for Sale' or 'Situations Vacant' and this general heading is what
is relied on by the advertiser to draw the attention of those who will be
interested. They are charged at a rate per line, and there is a premium
therefore on brevity, especially as this form of advertising is normally
used by firms only when economy is an important consideration.
Abbreviations are used sometimes to reduce the number of lines, but
these also reduce the effectiveness of the communication. Here are two
typical classified advertisements:

1 (under the section-heading 'Reupholstering'):
   Appledons of Pidderminster. Craftsmen Upholsterers. Workmanship
   guaranteed. Estimates free. Wide selection of patterns available. Market
   Place. Tel: Pidderminster 79.

2 (under the section-heading 'Auctioneers, Valuers, and Surveyors'):
Negotiations for rating. Survey reports and valuations. Sales by auction and private treaty. Mortgages. Harvey Drewitt & Co., Market Place, Pidderminster. Tel.: Pidderminster 84 and 617.

C *Public announcements and small display advertising*

Public announcements may be made exactly like a classified advertisement under a section-heading 'Public Announcements'; but as they are usually of some importance they are frequently treated similarly to a small display advertisement. Some public announcements are to fulfil legal obligations and the wording is circumscribed by legal requirements. Others are of a kind that comes very close to being advertising (announcements of lecture courses by the local education authority, for example) and the boundary between the two is not easily defined.

Small displays are achieved most convincingly in local papers by paying for two or three columns in the classified advertisements pages to a certain depth, using the resultant space for the advertisement. Simple devices of layout, headings, varying typefaces and sizes, can be used to increase the impact on the newspaper reader.

Here is an example of such a small display advertisement. It is in a

---

J. HARDY & SONS LTD
have vacancies in the counties of Wiltshire and Gloucestershire
for
SALES REPRESENTATIVES
Applicants should be between the ages of 22 and 32 years, and have proved selling ability. A background knowledge of agriculture would be an advantage.

Good salary and commission. Training given. Car provided with expenses paid.

The post offers outstanding opportunity to the right person in a highly competitive, but interesting, field, selling direct to farmers.

Write, in first instance, in confidence, to:
THE REGIONAL SALES MANAGER
J. HARDY & SONS LTD
BRISTOL ROAD, DELLWATER, GLOUCESTERSHIRE
GL33 2MS

dignified style – using sentences not just headlines – that would also suit a public announcement. A similar style could be used for publicity leaflets.

Many small display advertisements are, of course, very different from this and shriek at the reader with disjointed headlines and ugly, or haphazardly mixed, typefaces. There seems no point in illustrating these – you will be able to see a large number of them by glancing at your local newspaper – and no point in learning to write them.

IV EXERCISES

Exercise A

1 Criticise the following unsolicited sales letter.
2 Rewrite it, so that it will have greater selling power. Invent details that you think should have been included.

Dear Madam,

May we trespass upon your time to draw your attention for a moment to the GNOME High Speed Gas Kettle? Your time is what this kettle will save for you – and your money wasted on unnecessary gas. The kettle is manufactured from heavy gauge aluminium and the special system of flutings on the base ensures rapid and symmetrical distribution of heat from a gas-burner so that water boils faster. Laboratory tests have shown this kettle will boil 2 litres of water in 3.7 minutes.

With normal use the GNOME High Speed Gas Kettle should pay for itself within a few months of purchase and subsequently, a considerable reduction in gas bills should be a recurrent advantage.

The kettle is made in the 2 litre size only and the price is £8.25 net, including tax.

If you wish to purchase one of these you should be able to get it from your local Gas Showrooms, or if they have not received a supply perhaps you will be good enough to notify us and we will post one to you direct. If you would like to order direct from us kindly send a cheque for £8.25 and state what colour handle and knob you require. Your kettle will then be despatched to you by return, post free.

Yours truly,
GNOME KETTLES LTD

Exercise B

Prepare an unsolicited sales letter for HOUSE-HOT oil-fired boilers from the following notes:

Three models – outputs 8, 10 and 15 kW – priced £125, £185, £290 respectively.
Silent, odourless. Easy installation by our engineers. Attractive design and vitreous finish in white, cream, red, or royal blue to harmonise with kitchen. Technical representative will call to advise on installation free.

Exercise C

Prepare an unsolicited sales letter to advertise Oxbridge Encyclopedia. Use the following notes. You do not have to employ all the material supplied – appropriate selection is part of the exercise.

8 volumes. Total of 3600 pages. Illustrated with 205 black and white photographs (full-page). Price £78, Rexine binding; £92, half-leather binding. Many drawings and diagrams in text. Last volume consists of detailed index. Articles in alphabetical order. Revised throughout, this year. Intended for children aged 11–14. 125 separate contributors. All contributions edited by a board to ensure vocabulary and sentence structure suitable to children, and all illustrations clearly drawn and easy to understand.

Payment by monthly instalments available – £10 initially with 24 instalments of £3·25 (Rexine binding): £15 initially with 24 instalments of £3·65 (half-leather binding).

Exercise D

Prepare an unsolicited sales letter to be addressed to sales managers of companies employing travelling sales representatives. It is to introduce the REGENT Business Card Service. Selling points are: genuine copperplate engraving; fast delivery; advisory service for designs; special express service for new members of your organisation; packed in twenties in special slide-out packs – convenient and preventing soiling or damage.

Exercise E

Prepare an unsolicited sales letter to Managing Directors of production companies to introduce READICHEF Refreshment Machines. Selling points: fresh hot drinks twenty-four hours a day; time spent in 'brew-up' eliminated; queuing reduced; reduction of time and labour for canteen staff. Will serve tea (with or without sugar), coffee (with or without milk and/or sugar), hot chocolate, and soup (i.e. eight hot drinks). Will hold 800 cupfuls and delivers in six seconds into a non-tainting throw-away cup.

Exercise F

Prepare classified advertisements for *two* of the following situations. Do not exceed 30 words for each. Aim to include the maximum amount of material, but be careful not to make the advertisement unreadable. Do not omit information that would be essential in the real-life situation.

1 Selling a house.
2 Selling a secondhand car.
3 Advertising a situation vacant.
4 Advertising a small grocery shop.

Exercise G

Prepare a small display advertisement for *one* of the following purposes. Indicate your layout.

1 Seeking suitable lodgings for 400 workers coming into the area as a result of expansion of your plant.
2 Advertising a service for supplying foreign magazines – current subscriptions and individual back-numbers.

Exercise H

Prepare copy for one of the following:

1 A leaflet to be distributed from a supermarket to notify customers that it is now licensed for the sale of wines and spirits.
2 A leaflet to supply outline information about a weekend course at a residential college of adult education.
3 A leaflet for distribution to students, pointing out the facilities available to members of the students' association and appealing for their active support.

Exercise I

Below are given two advertisements, A and B, taken, respectively, from a 'quality newspaper' (QN) and a 'popular daily' (PD). (In both, the names of the advertisers and of their products have been suppressed.)

You are required to rewrite both advertisements, A in a form in which it might appear in PD, and B in a form in which it might appear in QN.

A

Agriculturally, many relatively small seeds are used to produce amazingly heavy crops; a ley, for example, can be produced by sowing as little as twenty kilograms of seed per hectare, but the crop grown from it may well yield fifty tonnes of greenstuff per year and, furthermore, continues to do so for several years.

To be completely successful in the field, seed rates as low as this demand an extremely high standard of analytical purity and germination. By scientific methods of seed production and seed cleaning, we are able to offer seed quality of the standard required. . . .

Wherever you see a fine field of corn or lush pastures, it is usually a sign that a wise farmer has been sowing X's seeds.

B

Budgies! Someone's doing right by us at last! They've found out what it takes to make us Budgies *bounce* with health. Result? A new food! Proper balanced food at last! Canary seed and millet, of course. But with extras. *Three* extras. Listen!

1st Extra: Concentrated Protein. Puts feathers on your chest, pal!

2nd Extra: Vitamins A and D. That 'A' is good for your tubes. The 'D' makes strong bones. Saves them adding cod-liver oil, too.

3rd Extra: Special Seeds against Enteritis. About time, too!
Clean? As a whistle! Budgies! You're entitled to it. Spread the word!

[*Royal Society of Arts, English
Language Stage III*]

Exercise J

Your firm (a retail store or a manufacturer) is shortly celebrating its 50th
anniversary. Prepare the following:

1 a letter to the heads of other firms with whom you have dealt for many
  years inviting them to a reception with buffet and drinks at a hotel;
2 a display advertisement for the press making a special jubilee offer;
3 a letter to the staff informing them of a wages bonus to mark the
  occasion.

[*Royal Society of Arts, Communication in the Office,
Clerical and Secretarial Examinations Stage II*]

Chapter 11

Written Communication – Special Applications

I INSTRUCTIONS

A *What or how?*

So far we have considered only the information-passing, or information-seeking, function of communication. Instructions, however, may tell the Rx what he is to do (or what he must not do). This involves the action-producing (or action-stopping) function of communication.

Instructions may, on the other hand, merely tell somebody how to do something (how to reach the college; how to write a report; how to take off the lid of a tin) when they are no more than information-passing.

It might be thought that it would be convenient if we made a clearcut linguistic distinction here, perhaps reserving *instructions* for the 'how' and using *orders* or *directives* for the 'what'. In practice we do not do this; and in fact the ambiguity in the meaning of *instructions* is not without its usefulness since we frequently have to tell people not only what they are to do but also how they are to do it.

There is a danger to good communication in this ambiguity, though – that the Tx (and sometimes the Rx) may forget whether the instructions are 'how' or 'what' instructions. This is particularly liable to occur since the same style can be used for both. For example *Insert a coin in the groove at the corner of the tin, and turn to release the vaccum* and *Check these figures by Friday next* are both imperatives; but their intention is very different. The first aims to help the Rx to do something. It is easy for the Tx to slip into an inappropriately mandatory tone when explaining how to do something. Similarly, the imperative, *Change the oil filter every 20 000 km* in a user handbook looks rather like an order to the Rx, although it is intended as advice by the Tx. It would be better rephrased as *It is advisable to change the oil-filter every 20 000 km* or *Changing the oil-filter every 20 000 km is recommended*.

B *Style*

The imperative is only one of many styles which can be used for instructions. When we are giving 'how' instructions orally we use the second person present indicative (*You turn to the right past the bus-stop and go on to the end of the road*) but this is not considered suitable for formal writing. All other styles are suitable for both speech or writing; which is the most suitable will depend on: the subject matter; the Tx and Rx; whether 'how' or 'what'; and the circumstances in which the instructions are given.

Here are the principal styles we can choose between:

> *You are to report this matter immediately*
> *You must report this matter immediately*
> *You will report this matter immediately*
> *You should report this matter immediately*
> *This is to be reported immediately*
> *This will be reported immediately*
> *This must be reported immediately*
> *This should be reported immediately*
> *The Supervisor*[1] *is to report this immediately*
> *The Supervisor*[1] *must report this immediately*
> *The Supervisor*[1] *will report this immediately*
> *The Supervisor*[1] *should report this immediately*
> *Report this immediately.*

The first task then in conveying instructions is to decide on the style that will best suit your purpose. Second person forms are direct and vigorous. They establish a bond between Rx and Tx. More distant and dignified are the impersonal forms; and the third person styles are the most formal of all (suitable for printed rule-books, standing orders etc). The style employing the verb 'to be' and an infinitive is suitable only for directives; it is smoothly mandatory, firm but not aggressive. 'Must' forms are not often used for 'how' instructions; they are strongly mandatory but a little overbearing. 'Will' forms are curious. By using the ordinary future in a context which is one of instructions the effect is produced of an exceedingly firm imperative. Their firmness is, in fact, often resented by the Rx. They are suitable only for directives in a situation where orders can be backed by disciplinary measures (as in the Forces). 'Should' forms, suitable for both 'what' and 'how', are more friendly than the last two styles but introduce a moral note of what *ought* to be done that some people find irrelevant and distracting.

---

[1] Where the Rx *is* 'The Supervisor'.

Most direct and certain for orders is the imperative. It is also the shortest form always. It does not disguise at all that orders are being given and sometimes this is a disadvantage. As we have seen, when used for 'how' instructions it can sometimes appear to bully rather than help. However, its advantages of clarity and brevity are not easily outweighed. It is particularly valuable when dealing with a rather lengthy procedure which is capable of being broken down into a series of comparatively simple actions.

It is, of course, possible to combine these styles, and over a sustained series of written instruction (as in a textbook) it is essential to do so, as circumstances change and to give variety. Fairly short self-contained passages of written instruction are, however, more effective if written in one style throughout.

C *Sequence*

Instructions, more than any other form of communication, require accurate arrangement in logical (usually chronological) sequence. The intimate connection between mandate and sequence is revealed by the double meaning of *order* as a noun. The verb *to order* originally meant 'to regulate, to arrange'. 'How' instructions equally require to be given in the correct sequence if they are to fulfil their purpose. Nothing is more confusing to the Rx than to be told halfway through a series of instructions that he should already have made certain preparations that he is now hearing of for the first time. This kind of sequence error – some vital stage has been temporarily forgotten by the Tx – is understandable enough in speech; unfortunately it is also common in written instructions, where it can only be a result of careless preparation.

D *Example*

Here are two reasonably satisfactory ways of expressing the same set of instructions. Would you prefer one to the other if you were the Rx? Can you think of any circumstances *(a)* when 1 would be better to use than 2; *(b)* when 2 would be better to use than 1?

1

Duties of staff responsible for
opening incoming mail

Registered letters should be recorded in
the registered letter log and a note made of

the person to whom the letter is passed for attention. Envelopes of other letters should be torn completely open to ensure that no enclosure is overlooked. All letters should be date-stamped as soon as opened and placed with enclosures in the appropriate departmental tray. All cheques and drafts should be crossed with the name of the Company's bankers immediately on extraction from the envelope, a note of the amount made on the covering letter, and the remittance passed to the cash department.

Procedure to be adopted when opening letters

1   Record all registered letters in the registered letter log. Enter the name of the person to whom the letter is to be passed in the column provided. Place the letter in the appropriate tray.

2   Tear open all envelopes completely. Check that no enclosure is overlooked.

3   Date-stamp all letters immediately on opening.

4   Place letters and enclosures in the appropriate departmental tray.

5   Cross all cheques and drafts with the name of the Company's bankers immediately. Make a note of the amount on the covering letter. Pass the remittance to the cashier's department.

E *Algorithmic instructions*

The term 'algorithm' – originally confined to use by mathematicians in describing a problem-solving procedure – has recently become much more widely (sometimes rather vaguely) employed, as a result of its application to computer programming. Specifically it is now frequently used to refer to a particular technique of giving unambiguous step-by-step instructions.

Detailed consideration of sequence involves breaking down instructions into discrete stages of such a kind that only one action is demanded of the Rx at each stage. If for each stage one (unambiguous) imperative is written and all these are then listed and numbered in the order in which the actions have to be performed we are coming close to the algorithmic method. Algorithmic instructions, however, also allow for alternative procedures according to certain factual decisions made at critical points in the sequence. These decisions may be generated by questions of the type demanding the answer *Yes/No* (e.g. *Has the applicant made a similar application within the previous twelve months?*). In practice such factual decisions are more often the result of the examination of a statement (e.g. *The applicant has made a similar application in the previous twelve months*) with indication of alternative procedures to be followed according to whether this statement is classified by the Rx as true or false. Thus the Rx may be directed (1) to one of two alternative branches in the sequence or (2) to an imperative later in the sequence, omitting intermediate stages or (3) to an earlier imperative, and required to repeat the sequence from that point.

It is possible to chart algorithmic instructions in the style of a flow diagram using rectangular boxes for the imperatives and rounded ones for the decision-generating statements. The path to be followed by the Rx after a decision-generating statement may be indicated by T (for *true*) and F (for *false*). Figure 9 represents instructions used as an example in the preceding section restated in algorithmic form and charted.

Diagrammatical presentation is not an essential of algorithmic instructions but undoubtedly a chart is easier to follow for most Rxs than a numbered list of instructions with alternative procedures indicated solely by words. Charts are not used as often as would seem desirable, however, as they are time-consuming to produce in a form suitable for reproduction.

A chart can, incidentally, be extremely helpful to the person setting out the instructions, clearly pinpointing the stages at which the Rx is likely to become confused. It can also bring to light confusion in the Tx's own mind; it is a salutary discipline to attempt to express in algorithmic form instructions that you thought quite clear and to chart the result.

The reader is urged to compare Figure 9 with the two conventional sets of instructions in the preceding section and to consider whether the advantages gained seem worth the additional effort.

Procedure sequence to be followed by staff opening incoming mail

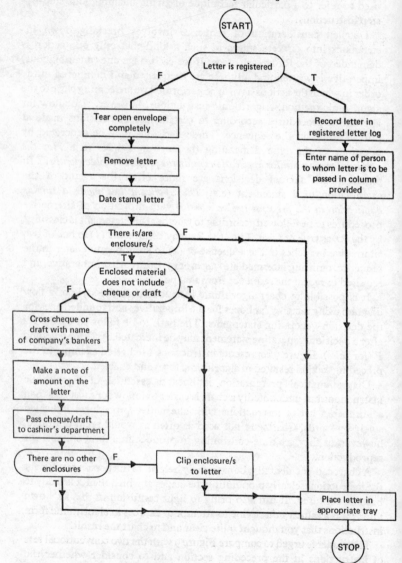

Figure 9 Algorithmic instructions in flow chart form

F *Personal instructions*

The preceding sections apply principally to instructions which are being issued generally or to a number of staff. Instructions which are intended for an individual can be more closely tailored for that person. His intelligence, his vocabulary level, his previous experience of this type of instruction, his personality and previous relations with the Tx – all these should be borne in mind in deciding the wording of the instructions.

Personal directives are often best worded as requests:

> *Will you check these figures and let me have your final estimate by Tuesday?*
>
> *Would you please investigate the cause of this excessive paper consumption?*

or favours:

> *I should be obliged if you would let me have full details of your departmental requirements before 31 March.*

Even the imperative can be softened by the use of 'please':

> *Please arrange lunch and a tour of the works for Mr Thomas Jackson (British Manganese) for Friday 10 March.*

These less direct ways of giving orders to individuals do not disguise from the Rx that they are orders, and that he has to do what is asked. But people do prefer being asked to being told; and the Rx is more likely to carry out instructions accurately, and with a good grace, as a result of a polite approach by his superior. Such touches do much to boost morale in an organisation.

II INTERNAL MEMORANDA

A The original meaning of *memorandum* was 'a note to help the memory' and the word is still often used in that way. It is, however, also applied in business to various types of written communication – nearly always internal – which do in fact provide an aid to memory in that they provide a written record, but whose primary function is to convey information or instructions, or to make proposals for the future.

B The longest and most formal memorandum is a document resembling a report. A junior manager may see a new way of increasing sales or an opportunity to improve office efficiency; as a vehicle for his ideas he prepares a memorandum to be submitted – unsolicited – to his superior. Memoranda of this kind have already been described in Chapter 9 (pages 162–3) and practice work provided on page 177.

C The term is also used to refer to a much simpler type of document which is sent to those concerned to remind of, or introduce, certain arrangements. Instructions, for example, of the kind discussed in the previous section may be circulated in this manner.

Such a memorandum is normally headed *Memorandum* or *Internal Memorandum* with the words *To* and *From* followed respectively by the name of the sender and the names of the recipients. In practice, the nominal sender – who may of course not be the person who actually writes the memorandum – is usually referred to by his rank or position, rather than his name.

Here is an example of a memorandum of this type:

FROM: Training and Education Officer

TO: Managing Director
         Works Manager
         Course members (as under)
         Mr Mayhew, Main Gate
         Mrs Paulson, 'D' Mess
         The Principal, Bromhill Technical
              College
         The Head of Department of Languages,
              Bromhill Technical College
         Miss M. Harcourt, B A

Foreign Language Course – French

Arrangements have been made with the Principal, Bromhill Technical College, and the Head of Department of Languages, to provide an intensive French course for executives of this company on company premises. The course is to be conducted by Miss M. Harcourt, B A. Enrolment forms will be available and should be completed on the first day of the course.

Details are as follows:

Courses will be held in 'D' Mess, Kentish

Street, on Tuesdays and Thursdays 17.30–18.30 hours, commencing Tuesday, 16 March 19..

The following have indicated their intention to attend:

Mr J. Aylett
Mr F. Baker
Mr D. Coombes
Mr L. F. Griffin
Mr J. P. Hollies

Mr J. Jackson
Mr L. M. Kneightly-Smith
Mr F. J. Lansdown
Mr T. Smithson
Mr I. Zarottini

D A very large number of brief internal communications between individuals are exchanged daily in most organisations. Although many of these will be informal and improvised (a message scribbled on a page torn from a diary and pinned to a man's desk in his absence, for example) it is desirable that as many as possible of these messages be conveyed on a standard message form, this marking them out instantly as official.

Most organisations provide pads (often interleaved with blank sheets for carbon copies) of headed message forms for this purpose. Such messages too are sometimes called 'memoranda' – or more often 'memos' – especially when written on printed standard message forms.

The printed section of the form will normally consist of the name of the organisation, a space for indication of department, the words *To* and *From*, and a space for the date. Here is a typical layout (but there are numerous variants):

COLLINGBURNE AND THOMAS LTD

Department ....

From .... To .... Date ....

The memo form is deliberately kept small so that wording will be held to a minimum. Good memos must be brief, unambiguous, without irrelevancies, yet friendly.

They ask for, or transmit, information; they convey personal instructions. Much of the day-to-day working of an organisation depends on them.

They represent a field in which communication principles can be applied to particularly good effect.

Such memos should not be signed. The longer type of memorandum (as the one about the French course) is, on the other hand, often signed by the sender.

III NOTICES

Instructions, announcements, appeals for cooperation etc are best directed to those concerned by means of memoranda. It sometimes happens, however, that too many people are involved for this to be practicable. To find a wholly satisfactory method of mass communication within an organisation is virtually impossible, but certainly the most widely used is the noticeboard.

To be effective a noticeboard must be:

1 well sited (large numbers must pass it daily)
2 big and attractively painted (so that it draws attention)
3 kept up to date (staff soon learn to ignore a noticeboard covered with old notices).

Even then, a large number of people will walk straight past it – this is its great defect as a communication medium. For notices of special importance, attention may be attracted by such devices as coloured tapes radiating outwards from the significant notice or a printed hand with pointing finger (of the type used as direction indicators in corridors) pinned beside it. Such devices lose their effect, however, if used frequently.

The quality of the notice itself is of great importance, not only in ensuring good communication on that particular occasion but also in encouraging staff in the habit of stopping to look at the noticeboard. Dull or incomprehensible notices will soon discourage even the most conscientious.

When a manager receives a memorandum (or other written instruction), that he considers affects his whole command, he is not usually doing his communication job properly if he merely pins it to the noticeboard. The memorandum will be one intended for *his* level of intelligence and experience in reading, and for quiet perusal in his office. For the noticeboard simpler and bolder presentation is necessary, and the message must be so worded as to be comprehensible to the lowest common denominator of intelligence and vocabulary amongst those likely to read it. The language should be vigorous and direct – aimed straight from Tx to Rx. Thus

NOT *The attention of management has recently been drawn to the increased use of motor vehicles by employees, which is causing progressive overloading of our already strained parking facilities.*

BUT *More and more of you are using cars to come to work. As a result, we are rapidly approaching a stage where we shall not have parking space for everybody who requires it.*

The message should be kept as brief as possible. This will involve not only concise wording, but also rigorous selection – only material that it is essential that everybody reads should be in the notice.

There is no harm in borrowing some of the milder devices of the advertiser. People who are screamed at all the time they are away from work by newspaper headlines, posters, and television commercials are going to take very little heed of a notice which consists of just a page of close typescript.

At least the heading and/or opening sentence should be of eye-catcher kind. An announcement of voluntary French classes sponsored by management is going to attract more attention if headed: *You can learn French free* than if headed *Voluntary French classes*.

Some element of display (such as the use of a felt pen) would make it more likely that the heading would attract attention.

There is no need for a notice couched in vigorous and lively language to be undignified or vulgar. It is simply a matter of remembering that: (1) you have got to start the Rx reading, and keep him reading, (2) on a noticeboard only simple clearcut sentences will carry much weight, (3) the Rx may be less intelligent, less knowledgeable, less used to reading, than you are; and it is your job to allow for that, (4) your notice is a waste of time for everybody if it does not produce the result you intended when you put it up.

EXAMPLE

You can learn French free

There is no catch in it. If you would like to start learning French next week, just hand in your name to the Personnel Officer before Friday. We will do the rest.

Classes will be held immediately after work in 'D' Canteen on Tuesdays and Thursdays. They will last one hour.

Remember 1   You have nothing to pay
        2   If you do not enjoy learning French, you can drop out whenever you like.

Places will be limited. Be one of the first on the list – hand in your name to Mr Lawton NOW.

NOTES

1 Material is whittled down to the minimum – further details such as precise times of meetings can be conveyed to those interested after names have been handed in.

2 Vocabulary is simple; sentences and paragraphs are kept short. Layout makes for easy reading.

3 Two advertising devices are used – the eye-catcher headline and the appeal to action at the end.

4 The Personal Officer, Mr Lawton, appears both by name and by title, in case some know him only by name and to reinforce who is the right person to go to.

Of course, such an approach is not suitable for everything. Important policy announcements, standing instructions, notices drawing attention to breaches of discipline – these require a more formal presentation. But they too will be more likely to be read and understood if the writer has taken some trouble to use a layout that will command attention and language that is well within the range of all potential readers.

IV FORMS AND QUESTIONNAIRES

A *Use of forms*

An increasing amount of business communication is now carried out by means of 'forms' – that is to say ready prepared documents with blank spaces to be filled in by the Tx. They are sometimes used for action-producing (as order forms, applications for share warrants, job cards etc) but are here considered chiefly in terms of information-passing.

Reference has already been made to routine reports (page 158) which are frequently submitted on forms; but the most interesting type of information-passing form is the one that is sent by an organisation that requires information, and which thus ensures that the information returned is exactly what is required, given in a standard order. A further refinement is so to arrange the wording on the form that the answers written in are of minimum length, thus making the task of both Tx and Rx easier. Forms may affect the young businessman in two ways – (1) filling them in (2) designing his own.

B *Filling in forms*

With a well-designed form, filling it in is one of the easiest acts of communication. All the Tx has to do is to read the instructions and obey them.

It is advisable to leave no part unanswered. If sections do not apply to you, draw a line through or write 'not applicable'. Sections left blank are worrying to the recipient who is never certain why you did not fill them in. Answer fully. If details are asked for, such as full Christian names, or names of, and dates of attendance at, all schools, these must be supplied – not a selection.

Unfortunately many forms are badly designed, and worded without regard to communication principles. Such forms are difficult for everybody.

C *Designing forms*

The increased use of computer processing has made the designing of many forms a specialised task requiring additional training, but firms do still devise their own without specialist advice if a computer is not to be employed. Readers of this book if called upon to undertake this task should bear in mind the following points.

1 The arrangement of the form should be free from internal contradictions, or apparent contradictions.
2 Instructions and questions should be arranged in a logical order.
3 They should be expressed in clear, simple, and direct English.
4 Direct questions and instructions are better than headings.

Thus

What is your surname? Answer in BLOCK CAPITALS	
What are your full Christian names?	
What is your full postal address?	

is to be preferred to

NAME (Surname first in block capitals)
ADDRESS

5 If there are several general instructions they should be introduced by some such heading as:
   Read these instructions carefully before completing this form.
6 Reference to explanatory notes should be kept to a minimum but where such notes are unavoidable they should be part of the form.

7 Where space is left for an answer it should be large enough for the kind of answer expected – it is extraordinary how many firms do not leave sufficient space for a country customer's full address, for example.

D *Questionnaires*

A questionnaire is a document, circulated in a sample of a group about which information is required, which is intended to obtain that information by a series of carefully designed questions. Such information is subsequently collated and permits deductions to be drawn about the group.

Originally such questionnaires were handed to the Tx to fill in himself, but increasingly today they are administered by a trained interviewer, who reads out the questions and fills in, or ticks off, the interviewee's replies. The compilation of questionnaires and the selecting of a true 'random sample' is skilled work that the ordinary businessman is not likely to be called upon to carry out.

It is, however, interesting to note how far the modern questionnaire has gone in removing the necessity for the Tx to write anything at all. The need to use computers in analysing results has been the principal cause of this development, but it has the additional advantages of time saving and increasing objectivity. The designer of forms could well take a few lessons from the designer of questionnaires.

Here is an extract from a questionnaire designed for the magazine *Encounter* and sent to all readers. Its purpose was to enable the magazine to assess the characteristics of its readership. The questionnaire was introduced by a letter from the editors, and the questions headed by the general instruction: *Please put a cross in the box beside the most appropriate answer, leaving the other boxes blank.*

9 *Do you own any of the following?*
- ☐ Record-player/radiogram
- ☐ Tape recorder
- ☐ Camera
- ☐ Cine-camera
- ☐ Typewriter
- ☐ Musical instrument

10 *About how many* hard-back *books do you buy each year?*
- ☐ Less than 5
- ☐ 5–10
- ☐ 11–20

☐ 21–30
☐ Over 30
☐ None

11 *About how many* paper-back *books do you buy each year?*

☐ Less than 5
☐ 5–10
☐ 11–20
☐ 21–30
☐ Over 30
☐ None

12 *About how many gramophone records do you buy each year?*

☐ 1–3
☐ 4–6
☐ More than 6
☐ None

13 *About how often do you go to the cinema?*

☐ Once a week or more
☐ Once in two/three weeks
☐ Once a month
☐ Less frequently
☐ Never

14 *About how often do you go to the theatre, opera, ballet or concerts?*

☐ Once a week or more
☐ Once or twice a month
☐ Three/four times a year
☐ Less frequently
☐ Never

V TELEGRAMS, CABLEGRAMS, TELEX MESSAGES

A Telegrams, cablegrams, and messages for Telex present an identical problem – to produce a clear unambiguous message in the minimum number of words – and the same technique is used for all three. Telegrams will serve to exemplify the method.

B Messages of this kind are usually sent to produce immediate action. Information-passing by these methods will be confined to extremely urgent material. Thus the first task for the Tx is to select from the material at his disposal relevant to the situation that which is essential to produce the correct action, or which must be transmitted to the Rx if the message is to be of any use.

C The content of the message having first been reduced to its minimum in this way, the wording of the message is next reduced. All minor words (such as articles, personal pronouns, and prepositions) are removed and normal sentence division is ignored (except in very long messages, where the word 'STOP' is inserted between sentences).

D EXAMPLE I The situation is that the Tx's car has broken down and he will be late for a committee meeting as a result. He decides to send a telegram to a friend who is attending the same meeting, but will not yet have left home. If the Tx were writing this message, he would probably put something like this:

> Dear Tom,
>   My car has broken down outside Luton and it will take at least an hour to get going again. I shall be unable to arrive at the committee meeting before eight o'clock at the earliest. Please apologise for me to the chairman.   Jack.

To reduce this message to its minimum, we would argue that all the Tx has to convey is: (1) what has happened – but not where (2) that his friend is to apologise to the chairman – the action the telegram is being sent to produce (3) the time he hopes to get to the meeting. Reduced in this way the message would run something like this:

> *My car has broken down. Please apologise to the chairman. I hope to arrive at eight.   Jack.*

Reducing this to the minimum, by omission of minor words and concentration on verbs and nouns, we arrive at the following as the best telegram the Tx can send:

CAR BREAKDOWN PLEASE APOLOGISE CHAIRMAN HOPE ARRIVE EIGHT JACK.

This is the best telegram because it is the minimum number of words that can produce the action required. It could be argued that the cause of the delay need not be mentioned, but it does enable the Rx to apologise more convincingly; however, if economy were very important it could be omitted. The 'please', on the other hand, cannot be omitted – politeness should not be sacrificed to economy.

E Since such messages are highly compressed and are transmitted without punctuation and capitalisation it is very easy to produce ambiguities. There are many variants of the anecdote about the businessman who instructed his broker to go on buying certain shares, and disappeared, far from telephones, into the grouse moors. In his absence, the price of the shares soared and the worried stockbroker sent a telegram, with a prepaid reply, that read:

SHARES NOW ABOVE TWO HUNDRED DO I CONTINUE TO BUY

only to receive the baffling answer:

NO PRICE TOO HIGH.

Before the message is sent, the Tx must check that it contains all the information asked for, or all the information permitting intelligent action to be taken; and that there is no ambiguity in the wording. It is sound practice to write out messages of this kind in block capitals so that the Tx sees for himself how it will appear to the Rx.

F Cablegrams are very expensive and those who use them frequently develop a somewhat bizarre English of their own in the constant attempt to keep costs down. Thus SEND SOONEST manages to say in two words what it is impossible to say with orthodox syntax in fewer than five.

G EXAMPLE 2 The following is a typical exchange of Telex messages between firms. The wording is identical with that which would be used for a telegram or cable in this example; but this is not always true of Telex messages. Since they are charged by time, not by the number of words used, there is an advantage in using abbreviations and contractions. As a result these occur much more frequently in Telex messages than they do in telegrams or cables where there is no advantage as the shortened form of a word is charged at the same rate as the full length form.

(a) VELOX BROMHILL
　　FURTHER　　DELIVERY　　DHP7　　MOTORS　　URGENTLY
　　REQUIRED　　PLEASE REPLY BY RETURN
　　TOMPKINSONS

(b) TOMPKINSONS　　BLEAK HILL　　WANNINGTON
　　DELIVERIES DHP7 HELD PENDING CLEARANCE OF £896·24 ON
　　OCTOBER ACCOUNT WHEN CLEARED WILL DESPATCH MOTORS
　　IMMEDIATELY
　　VELOX

Note that in addressing and signing telegrams, cablegrams, and Telex messages minimum wording is used – the firm's name without 'Ltd' or 'Messrs', a personal surname without Christian name or 'Mr', 'Mrs', or

'Miss' unless there is a real risk of confusion between members of a family. Frequently the simplest and friendliest way of signing is a Christian name only, provided the Tx is confident that the Rx will be able to identify from the message which of several people with the same Christian name is sending the message. Addresses and names are paid for by the word at the same rate as the message.

VI EXERCISES

Exercise A

Write out instructions how to get to your home from your technical college (1) in colloquial style as you would tell a friend (2) in formal written style.

Exercise B

In each of the following groups say which instruction seems to you the most appropriate in style for the subject matter and which the least, and why:

A
1 You are to empty the contents of this can into a saucepan and heat to boiling point.
2 Empty the contents of this can into a saucepan and heat to boiling point.
3 The contents of this can should be emptied into a saucepan and heated to boiling point.

B
1 Please complete this form in ink. Use block capitals. Use a typewriter for name, date of birth, and sex only.
2 You should complete this form in ink, using block capitals. You should use a typewriter for name, date of birth, and sex only.
3 This form should be completed in ink, using block capitals. A typewriter may be used for name, date of birth, and sex only.

C
1 You are to arrange transport Leeds to Manchester for Mr Tompkins and book accommodation for him in Manchester for the night of 25th June.
2 Transport is to be arranged by you Leeds to Manchester for Mr Tompkins and accommodation booked for him in Manchester for the night of 25th June.

3 Please (1) arrange transport Leeds to Manchester for Mr Tompkins (2) book accommodation for him in Manchester for the night of 25th June.

Exercise C

Which of the following imperatives, in your opinion, *(a)* tells how to do something, *(b)* gives an order, *(c)* gives advice? Are there any where you are not sure – if so, why is that?

1 Catch the 10.10 from Liverpool Street. Bring the documents with you.
2 Remember that the 10.10 from Liverpool Street is usually ten minutes late at Ipswich. Don't forget the documents.
3 Check that there still is a 10.10 from Liverpool Street on Saturdays.
4 Let me have your detailed report by Monday next.
5 Please send me a copy of your illustrated brochure, as advertised.
6 Insert coin and slide the knob to the right.
7 Give to each telephone call, no matter how trivial, the same attention that you would give to the caller in person.
8 Do not lean out of the window.
9 Ask your chemist for NERVORITE.
10 Answer all the questions.

Exercise D

1 Make detailed comment on the following standing instructions observed by the author in a classroom at one technical college.
2 Rewrite them.

FIRE PRECAUTIONS

In the event of a fire alarm all students are to observe the following instructions:

1 Follow the advice of your tutor as to whether to evacuate the room or not.

2 From this room the quickest exit route is via the east staircase rear exit to the yard.

3 Students leaving this room please assemble for checking at the rear yard.

If the east staircase is affected students are to proceed along the corridor to the west staircase.

Lifts must not be used.

Exercise E

Prepare algorithmic instructions for one of the following in flow chart form:

1 starting a car (or motor cycle)
2 playing a 45 rpm record on a record player
3 making a call using a domestic (or office) telephone.

Exercise F

Prepare *one* of the following memoranda:

1 to office staff on answering the telephone
2 to members of a tennis club on care of the (grass) courts
3 to new students outlining their responsibilities to the students' association.

Exercise G

Write the following messages for use on message forms ('memos'):

1 Notifying a junior member of staff that his holiday choice of 26–9 July August has been asked for by too many, and only 15–29 March is available for him.
2 Asking another department whether a parcel of GPO pamphlets on the use of the telephone has been delivered to them by mistake.
3 Instructing a senior member of your staff to prepare a roster for overtime duty after consultation with other members of the office. Give a time limit for completion of this.

Exercise H

Write out notices, about 100 words in length, suitable for display on a notice board, for *two* of the following:

1 Drawing attention to the facilities of the college library.
2 Soliciting support for ONE of the following college activities – rambling group; chess club; wild life preservation society.
3 Announcing a distinguished visitor (specify) to works, office, or college, and calling on all for support in making his visit a success.
4 Introducing a system of staggered tea-breaks for various departments of college or office.
5 Drawing attention to *either* health hazards *or* fire hazards caused by cigarette smoking.

Exercise I

Your firm is mounting an exhibition for a week to show the history of its products over the last hundred years. There will be an official opening ceremony on the first day, followed by a buffet lunch for special guests.

(a) Design a poster advertising the exhibition to the public.
(b) Prepare an invitation card to be sent to special guests.

> [*Royal Society of Arts, Communication in the Office,*
> *Clerical and Secretarial Examination Stage II*]

Exercise J

Prepare a short questionnaire on one of the following topics, or one of your own choice.

The exercise can be made more realistic (and more interesting) if you are working in a group. You can then arrange amongst yourselves to choose different topics, duplicate your questionnaires, fill in each others, and analyse results. With a large group some will have to think of subjects of their own, similar to the following suggestions.

1 Newspapers
2 Reading
3 Motoring
4 Leisure activities
5 Careers and ambitions
6 Shopping habits
7 Holidays
8 Television viewing
9 Amenities of local town (or district of large city)
10 Communication in business

Exercise K

Write telegrams for the following situations. Include name and address of the Rx each time. Invent necessary supporting detail. The aim is to produce a practical message with all detail the Rx would need. Use block capitals throughout and no punctuation marks.

1 The estate agent who is selling your house has notified you of an offer of £14 000 and your immediate reply is required. Refuse this offer and give £15 500 as the minimum you will consider.
2 You are secretary of the college or office football team. On the morning of an away match your centre half phones you to tell you he sprained his ankle the previous evening. Your most useful substitute in this position is not on the phone but you would like him to play rather than the reserve.
3 You are on a walking tour, and have run short of cash. You will have to shorten your holiday if you cannot obtain a little more. Ask parents or a good friend to wire ten pounds to you at the next place you are stopping at.
4 You are expecting a firm to collect and replace a defective duplicating machine they have supplied, but they have not called. You wish the matter to be dealt with quickly but you have no telephone number for the firm.
5 You have written to a firm complaining of non-delivery of goods (specify) and within an hour of your posting the letter the goods arrive.

Exercise L

The sales manager of a motor car factory in England receives this cable from Eagle Motors Inc., the agent in Chicago:

AUTOMOBILE 426967 FITTED WITH RIGHTHAND DRIVE STOP PLEASE ADVISE

N.B. In the USA cars should have lefthand drive.

Write the following:

(a) A cable in reply, telling them to sell the car at a reduced price and that the correct car will be sent;

(b) a confirmatory letter, giving a full answer;

(c) a memorandum to the export manager.

> [*Royal Society of Arts, Communication in the Office,*
> *Clerical and Secretarial Examinations Stage II*]

Exercise M

One alarming feature of the past decade has been the increase in damage done to property by apparently wanton acts of vandalism. Many of the most vulnerable targets are items of public property (e.g. public telephones) and a large proportion are the responsibility of local authorities. Recently, for example, almost all the movable fittings in a public park were destroyed or taken away in one night.

You have been asked to devise a short notice or advertisement for your Authority, *either* discouraging acts of vandalism in general, *or* discouraging vandalism against a particular public amenity or item of property.

(a) Design the notice/advertisement in whatever form you consider appropriate, and *(b)* write a passage (not more than 200 words) stating your view on vandalism as it affects local authorities. Consider how serious the problem is and what steps local authorities ought/can take to combat it. Write as far as possible in relation to your own experience and to the area in which you live.

> [*Local Government Training Board –*
> *Clerical Examination*]

Exercise N

Draft the memorandum referred to in the following transcript of instructions from a senior officer.

There have been far too many minor accidents recently in our offices. I'd like you to draft a memorandum on this subject to all members of staff.

Here are some examples of the sort of accidents I mean and the dangerous practices which can cause accidents.

Secretaries and other people tend to leave cabinet drawers and desk drawers open. This is not just a nuisance for those who have to shut the drawers; it's positively dangerous. And in this connection I was taught never to open more than one drawer of a filing cabinet at one time.

At least two members of the public have been involved in incidents which were the fault of our staff. In one case, someone was badly bruised when a swing door was pushed right into him, although the door was clearly marked PULL TO OPEN. The other incident involved an old lady who was knocked over by a member of staff who was running down one of the passages.

The other day, one of the staff fell down some stairs and broke an ankle because he didn't look where he was going while he was carrying a lot of files. And while we're on the subject of carrying things, I'm really worried whenever I see one of the girls carrying a typewriter or trying to lift something too heavy for her. Actually, it's the same for anyone. You shouldn't try to lift or carry anything on your own if it's too heavy or bulky for you to manage.

Last month we had a minor fire when someone dropped a cigarette end into a wastepaper basket. The excuse I was given was that it was a metal one. That doesn't matter. We work in offices in which there's always a lot of paper about. That's why there are plenty of ash-trays.

Still on the subject of fire hazards – people should not put materials on or against any sort of heating apparatus.

It might sound ridiculous but some of us manage to injure ourselves even when we use pins and stapling machines. And of course there's the occasional mishap with other bits of office machinery, such as guillotines.

Lastly, I'm convinced that it's extremely important to be tidy in an office. Don't leave things lying about when you finish a job. And if you spill something or break something, clear it up straight away. If you want to get rid of broken glass or razor blades, don't leave them in the waste-paper receptacles. Wrap them up and label them clearly.

That's about all, though you may well think of something important that I've left out. If you do, then put it in.

The essential thing about your memorandum is that it should encourage staff, in the friendliest way possible, to be genuinely safety-conscious. You should not just give them a list of accidents that have happened or might happen. And remember it's for all office staff, not just those in your own office.

[*Local Government Training Board –*
Intermediate Examination]

Exercise O

1 Imagine you are employed in the Chief Executive's Department at Blenkinsop. The following letter has been received:

5 Pudding Rise,
BLENKINSOP, Yorkshire
YO53 7BM

15 April, 19..

The Chief Executive,
Civic Offices,
BLENKINSOP, Yorkshire
YO53 1AF

Dear Sir,

The garden of my house, in this area of high rateable values, abuts upon the Gracing Green Corporation Allotments. Last year it became the practice of several allotment holders to bring their transistor radios on to their plots to provide music while they worked, to the considerable annoyance of those of us who wished to enjoy the peace of our gardens.

This nuisance has already started again this year. Is it possible for you to write to these people pointing out the annoyance to others? Perhaps your powers can permit you to ban their use altogether on allotments.

Yours faithfully,
John Studwick

The Chief Executive's comment is: *I think we should do something about this. I don't know whether our present powers permit us to go so far as banning radios on allotments. It is an offence to play one in any park or open space under our bye-laws, but I'm not sure whether an allotment would be considered a park or open space. Better try Mr Studwick's letter approach with perhaps a vague threat of further action. Send the letter across to Mr Williamson[1] with a memo as from me telling him to send a circular letter on those lines to all allotment holders.*

Write *(a)* this memo, *(b)* a reply to Mr Studwick for the Chief Executive's signature.

2 Now imagine you are on Mr Williamson's staff. Draft a suitable circular letter.

---

[1] Mr Williamson is Director of Arts and Recreation for Blenkinsop.

Chapter 12

Essays, Projects, and Papers

I ESSAYS IN EXAMINATIONS

A *Examination essays and communication principles*

Time should not be devoted to Section I of this chapter unless you are preparing for an examination which requires you to prove your ability to write successfully at some length by producing an essay (i.e. an extended piece of continuous prose on a set subject) under examination conditions.

Such essays present you, as an examination candidate, with special difficulties arising from the unnatural circumstances of the piece of writing required. The Rx is faceless and unknown. Unlike the Rx of everyday life he is not really interested in finding out what you have to tell him, but principally in how you tell it. Communication principles cannot, therefore, be fully applied, and the essay will be judged not only for its linguistic but also for its literary achievement. Further, under examination conditions you are frequently forced into writing about something you know little about, and this affects the kind of planning you can employ.

You will have met these problems before in previous English examinations. What follows is not, therefore, intended as a comprehensive guide to examination essay-writing but to draw your attention to particular points of importance concerning essay-writing at the post 'O' level stage.

B *Choosing the topic*

An essay may consist of (1) narrative, (2) description, (3) exposition, or (4) discussion.

Certain essay titles confine you to one of these treatments at a time – for example *The life of a notorious pirate* (narrative) *A walk in winter* (description) *Uneasy lies the head that wears the crown* (exposition) *A woman's place is in the home – discuss* (discussion). Those that limit you to narrative or description are not likely to be set at this level.

Other titles leave you to select your treatment or to blend several treatments. Thus the title *Advertising* leaves you free to handle it as narrative (history of advertising) description (the forms advertising takes, with examples) exposition (the various media of advertising, with their relative effectiveness), or discussion (do the advantages to the customer outweigh the addition to the cost of the product and the extent to which our lives are dominated by advertising?). Or a combination of two or more treatments is possible – thus a brief history of advertising or a brief survey of the forms advertising takes may lead into a discussion of its advantages and disadvantages to consumer, retailer, and manufacturer.

Exposition and discussion are more difficult to handle than narrative and description, but they give you much more opportunity to show that you are capable of logical thought. At this stage, that is what an examiner is looking for, and a very high level of writing indeed would be necessary to compensate for the comparative simplicity of narrative or descriptive treatments. Topics should, therefore, be chosen which permit predominantly exposition or discussion treatment.

C *Timing the essay*

Timing is very important in English examinations. You are always working against the clock and if you fall behind you may have to leave a question out – almost the only way of scoring nought for a question in a conventional English paper. The essay must therefore take not a minute more than is provided for it. On the other hand, an essay that occupies less than the allocated time, or is short of the required length, is bound to be marked down.

Some examining bodies indicate essay length by time, others by the number of words required. It is useful to have a conversion formula for these and the following will give an approximate indication of what is required.

1 TIME TO WORDS. Allow one-sixth total time for plan – then assume 10 words written per minute of remaining time. Thus a one-hour essay works out to 10 minutes planning and 500 words written.

2 WORDS TO TIME. Allow 10 words per minute and add one-fifth of this time as planning time. Thus a 300 words essay requires 30 minutes writing and 6 minutes planning.

D *Planning the essay*

A plan – that is to say brief notes of the points to be made with an indication of the order in which you propose to make them – is essential to success. A plan serves you in three ways:

1 It prevents 'drying up'. Time spent staring at the ceiling is time wasted. When you start again there is inevitably a hiatus at that point which shows to the examiner. Often you go off at a complete tangent.

2 It enables you to check your timing. If you have a plan, you know if you are going too slowly or using up your material too fast; and you know early enough to be able to make adjustments that will not show in the final product.

3 It gives shape and development to your essay – the most important advantage. A good essay has form. It should lead the reader point by point to a predetermined conclusion. At the end the reader should feel he has arrived at a destination, not that the essay has suddenly expired because all the material has been used up.

Two types of plan are of use. These could be called the *Imposed Plan* and the *Organic Plan*.

THE IMPOSED PLAN can be used only when you are fortunate enough to have plenty of material to write about. It is a limiting plan whose chief purpose is to ensure that you provide a balanced coverage of your subject matter and do not try to squeeze a quart of material into a pint-size essay. Decided upon by the principles of logical organisation discussed in Chapter 2, this plan edits, selects, and arranges.

The best essays spring from the Imposed Plan but the examination candidate does not always have the necessary depth of material to draw upon. In such a situation the ORGANIC PLAN will help. The method is as follows:

1 Scribble down as quickly as possible all the ideas that come into your head as you decide your essay topic. These are got down without editing or arranging, before the stream (or trickle) dries up.

2 Read through the list of points and strike out any which are too weak to be of use or which do not fit in with the others.

3 Note points that are connected with each other (these will often be close to each other in the list because an association existed in your mind when you wrote them down). These can be looped round in pencil, and tails coming from the loops joined to show connection (see Figure 10). These looped and joined points are to form your paragraphs, so it is worth

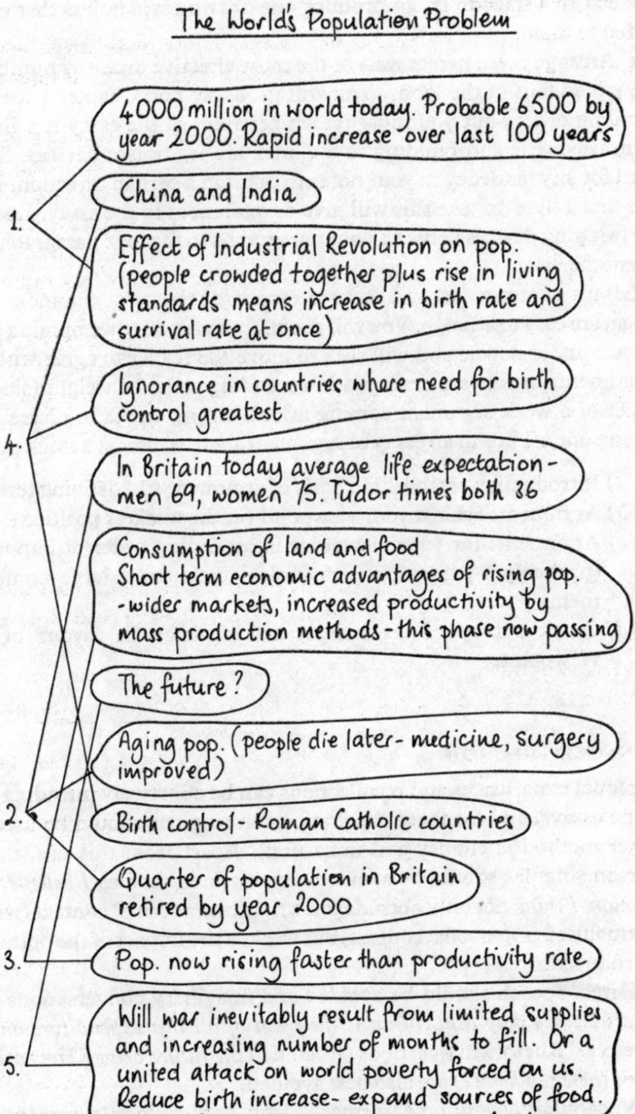

The World's Population Problem

4000 million in world today. Probable 6500 by year 2000. Rapid increase over last 100 years

1.

China and India

Effect of Industrial Revolution on pop. (people crowded together plus rise in living standards means increase in birth rate and survival rate at once)

4.

Ignorance in countries where need for birth control greatest

In Britain today average life expectation— men 69, women 75. Tudor times both 36

Consumption of land and food
Short term economic advantages of rising pop. - wider markets, increased productivity by mass production methods - this phase now passing

The future?

Aging pop. (people die later - medicine, surgery improved)

2.

Birth control - Roman Catholic countries

Quarter of population in Britain retired by year 2000

3.

Pop. now rising faster than productivity rate

5.

Will war inevitably result from limited supplies and increasing number of months to fill. Or a united attack on world poverty forced on us. Reduce birth increase- expand sources of food. Future of world depends on quick solution

Figure 10 An organic plan

while at this stage to try to produce one or two extra points that can be added to them.

4 Arrange these paragraphs in the most effective order by numbering the joined tails of the loops. You will probably find Chapter 2 useful in deciding order; but you must remember that, as the essay is a literary form, suspense and building to a climax are legitimate devices. Search hard for any tendency in your notes to point in a certain direction. If you can find a 'line' to take this will give development to the essay. Look too for bridging devices between your paragraphs so that one paragraph leads to another.

Essays of argument, and these are amongst the most common at this stage, are easy to arrange. You will probably have your own opinion on the matter under debate and will seek to move the reader to agree with you. Arguments are always arranged in ascending order of weight (since the effect of a weak argument coming after a strong one is to discredit the strong one). Thus in an essay of argument there is almost a stock plan:

(a) Introduction establishing basis of argument and defining terms
(b) Arguments against your viewpoint (in the weakest position)
(c) Arguments for your viewpoint in ascending order of importance (probably a paragraph each, unless there are a large number of them)
(d) Quick survey of arguments, and decision in favour of your viewpoint.

D Some points of style

Personal experiences and recollections can be effectively introduced into some essays, and for these the first person singular should be used (any other method is clumsy and unnatural). Apart from this use, the first person singular should be avoided. Expressions such as *I believe, in my opinion, I think* not only obtrude the writer into a formal context (which is normally an impersonal context) but weaken the impact of the opinions so introduced.

Direct speech should be avoided and imaginary conversations of the kind: *People may ask, 'What is the point of all this expenditure on social services?'* Rhetorical questions (*What will the future bring? How are we to solve these problems?*) are also best avoided.

Vocabulary should be formal. Slang and colloquialisms must be avoided, and all abbreviated forms such as *don't, can't, won't.*

Abbreviations generally should be introduced only when essential. A list of examples which trails off in a vague *etc* produces a particularly slipshod effect.

Some attempt should be made to vary sentence length and sentence structure. If your vocabulary is wide you should demonstrate this fact provided this can be achieved with tact – thrusting unusual words at the reader is ostentatious and impolite in an essay, as in other forms of writing. Above all, you should aim at crispness and originality of expression.

E *Practice essays*

The following groups of essay subjects are designed so that each gives a balanced representation of the types of topic set in post 'O' level English examinations. You should write for the time, or the length, prescribed in the examination you are preparing for. As a variant you can, especially in the early stages, prepare plans for, say, three essays in one group; then decide which is the most effective of your outlines and write an essay based on that one.

1. Early marriages
   Alcohol and the motorist
   The ideal companion
   North Sea oil
   'This is still the best country in which to live, even in which to live pretty close to the breadline' – *Clement Freud* (1975)

2. Student protests
   The preservation of wild life
   Why I consider Pop inferior to some other kinds of music
   What Pop gives me that no other sort of music can
   'The ability to laugh together is the essence of love' – *Françoise Sagan*

3. Families under stress
   Country pleasures
   Fashion
   Has Christmas become nothing more than a festival of commerce?
   'All men are created equal' – *Thomas Jefferson*.

4. Violence as a political weapon
   Government intervention in industry
   Waste

Making a house a home
'Any man can make money if he has nothing else in his head' – *Hazlitt*

5 Child vandalism
The do-it-yourself movement
Choosing a present
What is work?
'Britain has become a multiracial society and the sooner people accept that the better' – *Sir Geoffrey Wilton*, Chairman of the Race Relations Board (1975)

6 The pleasures of eating out
Are British workers lazier than their continental equivalents?
Is local government spending to support the Arts justifiable?
The world's food problem
'The less people know about what is really going on, the easier it is to wield power and authority' – *Prince Charles* (1975)

7 Britain's health service
Unusual hobbies
Examinations as a test of ability
The right to strike
'Educate a woman and you put a knife in the hands of a monkey' – *Indian proverb*

8 Organ transplants
Do we still have class distinction in Britain?
Should all tobacco advertising be made illegal?
Film societies
'The car is going to contribute very largely to wrecking our civilisation' – *Sir Alex Issigonis*

9 Do local government elections matter?
Are we happier now than we would have been 100 years ago?
Consumer organisations
Worry
'The liberty of the Press is the birth right of a Briton' – *John Wilkes*

10 What do you consider to be the most urgent problems facing Britain today?
Teenage morality
Incentives
Is private charity an anachronism?

'Economy does not lie in sparing money, but in spending it wisely' –
T. H. Huxley

II EXTENDED ESSAYS

A *Choosing the topic*

Some course schemes require an extended essay to be written for assessment. These are usually expected to be 3000–5000 words in length and most schemes require the subject chosen to show some relevance to the student's main area of study.

A common mistake is to choose a topic that is too big; 3000–5000 words seems very long if you are used to essays only a tenth of that length, and it is natural to want to make sure you have sufficient material to last the distance. However, large general themes such as *Oil* or extended historical treatments such as *The Development of the Merchant Navy* provide too much material and the essays inevitably become a breathless catalogue. *Recent Trends in Oil Marketing* or *The Development of Merchant Shipping during the Seventeenth Century*, at first more forbidding titles, will in practice serve the candidate much better, as the subject matter can be kept under control and sufficient space is available to permit something interesting to be said.

You should first decide upon your field of interest, and subsequently limit the area in this field which you are going to explore thoroughly. What you finally choose to write about should represent a still further reduction of this area, since the best extended essays are produced when you know more about the subject than the part you are selecting for your essay. It is sound policy to decide upon your detailed topic only when you have already carried out some investigation into the subject generally and are able to see what particular part or aspect of your material will make a self-contained and easily handled topic.

Local interests should not be neglected. A lively essay could, for example, arise from the study of some local industry about which little is known nationally. Commercial or industrial history limited to your own area will be more compact and controllable than similar themes treated nationally.

Provided no breach of confidentiality is involved your own firm or organisation may offer suitable subject matter – the development of a new product or process, for example. For government students, the investigation of some aspect of the work of your own authority or civil service department might provide admirable material not generally available.

B *Preparation*

1 RESEARCH. You will not be expected to attempt much in the way of primary research (i.e. obtaining information firsthand or examining original documents). The bulk of your research will be secondary – you will be drawing your information from the writings of those who have carried out primary research or who have at least assembled conveniently the product of secondary research on a scale you could not hope to emulate. Your principal sources will be books, magazines, and newspapers. This is not to suggest that your essay will be a mere matter of copying or rehashing what others have written. Having obtained the information you require from your sources, you will then have to collate it (one source against another), assess it, and attempt to form your own opinions and viewpoint. The facts in your essay may come from your sources, but not the way those facts are expressed or the conclusions drawn from them.

For certain subjects you may be able to draw upon what you have been told (oral reports) if the source is a reliable one. Many firms and institutions are willing to cooperate by supplying pamphlets dealing with their work and will sometimes supply information that is not generally available if you explain your request in a courteous letter.

Your first task, then, is to prepare a reading list. Starting is difficult sometimes, as there are only a limited number of subjects for which libraries hold readymade bibliographies, and those they do have may be out of date. Your tutor will probably be able to make some suggestions to start you off; the college librarian or local public reference librarian will also be prepared to offer advice and direction. Once you have started, you begin to find out for yourself what you should read next. For example, a good start is often an encyclopedia article, which will not only outline your subject but also list books that you can then refer to. These books in turn will provide further bibliographies. The only danger about this way of assembling your reading list is that it tends to be out of date, as you are working backwards and no reference can be more up to date than your original encyclopedia article. Some subjects date more than others, but it is always important to note the date of publication of a book referred to – if it is an old one it may still be the best there is, but it may be one that has been superseded and much of the material in it discredited by a more recent work. It is best to avoid topical subjects because of the danger of some political change, for example, suddenly making your essay out of date just as you have completed the work on it.

The most topical source is the newspaper, but it is also the least reliable. Specialist periodicals include material that is normally more up to date than that in a book, since the delay in writing and publishing a book is considerable. Material sent by firms may be assumed to be as up to date as a magazine article, if in the form of printed pamphlets, and completely up to date if provided specially for you.

To find out what are the latest books dealing with your subject you should:

(a) Check the subject catalogue of all libraries to which you have access.
(b) Watch book reviews and switch on for TV and radio programmes relevant to your subject.
(c) Study the annual volumes of the *British National Bibliography* for the last two or three years. This is arranged under subjects, but will, of course, show only works published in the year of that particular volume.

2 KEEPING NOTES. As you read you will make notes indicating the exact source, including page references, in case you wish later on to refer to the original again. Material which you intend to quote must be copied out accurately with a full note of the source. Distinguish between facts and opinions. You are bound to have to draw your facts from your sources; but you should try to form your own opinions, or at least weigh one writer's opinion against another's.

It is useful to keep your notes on separate pieces of paper in a loose-leaf folder, so that they can be shuffled about and rearranged as necessary. If as you make the notes you try to arrange them under headings this will help you when you come to the planning stage.

3 PLANNING follows broadly the principles laid down in Chapter 2, and the hints on the imposed plan earlier in this chapter. Paragraphing alone does not usually provide sufficient organisation for an essay of this kind and you are recommended to divide the work also into sections or 'chapters' each with its own heading. It is then a matter of deciding the best order for these chapters and the best order for the paragraphs within the chapters.

Subjects which have a chronological sequence present few problems, but others may involve much thought before the best order reveals itself to you. Planning an essay of this length is not a ten-minute matter. You need to familiarise yourself with your material and live with it over a period – a weekend for example – continually returning to the problem of how best to order it. The recommended notes on separate sheets grouped under headings will save you much trouble at this stage. It is much easier to try over various arrangements by moving these notes about physically than it is to carry all the ideas in your head or to write out several experimental outline plans.

4 THE ROUGH DRAFT of your extended essay must be fully written out in the form that at that stage you intend as the final form. It must be legible, because your tutor will have to read it and discuss it with you. He will be able to draw your attention to errors of fact, unsubstantiated opinions, faults of arrangement, and imperfections of style. After discussion with your tutor you will either write out the final version correcting the flaws that have been pointed out to you, or prepare a modified rough draft for further discussion with him.

C *Presentation*

You should try to make the final product as handsome as possible. If you can type, it should be typed. If it is handwritten, it should be neat and legible. You should supply a thin cover of some kind (heavy covers should be avoided as the essays may be posted) and a title-page. If the work is divided into chapters with headings, a table of contents listing these chapters and the pages on which they start should appear immediately after the title-page. The whole essay should be sewn or stapled together.

You should not 'lift' passages from your sources, but must re-express the material in your own words. Short quotations may be employed where you consider the original wording particularly striking or where it constitutes important evidence about a point you wish to make. Such quotations should be enclosed between inverted commas and the source of the quotation made clear. There are several ways of doing this. The simplest is to introduce the quotation by a form of words such as: *James Codd in 'Frying More Fish' says* ... Alternatively, after the quotation you can add: (*James Codd*, '*Frying More Fish*'). Footnotes can also be used to indicate the source of a quotation. You should keep to one system throughout the essay.

A modest number of such short quotations (say six to eight) may be counted towards your total of words.

You should make a similar reference to your source when you are not quoting but are nevertheless paraphrasing or summarising material pretty directly.

In short, the reader should be put in a position where he is able to distinguish what is your own original contribution – ideas and interpretations – from what you have extracted from the books, articles, and pamphlets you have been reading.

At the end of the essay all sources of information should be listed and your main sources incorporated in a bibliography (i.e. a list showing for each the author, name of work, and date of publication, as above). Where field work has been undertaken, brief details of this should be added.

The method recommended by British Standard 1629 for listing (abridged) bibliographical detail is illustrated below:

CODD, JAMES. Frying more fish. 1977

(when we are listing a separately published book, pamphlet etc)

HADDOCK, HARRY. Low carbohydrate batters. *Journal of the Association of Fish Friers*, vol. 16, May 1977

(when we are listing an article from a periodical, newspaper etc).

III PROJECTS

The term *project* is used in commerce and technology to refer to a planned investigation intended to lead to change or development. It is more familiar to students as the name of an increasingly popular learning method. A student project will involve (1) selection of a suitable undertaking (2) experimentation, investigation, fact-finding (3) writing the project up.

The distinction between the student project and an extended essay is a fine one, but it is clear that the investigatory element is much stronger in the project. Most of the advice on the extended essay given in the previous section is, however, relevant. Writing up involves less continuous writing and more use of sketches, diagrams, charts, tables of readings etc. Sometimes illustrative material cut from magazines and newspapers may be inserted (but discretion must be exercised here or the final product will look like a schoolchild's effort).

IV PAPERS

A paper is essentially an account of original research or the discovery of new data or the exposition of a fresh interpretation of already established data. It is prepared for the consideration of those best qualified to judge the value of the work and findings it describes and is seen in its most typical form in the paper read before a learned society and subsequently published in the society's journal.

Confusingly the term is sometimes applied to material not intended to be read to an audience. (It would seem preferable to employ *article*, *report*, or plain *account*, for material intended for readers only.)

Transatlantic usage employs the term 'research paper' for a written report of a research project and this meaning is increasingly met with nowadays in the United Kingdom too. A research paper in this sense, if involving genuine original research, is prepared on exactly the same lines as a detailed report (see Chapter 9). If the term is used to refer to no more than a student exercise what is required is virtually indistinguishable from a student project or extended essay.

Students are also sometimes asked to prepare a paper to be presented orally to their fellow students. In this context original work is not, of course, expected from them; only an exposition of some subject they have studied. This provides a useful exercise falling between a project (or essay) and a talk; more formal than the latter since it has to be in the language of writing rather than that of speech, but – unlike the project – unable to rely on sketches, pictures, graphs, tables etc.

Both genuine papers intended to be read aloud and the ones prepared as student exercises should be written out in full in advance in the language of written communication rather than of oral. Accuracy, objectivity and a consistently dignified register are essentials.

Part III

Chapter 13

Oral Communication

I SPEAKING VERSUS WRITING

Figure 11 indicates the principal advantages of face-to-face communication. Communication by telephone shares these advantages but the feedback situation is less than ideal as the facial expression, posture etc of the Rx cannot be seen and the Tx is therefore deprived of valuable indicators of the success or otherwise of his attempts to communicate. (This situation will, of course, improve with the gradual introduction of video-telephones.) An additional advantage of both types of oral communication is that the Tx does know that the message has been, at least, delivered. With written communication there is often a measure of doubt whether the message will reach the Rx at all – and a further doubt whether he will read it if it does.

It would seem therefore that oral communication is to be preferred whenever practicable (i.e. whenever access to the Rx in person, or failing

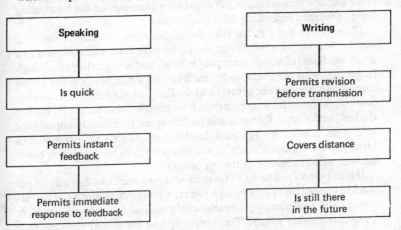

Speaking	Writing
Is quick	Permits revision before transmission
Permits instant feedback	Covers distance
Permits immediate response to feedback	Is still there in the future

Figure 11 Speaking versus writing

that by telephone, is feasible). The great disadvantage of oral communication is, of course, that there is no record of what was communicated. Thus the Rx has no opportunity for future study of what may be an extremely complex piece of information: nor has the Tx any way of proving what he told the Rx, in the event of a dispute. There will be many situations where the extra effort of communicating both ways is well worth while. Thus we may give the Rx a full explanation of some point and follow this up with a brief confirming letter or memo. With complex material the opposite process is frequently employed: a short oral briefing is followed by detailed written material for leisurely study and future reference.

Decisions whether to use speech or writing for specific verbal communication tasks are frequently made on a quite irrational basis. Instead of consideration of the nature of the information to be conveyed or whether a record of the information for future reference is likely to be needed, the decision is often made on the basis of the Tx's convenience (more rarely the Rx's if he is considered very important or excessively busy). The position of the Tx on the communication ladder seems to affect the decision too. People near the bottom often fail to put complaints and suggestions in writing because they are frightened of committing themselves to paper. At the top the fear is more usually of personal contact with subordinates; memos or notices on noticeboards are used to convey information that the Tx thinks may not be favourably received whereas a much better communication job could have been carried out by meeting those concerned and telling them face-to-face.

There is one more factor that should be borne in mind in deciding whether to speak or write. When we speak we are not communicating by a single medium (although most people think that is what they are doing). In parallel with the main verbal medium are a number of other media conveying a message about the Tx to the Rx. Such media include: his/her posture, gestures, facial expression; how good-looking he/she is; his/her clothes (with a man, footwear and neckwear are particularly important), hair style, accent; his/her rank in the organisation; his/her previous history in the organisation (is he/she reckoned to be honest, frank, clear-headed, well-informed – or the opposite?).

It is important to line up all these subordinate media so that they do not work in opposition to the message you are attempting to convey. If you are trying to lift staff morale your melancholy worried face may give the lie to your encouraging words. The very way you stand may indicate your contempt for the person you are speaking to although your words are polite. Your accent, clothes, and hair style may be opening a communication gulf between you and your Rx while your words are attempting to build a bridge. On the other hand insincerity is quickly detected. We all know the salesman who can clip on a false smile to match his friendly words.

Sincerity and sensitivity are much more important for success in face-to-face communication than any special skill with words. Awareness that other people have feelings; that they can be easily offended; that they can sometimes be (by our own standard) unbelievably slow in getting the point – that is what is needed. And a sense of humour.

II DIFFERENCES BETWEEN SPOKEN AND WRITTEN ENGLISH

Some American communication consultants recommend, 'Write as you talk'. During recent years there has certainly been a considerable blurring of the boundary between speech and writing, but in England at least we are not yet in a position where we can assume that the spoken and the written forms of the language are completely interchangeable.

We have already seen (in Chapter 5) that some words and expressions are at any one time in the history of the language considered suitable for speech only (colloquialisms) although these may subsequently be accepted into the written language. The existence of colloquialisms constitutes an important vocabulary difference between speech and writing. On the other hand, there is a considerable vocabulary traditionally associated with the most formal kinds of writing that sounds strained and unnatural in speech. Of a man who uses this vocabulary when he is talking people say, 'He talks like a book' or 'He's swallowed a dictionary.'

As well as vocabulary differences between speech and writing, there are differences of syntax. In speech we have greater licence. We do not, for example, speak in perfect sentences. *Just going down the road for a bit*, we say – with no subject and no finite verb. *I am just going down the road for a bit* would sound a little pedantic in most situations. This is the kind of lesson that the tyro at playwriting has to learn. Dialogue – which has been written – sounds unnatural when spoken if the writer has failed to allow for the greater freedom of the spoken language, and often has to be altered by a producer before the actors can speak it effectively. The same lesson has to be learned by the manager preparing his speech or his oral report.

There are a number of minor grammatical imperfections which are accepted in the spoken language – partly because the difference between the forms is not easily detected by the ear. Thus *who* is widely used for *whom* and the accusative instead of the possessive before the verbal noun (*Do you mind me asking a question?*) Accusatives after the verb 'to be' are so well established in speech (*That's them!*) that the formally 'correct' version sounds wrong. In such examples, to follow the rules that apply to formal writing is to make our speech sound pedantic and to alienate our Rx.

In speech we can produce shades of meaning by stressing one word rather than another in a sentence. There is no satisfactory equivalent to this in writing, though in informal writing underlining of the stressed word is sometimes possible. Consider the words: *You might have known me better*. Probably the most usual stressing of this sentence is to put a slight emphasis on *known*. Variations on meaning arise with shift of stress, as follows:

1 Stress on *you* : 'You of all people might have been expected to have known me better.'

2 Stress on *me* : 'You might have known that I at least would not have done such a thing.'

3 Stress on *might* : 'It is possible that you could have known me better.'

4 Pause before, and slight stress on, *better* : 'You might have known me when I was a better person.'

Two important observations must be made about this example (1) The written versions have to be longer than the spoken if they are to avoid ambiguity – stress emphasis permits greater economy of words in speech. (2) The six words written down might be capable of any of these interpretations. A prime cause of ambiguity is failure to notice that words written down, and thus deprived of the stressing you give them in dictating, or even just in your mind, may to a reader carry a meaning that you did not intend.

Similarly in speech we can convey, by gesture and facial expressions, a shade of meaning, an emphasis, a hint of mockery, humour, irony – a whole range of delicate modifications of our words denied to us when we write. This is something that must be remembered all the time when we are dictating material. It is to be borne in mind too when we are on the telephone, and therefore invisible to our Rx.

Finally, the separations of word from word, sentence from sentence, paragraph from paragraph, that are characteristic of writing, do not apply in speech. Words are run together into convenient speech groups: we do not necessarily pause at the end of a sentence: there is nothing in speech which is equivalent to division into paragraphs. The first of these three points affects the oral Tx. It is a mistake to believe that slowing up delivery by putting a pause after every word improves communication (adults frequently address children in this way). In fact the breaking up of the familiar speech groups that results is a source of confusion and irritation to the Rx, as will be quickly recognised by all who have ever listened to an old-fashioned headmistress addressing pupils and parents on Open Day.

That we do not normally divide spoken material into sentences and paragraphs affects the dictator – who has to do just this when he is dictating – and also the man who has to talk a great deal in his job but seldom writes. When such a man does have to write he tends to run his sentences into each other, with a comma between, and to forget about paragraphing until he has gone well past the place where he should have started a new paragraph.

III PHATIC COMMUNION

The term *phatic*[1] *communion* was coined to provide a convenient way of referring to what takes place when we employ speech to convey an attitude or reaction to another human being but the meaning of the words we use is unimportant.

Here is an example. The head of the firm is about to pass young Jackson (who has been away on a short course) in the corridor. He stops and says, 'Hullo, Jackson, I see you're back again.' The apparent message is here completely pointless. Jackson knows he is back and does not need telling he is; clearly the boss can also see he is back since he is standing in front of him. The observation is, however, not so worthless as communication as it at first appears. The boss's words carry a hidden meaning – something like: *You see, I know you are called Jackson and I know you have been away on a course. I keep in touch with what is happening to all members of my organisation – even quite junior ones.*

If we watch for them we become aware of innumerable examples of phatic communion in our daily social and business life. The cross-examination that one has to undergo about the route used when one has travelled to a meeting has nothing to do with trying to find out the quickest route. It is talk for the sake of talk (or for the sake of ice-

---

[1] From the Greek *phasis*, an utterance.

breaking). It is purely phatic. The traditional British habit of commenting on the weather to strangers is similarly phatic. The real message conveyed by such words as 'Looks as if it's going to be a bit brighter today' is: *I'm friendly towards you in a mild sort of way.*

In its more extreme manifestations phatic communion becomes virtually ritual. The custom amongst the well-bred of asking 'How d'you do?' when meeting somebody for the first time is an example. The last thing expected is a reply to this enquiry along the lines perhaps of: 'Well, not too badly on the whole; but I'm having a spot of trouble with my ingrowing toenail again.' The ritual answer is a simple repetition, a second 'How d'you do?'

Although endless empty chatter can be irritating, phatic communion is not to be despised. There are many social and business occasions when the capacity to keep a meaningless (but also harmless) conversation going is of value. The English are supposed to be particularly good at this – an American has compared English small talk to a game of first-class tennis played with imaginary balls. The man who will not talk is classed as unsociable, a poor mixer; he is distrusted. Phatic communion can build an emotional bridge between two strangers, or two men who have to do business together but are a little suspicious of each other, across which genuine communication can subsequently take place which would not have been possible without the early meaningless exchanges that produced a more friendly and relaxed atmosphere.

IV INTERCALARY EXPRESSIONS

Intercalary expressions are superfluous speech units inserted between the words that carry the meaning of an oral message. The most common are: *I mean; really; well; sort of; in fact; you know.* One becomes sharply aware of the repeated use of these unnecessary words whenever anybody of limited educational background, unused to speaking at any length in a fairly formal situation, is called upon to give an oral explanation, eye-witness account, or report. Television provides daily examples when witnesses of events covered in the News are asked to describe what they saw. More assured and better educated people than these also pad out what they have to say with intercalary expressions. They do not make so much use of the expressions already listed (which are particularly associated with the less well educated) but have their own specialities which would include: *actually; as a matter of fact; not to put too fine a point upon it; to tell you the truth; speaking quite frankly; Well, now; between you and me* etc.

It is far from clear why intercalary expressions are so popular. Some of them (such as *sort of; I mean; you know*) seem to seek support from the Rx; it is as if the Tx were apologising in advance for any inadequacies in what he is saying. Others stress the truth or factual accuracy of what is being said – another defensive move. Experiments at Oxford University in 1975 indicated that the use of *Well* and *I mean* increases in anxiety situations. Intercalary expressions also serve to fill in time while the speaker is thinking what to say next or to make a short bald statement seem a little longer and more important (in the mind of the Tx only: the Rx is usually simply irritated by the padding out of the message with superfluous wording).

There does not seem to be much of a case for intercalary expressions; on the surface they would appear to be a waste of energy for the Tx and a source of irritation to the Rx. (It is possible, however, that the less educated, less intelligent, Rx is not irritated by them but subconsciously welcomes the slowing up of the message, which gives him more time to understand it.)

It would seem to be sound advice to recommend young men and women hoping to rise to managerial or senior technician roles to start cutting out intercalary expressions from their speech as quickly as they can. It is certain that what they subsequently have to say will appear crisper, more incisive, more professional, as a result.

V DICTATING LETTERS

Two special difficulties confront you when you have to dictate a letter or indeed any other material.

1 Although you are speaking, your Rx will read your communication and therefore consider it writing, and expect it to conform to writing standards. You are therefore 'writing' by speaking, an unnatural activity bound to produce problems since the spoken and written language are, as we have seen, not identical.

2 It is impossible to see what you are 'writing' or what you have 'written'.

The following recommendations will be of use to you when you dictate and will help you to meet these two special difficulties.

(a) Prepare ahead. Have ready the letter you are answering and any other document you will need to refer to. Think before you start to speak, and rough out your letter in your mind. If the letter is likely to be at all complicated, jot down headings to remind you of the principal points. If it is likely to be very complicated, write out a full rough draft before you start to dictate (this is easier if you are using a dictating machine than if you have a shorthand-typist waiting for you to start).

(b) Dictate slowly and clearly. Do not mumble, or speak with cigarette or pipe in your mouth. Spell out personal names, brand names, and obscure technical words that it is unreasonable to expect a typist to know.

(c) Indicate sentence division by saying firmly, 'period' or 'full stop' at the end of every sentence. Indicate each change of paragraph by saying, 'paragraph'. Less familiar punctuation (such as dashes to mark a parenthesis) should also be indicated. How far you go in dictating punctuation may depend upon your previous experience of a secretary's knowledge of punctuation, but it remains your responsibility to see that the letter is punctuated the way you want it to be.

(d) Keep your sentences and paragraphs short.

(e) If you do lose track of what you have 'written', do not hesitate to ask the shorthand-typist to read back (or play back to yourself, if using a machine). Do not hesitate to make corrections – though you should try to avoid dictating material that needs correction.

(f) Remember all the time that your vocabulary and syntax must be that of writing, not speech.

(g) Try to avoid emphasis by stressing.

(h) Avoid facial expressions and gestures that modify meaning in a way that cannot be conveyed on the typed page.

(i) Avoid intercalary expressions.

(j) With all but the most simple letters have a read-back or play-back at the end, to check that the letter is all that you wish it to be.

(k) Remember to observe communication principles. The recommendations for business letters made in Chapter 8 apply just as much to dictated letters as to any other kind.

VI USING THE TELEPHONE

Some of the difficulties that confront the dictator are also relevant to the use of the telephone, particularly that gesture and facial expression are invisible to the Rx. Certain tones of voice, especially those conveying irony or humour, seem to get lost in transit; jokes misfire and flippancies are easily taken as serious comment.

Calls should always be kept short as this helps to clear the firm's lines.

There has been an additional demand for brevity since the introduction of STD. STD trunk calls are charged on the basis of very short time units, but to obtain the maximum benefit from STD the greatest possible number of calls should be confined to the minimum unit. This permits no social chatter or digressions; every word must be a necessary one. To compensate for inevitable curtness it is necessary to cultivate warmth and friendliness in your voice. Although the seconds are ticking past you must seem to your Rx calm and assured. The key to success will be (as so often with communication problems) good preparation; know precisely what you have to ask before you dial the number.

When it is your turn to be the Rx, seek to aid the Tx in making his call as economical as possible. When you answer, give your name and department (*Mrs* or *Miss* is sometimes added to the name by women, but there is never a need for *Mr*). Give an answer if you possibly can; otherwise take a message or offer to ring back. Do not ask unnecessary questions or waste time trying to find out about something while your Tx is still on the line. Be pleasant; keep calm; avoid waffle.

VII SPEAKING IN PUBLIC

A *Preparation*

Preparation is also the key to successful speaking in public. The surest protection against nervousness is the consciousness of having good preparation behind you. The first consideration is the audience – how many are there likely to be; what will their attitude be; how much will they know already; how will they compare with you in education and intelligence? As in all communication, know your Rx and plan accordingly.

Next the purpose of your talk must be considered. Is it only to put the Rx in the picture; to supply detailed information, as in a lecture; to put forward new ideas; to teach a skill; to introduce a new policy, or a new line of action?

Finally you collect and assemble your material – from previous knowledge or experience, from discussion with others, from documents and reference works – and set to work to organise it. The principles governing organisation of material presented in Chapter 2 will assist you, but remember that beginnings and endings are of particular importance in a talk. Your beginning must arouse interest in your material or enlist sympathetic attention to your viewpoint. Allow your own enthusiasm to show from the start; if possible, show too that your subject is of personal importance to the audience. Your ending must be carefully thought out. Do not go on too long. Many a speaker, having made a number of points effectively, has destroyed his impact on the audience because he felt that he had not talked long enough. What comes last is best remembered by the audience. Your natural ending is therefore either a rapid summary of your principal points or a forceful presentation of the point that you particularly wish the audience to carry away with it. The old dictum: *Tell them what you are going to say ; say it ; then tell them what you have said* has much to command it. Repetition is an essential part of good spoken communication; the Rx has no second opportunity to grasp what you are saying unless you provide it.

Some speakers find it helpful to write out their opening and closing sentences in full and to have these with them. You should certainly not write more of your talk than that – a talk which is read, or is writing memorised, carries no conviction, unless you are exceedingly skilful in writing in such a way that it sounds like speech (as in broadcasting, for example).

Even full notes are more of a handicap than an aid. The speaker who is continually referring to his notes is speaking most of the time to his chest rather than to the audience, and presents the top of his head for inspection rather than his face. Ideal as a stand-by during a talk is a list of the principal topics of your discourse, clearly printed (so that you do not have to peer) on a half postcard held in the palm of the hand. If you have prepared thoroughly, these headings are all you will need.

B *Delivery*

You are bound to feel a little nervous before you start, especially if you are a beginner. One or two very slow, very deep, breaths help to calm you down. Then go straight into your talk with something to interest your audience. Nervousness and selfconsciousness will soon disappear as you sense your hold on the audience tightening.

Speaking directly to the audience increases your hold over it. You should, however, avoid fixing your gaze on any particular face. Your eyes should focus just above the heads of the back row of your audience (assuming a level seating arrangement). You should keep still – not rigidly to attention but not walking up and down or twisting your fingers together, or turning one foot over and back continually. Mannerisms distract the audience from what you have to say – if you throw up the chalk almost the entire concentration of the audience is on whether you will catch it.

Speak clearly, with adequate volume for the size of room (but no more – audiences do not like being shouted at). Speak slowly enough for your points to have their full impact. Pauses between sentences are a better way of slowing your delivery than pauses between words. Regular pauses between sentences disguise too the moment when you have to pause a little longer than usual because you are not quite sure how to put the next point. If you remain calm, an audience will in fact accept your remaining silent for a considerable time while you think out what to say next – silences never seem so long to the audience as they do to you. Noises such as 'um' and 'eh', at moments when you are at a loss for a word, and intercalary expressions irritate the audience; they should be eradicated from your delivery.

Make full use of the advantages of spoken communication over written. Use gesture, facial expression, stress emphasis, pauses, and variations of pitch and speed of delivery to draw attention to your main points and to avoid monotony. Many beginners deliver their talks in a dreary monotone as if they themselves were bored; you cannot hope to interest an audience if you do not even sound interested yourself.

C Timing and feedback

There are two types of timing that affect the public speaker.

First he must ensure that his talk lasts for approximately the time expected of him. If he runs out of material considerably earlier than the organisers had expected he causes embarrassment to all, including himself. On the other hand, to go on after time throws a strain on the audience and is often resented. Accurate timing of this type comes only with experience but during preparation the time that the talk is to take must be borne in mind. Speeds of delivery vary considerably but as a very rough guide you can assume you will probably speak at about 150 words a minute. During the talk an eye should be kept on the time so that adjustment can be made as the talk goes on.

The second type of timing is a matter of adjusting your speed of delivery to the reception speed of the audience. If a second point is made before the first is fully absorbed, both points will be inadequately communicated. Long pauses between points when the audience is absorbing the points rapidly and easily lead to boredom and distracted concentration. Successful timing of this kind depends partly on previous experience and partly on rapid reception of feedback from the audience. The glazed eye, the restless movement of feet, even the way people are sitting on their chairs – these are the indicators that you are going too fast or too slow. They are more easily 'read' with a small group, but even with a very large audience the alert speaker is aware of feedback; he knows whether the audience is with him or not.

Lack of response from the audience may be caused by other faults than those of timing. Your vocabulary may be unsuitable; your assessment of their previous knowledge of the subject wrong; your manner of delivery monotonous or infectiously sleepy; perhaps they just cannot hear you. It is part of your job as an oral communicator to try to find out the cause of an unfavourable feedback and correct this as your talk goes on. This will often be a matter of trial and error, and sometimes you will not succeed; but the attempt to amend what is displeasing the audience must always be made.

VII ORAL COMMUNICATION TO INDIVIDUALS AND SMALL GROUPS

A substantial amount of the day-to-day communication that goes on in any business is spoken communication between individuals (face-to-face communication) or between an individual and a small group (committee work, oral reporting to a board, instructions given to a group of subordinates, etc.).

As was noted on page 232, it is written communication that is feared and avoided by the lower ranks of an organisation, oral communication by those nearer the top. It is easier to dismiss a man in writing than face to face; a proposal can be turned down in a memo without giving the proposer a chance for last-minute arguments; unpopular decisions and rulings are more easily pinned to a noticeboard than told to the men concerned in person.

Where the communication chain consists of one Rx and one Tx only, the advantages of oral communication probably outweigh the disadvantages, though even with a line as short as this it is desirable to confirm the more important oral communications by memos. With longer lines distortions creep in as oral messages are conveyed down, or up, a communication chain. American experiments indicate that the greatest loss of detail in oral communication occurs at the second stage (i.e. when the first Rx becomes a Tx and passes the message on), and that false additions to the message and distortions of what remains of the original message become very marked by the fourth stage of a chain.

The principal problem in oral communication is ensuring that the Rx continues to listen. A brisk lively voice helps, and you should watch the face (or faces) of the Rx to detect first signs of misunderstanding or loss of concentration. Vigorous language with avoidance of clichés also helps.

Barriers between you and your Rx may include: your face, your clothes, your accent, your tone. Only the last of these is much within your control. If the Rx does not like your face this is a serious disadvantage to your power of communication; you can reduce it by at least trying to look friendly. Your clothes may mark you out as earning more money, doing a more sedentary job, or being of higher rank, than your Rx, and this may antagonise him (them). With some Rxs a sports jacket may not carry as much authority as a lounge suit. A beard, long hair, trendy clothes, not wearing a tie – such things may arouse quite sharp opposition in the Rx. You can do little about this but to avoid extremes, and to dress fairly conservatively. Your accent may mark you out as public-school educated or of working-class origin, and with certain Rxs either can be a handicap. It is difficult to eradicate class accents of this kind and attempts to do so often sound ridiculous.

Tone, however, you can control. An overbearing bullying tone, or a patronising one, is very harmful to communication. Friendliness, helpfulness, reasonableness, patience – these are what your tone should convey, and, above all, sincerity.

Small groups are in some ways more difficult to talk to than a large audience. The large audience is anonymous and develops a group response to you that is usually predominantly cooperative. With small groups, individuals stand out; a single antagonistic element in a small group can be very harmful. Differences between members of the group become apparent and are threatening all the time to break the group into a number of separate people difficult to communicate with equally at the same time. A blanket treatment for all will not work and you have to be alert for feedback from individuals and deal with this individually, while not allowing any one person to dominate the group that is your Rx. Usually a much more intimate and relaxed approach is possible than with a large audience, and some informality of manner and language is often helpful.

Face-to-face communication with individuals is the simplest form of oral communication. You have only one Rx to think about and the feedback indications from him are comparatively easy to read. Your Rx has also plenty of opportunity (provided you do not insist on talking all the time yourself) of becoming a Tx in his turn; complete two-way communication is possible as it never is with a group. When it is your turn to be the Rx do listen; do not merely wait for the other man to stop so that you can start again – that is the commonest cause of communication breakdown between individuals. When he is talking, continue to watch his facial expression, while concentrating also on the subject matter of what he has to say; do not spend so much time thinking how to reply to his first points that you do not even hear his subsequent ones. If he looks like bringing up more points than you can easily carry in your head, stop him for a moment while you deal with what he has said so far. This does not mean that you can feel at liberty to interrupt him whenever you like. If you do this, he will forget what he was going to say and your mutual communication will be that much the less complete.

IX ORAL REPORTS

Oral reports should present little difficulty if the recommendations of the last two sections are borne in mind. The more formal oral report, such as the report of an officer at a meeting of an organisation, offers problems similar to those confronting the public speaker, and the problems are met in the same way. Fuller notes than for a speech are, however, necessary and this could be one occasion when the whole thing is written in advance and merely read out.

The less formal oral report (as when you are called in by the boss to give him your version of what happened or are required to report progress to a committee) should be treated as no more than a special example of oral communication to an individual or group.

X EXERCISES

Exercise A

1 Give as many meanings as you can to the following sentences by varying the stress emphasis.
2 Write out sentences which fully express these variations of meaning.

(a) What are you doing here?
(b) The complete sales figures will probably not be published this year.
(c) Your action has not been entirely justified by this letter.
(d) The whole course is not essential for men employed full-time in advertising agencies.

For Exercises B, C, and D the tutor or a member of the group should act as chairman and introduce you briefly. Start your talk with 'Mr (or Madam) Chairman, Gentlemen' or Mr (or Madam) Chairman, Ladies' or 'Mr (or Madam) Chairman, Ladies and Gentlemen' as appropriate.

Exercise B

Prepare and deliver a three-minute talk on the town or village you come from (or district, if a large town or city). Comment from group and tutor.

Exercise C

Prepare and deliver a four-minute talk on a hobby, sport, or similar activity that you are interested in. This should be tape-recorded and played back to you. Your own comments first, followed by those of group and tutor.

Exercise D

Prepare and deliver a six-minute talk on a subject of your choice. If you say 'um' or 'eh' your audience is to repeat this after you each time, or – if this is considered too noisy – raise their hands each time.

Exercise E

1 If you have a job, explain to the group what your duties are. Imagine the group are new members of the firm who will have to carry out the same duties. If you are a full-time student without a job, explain the rules of a game, or the rules of a club you belong to, as you might to those new to the game or club.
2 Answer questions from the group.

Exercise F

If you are working in a group, each member should produce a letter on some business topic requiring a reply. The subject matter should be simple and non-technical. These letters are then distributed at random through the group and replies 'dictated' by those who receive them. It is advantageous if replies are made onto dictating machines, or tape recorders in a language laboratory, so that you can play your recording back to yourself, note your own faults, and rerecord to improve clarity of diction. If you are on your own, you should practise dictation into a tape recorder, so that you become aware of your own faults, and can check if you are correcting them.

Exercise G

The group should divide into pairs and perform the following telephone roles:

(a) Student and registrar – enquiring what room a certain subject will be taught in that night.

(b) Businessman and hotel receptionist – booking a room for an overnight stay.

(c) Customer and dry cleaners – enquiring why a suit for dry-cleaning (quote receipt number) promised for the previous Saturday has not been delivered.

(d) Sales representative and sales manager – confirming a delivery date.

(e) Two businessmen, Tompkins and Smethers – arranging for Tompkins to be met by Smethers off a certain train.

The member of the pair initiating the conversation should work out details such as times and dates in advance, but should not let his partner know these before the conversation takes place. Members of each pair should take it in turns to initiate the dialogue. The aim is to complete the conversation in the shortest possible time without gabbling, or sounding impolite. It is desirable to have a third person time the pair (a watch with a good seconds hand is all that is needed). Alternatively dialogues can be recorded and timing worked out from the rev-counter of the tape recorder.

Chapter 14

Meetings

1 GROUP DECISIONS AND MANAGERIAL DECISIONS

Apart from face-to-face communication with individuals, the most important application of oral communication in business is the meeting.

The range of meetings that readers are likely to be concerned with (if not as organisers at least as amongst those present) extends from such extremely formal occasions as the annual general meeting of a company to the informal meeting called by a manager in order to discuss some aspect of their work with members of his command. This range may be divided into three principal categories – formal meetings, committee meetings, and command meetings.

Formal meetings and committee meetings have this in common – they are intended to produce group decisions, by some method of voting. The person controlling such meetings (usually called the 'chairman') is bound by prescribed or traditional rules of procedure. Command meetings on the other hand are called by managers as a communication device, to enable them to obtain information from their subordinates or convey information to them. Opinions may be sought but the manager alone is responsible for making decisions and there is no point therefore in taking a vote. The manager is free to devise his own procedure.

It is most important to distinguish clearly between the group decision meetings and the command meetings that you attend. In the first the decision is a joint responsibility decided by a majority vote, and once the decision is made you must give it support even if you had previously voted against it, or cease to be a member of the organisation. In the second you may state facts or express opinions as required by your manager, but you are not able to influence the decision in any other way. The decision is binding on you not because it is a group responsibility, but simply because you are the subordinate of the man who makes the decision.

As for organising meetings, it will probably be several years before readers will be in managerial positions requiring them to communicate with subordinates by means of command meetings. Their immediate chances of experience in organising meetings are much more likely to be in connection with the formal or committee meetings of societies and clubs of which they are members – group decision meetings. For this reason, although the command meeting plays such an important part in business communication, this chapter gives primary attention to the group decision meeting.

II FORMAL MEETINGS

Formal meetings follow set procedures which may be for public meetings those established by custom and precedent, or for private meetings those prescribed by standing orders of public authorities, by articles of association of bodies registered under the Companies Acts, or by the rules of organisations not trading for profit (i.e. social, educational, or recreational clubs and societies). 'Public' meetings are those on matters of public concern, or held in a public place, or to which the public or a section of the public is admitted (with or without payment). 'Private' meetings are ones which are of sectional concern only, or held on private premises, or to which admission is restricted.

By far the commonest type of formal meeting is the private meeting where attendance is limited to membership – this would include the meetings of registered bodies such as joint stock and other companies, or trade unions, and the business meetings of clubs and other special interest organisations.

Although some readers of this book doubtless aspire to becoming secretaries of registered bodies, it will be many years before they succeed. All readers are, however, quite likely to be able to obtain practice in the art of being a secretary by becoming secretary to an organisation not trading for profit (for example a college club) and are advised to seize such an opportunity if offered. It is for this reason that material in this chapter pertaining to formal meetings is illustrated rather from the meetings of such organisations than from those of registered bodies.

III COMMITTEE MEETINGS

A committee may be defined as a small body of people appointed by a parent body to meet to discuss certain matters (defined by terms of reference) with a view to making group decisions on behalf of, or group recommendations to, the parent body. Such committees may be homogeneous – that is to say with all members of similar interests or perhaps similar status – mixed, or joint. The joint committee which represents both management and staff is of special value in improving communication within a firm.

That one's full range of oral communication skills is called for in committee work is obvious; but there is much more to successful committee work than communicating, and the art (and occasional guile) is learned only by experience. For those starting off (and service on student committees is an admirable way of obtaining a first inkling of what is involved) here are a few key points to bear in mind.

1 You are part of a team and the idea is to come to the best possible decisions by group discussion. Soloists, prima donnas, and those who will never allow themselves to be persuaded to a shift of viewpoint are valueless to a committee. A group of individualists like that will continually come up with compromise solutions that endeavour to incorporate a little of everybody's viewpoint (the origin of the old joke that a camel is a horse designed by a committee).

2 Listen more than you speak. Listening time = speaking time × number of members of the committee.

3 If you have nothing to say on an item under discussion, say nothing. (Surprisingly difficult for some.)

4 If you have no special interest in an item use your influence to speed up a decision. (Beginners at committee work usually talk all evening and decide nothing.)

5 If you do have a special interest in an item and wish to persuade the committee to adopt your viewpoint

(a) try to talk last; let the opposition have first go.

(b) try to influence a few members to support you *before the committee meets*.

IV COMMAND MEETINGS

Within any firm or public authority where managers are aware of the importance of communication a large number of informal meetings will take place between managers and their subordinates (or *commands*). Such meetings have various names in various organisations – *staff meetings*, *conferences*, *manager's meetings* etc – but in this book are called *command meetings*.

Two types of command meeting can be distinguished – the extended command meeting, and the immediate command meeting.

THE EXTENDED COMMAND MEETING is a meeting called by a

manager so that he can communicate orally to all those he has under his control. Except at the lowest levels of management, this will mean a large meeting where the manager can do no more than address all present and answer questions. It is therefore essentially public speaking that is required of him; considerable attention was devoted to this subject in the preceding chapter, and no more need be added here.

IMMEDIATE COMMAND MEETINGS are between the manager and those directly responsible to him. These will be small meetings, permitting two-way communication. They will be called whenever a manager feels the need to explain, or to sound opinion, or to exchange information more rapidly than is possible by writing. In departments where there is a tradition of consultation and good communication, such meetings may, in fact, take place as a result of a request to a manager by his subordinates for clarification of certain points.

Before calling an immediate command meeting a manager must be clear in his mind whether he is calling the meeting to tell, or to discuss and consult. It should, of course, as often as possible be for the latter purpose, to permit feedback, and the inclusion of staff suggestions in the final version of a project. Discussion and consultation must take place before the manager has reached his decision. To invite discussion, for example, of a scheme after he is fully committed to it, is to invite trouble. If the scheme meets with reasoned opposition, or hostility, he must either make a mockery of the whole concept of consultation by ignoring criticisms, or appear indecisive to his own manager by a reversal of his previous opinion – the latter being much the less harmful of the alternatives open to him.

Informal meetings of this kind are often not minuted and the agenda may well exist only in the mind of the convener. The latter should make every effort to produce a relaxed and friendly atmosphere where the difference of rank between himself and the group is not permitted to stifle the free airing of views. At the same time he should see that discussion is relevant and that it never moves outside the area in which he is the appropriate person to make decisions.

The higher the level of manager who is convening the immediate command meeting, the more formal it tends to become. Meetings between the principal executive and his departmental managers, for example, will usually have a typed and circulated agenda, and be minuted by his secretary.

Minuting of command meetings is, in fact, desirable at all levels since it preserves a record of decisions reached. In recognition of the fact that such decisions are not group decisions a form of words such as *The Sales*

Manager decided that ... should be used rather than the styles shown in Section IX of this chapter, which refers to minuting of group decision meetings only.

V NOTICE

For all meetings, adequate notice must be given to those who are to attend; the meetings of registered bodies, indeed, will normally be considered invalid if every member has not been notified.

Notice may be oral, written, or by public advertisement. For informal meetings oral notice is often sufficient, but for formal private meetings and committee meetings written notice is desirable. For public meetings advertisement, combined with oral and written notices to those thought to be interested, is usual.

The notice must state the date, time, and place of meeting. It is essential that it be given early enough for the recipient to have a reasonable chance of attending, and desirable that it should be early enough for him to be able to keep the occasion free of other engagements. Notice of formal private meetings must be sent to every person entitled to be present; the rules of the organisation usually specify how many clear days before the meeting.

The form of written notice ranges from a friendly memo for an informal meeting to the strictly controlled legalistic language of the notices sent out by registered bodies. The notice for the annual general meeting of a large limited company (usually printed) will read something like this:

ADPRESS ENGINEERING LTD

Notice is hereby given that the Tenth Annual General Meeting of the Shareholders of the above named Company will be held at The Assembly Rooms, High Street, Bromhill, on the 19th day of August 19.. at 11.00 hours for the purpose of considering the Directors' Report and Statement of Accounts for the year ending 31st March, 19..; of declaring a dividend; of electing Directors and appointing Auditors; of transacting any other general business of the Company requiring transaction. A member entitled to attend and vote is entitled to appoint a proxy to vote instead of him; such proxy need not be a member of the Company.

Dated this 27th day of July, 19..
By order of the Board,
James Harrington
Secretary

Social and recreational groups are less formal than this and the notice usually takes the form of a letter:

BROMHILL DRAMA GROUP

10 Croft Road,
Bromhill, Kent.
BRO45 5TA

27th July, 19..

Dear . . .

The Annual General Meeting of the group will take place at The Assembly Rooms, High Street, Bromhill, on 19th August 19.. at 19.15 hours, and I hope you will find it convenient to attend.

A copy of the agenda is attached.

Yours faithfully,
Sheila Lavington
Secretary

VI AGENDA

An agenda is simply a list of items to be considered during a meeting. It is particularly associated with the formal private meeting, though the more formal type of committee meeting or command meeting may also have an agenda prepared in advance. For most informal meetings no written agenda is prepared, though the convener is well advised to write down for his own benefit a list of points he wishes to deal with. Agenda for private meetings are prepared by the secretary of the organisation in consultation with the chairman. Agenda for committees may be similarly prepared by the clerk or secretary to the committee; or, for small committees, by the chairman himself.

The purpose of the agenda is to guide the chairman through the meeting and to give prior indication of what is to be discussed at the meeting to those attending. The agenda should therefore be circulated with the notice or incorporated with it. Even in the most informal circumstances the convener of a meeting should normally let those attending know what the meeting is about, so that they can prepare their ideas in advance.

In its simplest form the agenda will consist of a list of items, typed underneath each other, and numbered in the order in which they will be taken by the chairman. More elaborate agenda will include brief notes on the items. Items for discussion should, as often as possible, be already in the form of motions at the agenda stage and their proposers and seconders known.

Meetings vary greatly in character but the following is the most usual order of events at formal private meetings. Of course, not all these items will necessarily appear on every agenda.

1 Election of chairman (if necessary)
2 Reading of notice of meeting by secretary (optional)
3 Reading of minutes of previous meeting by secretary
4 Points arising from minutes
5 Reading of correspondence by secretary
6 Chairman's opening remarks
7 Business adjourned from last meeting (if any)
8 Financial matters (treasurer's report, circulation of accounts etc)
9 Reports by committees
10 Election of officers (if necessary)
11 First motion moved and seconded (the wording of the motion should, if possible, appear on the agenda)
12 Further motions and points for discussion of which prior notice has been given (specified on the agenda)
13 Date of subsequent meeting
14 Any other business (this item is included to permit minor points to be raised; it is not intended for important matters of which prior notice should have been given)
15 Vote of thanks to chairman
16 Reply by chairman
17 Meeting declared closed by chairman.

The last three items do not always appear on the agenda sheet that is circulated, and in fact the chairman is not always formally thanked.

The agenda is sometimes worded as a series of titles for the stages of the business transacted (as above); sometimes as imperatives to the chairman (*Declare meeting closed*); sometimes as future tense constructions (*The chairman will declare the meeting closed*). The method used should be consistent within the one agenda.

VII DRAFTING MOTIONS

In a formal meeting of group decision type no matter should be debated that has not been proposed in the form of a motion. It is usual also for such a motion to be seconded; few chairman would permit the discussion of an unseconded motion, since it so clearly has no support.

For the meetings of large deliberative bodies it is necessary for all motions to be in writing, signed by the proposer, and submitted in advance. In less completely formal circumstances, such as the business meetings of social and recreational organisations, it is common for the wording of the motion to be submitted orally at the time of raising the matter. In the meetings of committees, matters are often discussed before a motion is formulated, the stimulus for discussion being a letter, a report, or simply the wish of a member to sound opinion on a certain point.

The wording of a motion is traditionally introduced by the word *That*. Thus a motion to a Joint Consultative Council might read:

> *That a committee be formed to consider methods of staggering working hours to avoid traffic congestion and overloading of public transport at 09.00 and 17.30 hours.*

It is very important that the wording should be clear and unambiguous so that nobody is in any doubt what he is voting about.

Proposals to amend the wording of motions before the meeting are drafted similarly. Thus if it was felt by a member that congestion at lunchtime was also important he might propose the amendment:

> *That the words '12.30, 13.30' be inserted between '09.00' and 'and 17.30 hours'.*

Amendments are voted on before the original motion. If the amendment is lost, the meeting proceeds to discuss the original motion. If it is carried, the modification in the wording suggested is made by the chairman and the meeting then considers the motion (now called 'the substantive motion') in its new form.

When a motion is carried it becomes a 'resolution'.

VIII REPORTS AND MINUTES DISTINGUISHED

When discussing meetings, it is important to distinguish between reports and minutes.

Reports in this context may be of three kinds:

1 A report by an individual (officer, official, expert witness etc) to a meeting
2 The specific report by a committee to its parent body on the matter the committee has been required to investigate
3 A general account of what occurred at a meeting. This may be a verbatim report (as Hansard) or, more usually, a selective survey intended perhaps for the Press or for absent members who require more detail than minutes provide, or one prepared by a representative for the benefit of those he represents at the meeting.

Minutes are primarily a record of decisions reached. Once signed by the chairman – at that or a subsequent meeting – minutes of formal meetings are legally binding, may not be altered, and may be submitted in court as evidence.

Essentially, minutes constitute a briefly worded record of the following:

1 Date and place of meeting
2 The names of those present (only number for a large meeting)
3 The items of business transacted, with the decisions reached – these will of course be in the same order as the agenda (unless the chairman sought the meeting's permission to vary the order); the agenda is therefore a most useful guide to the secretary in preparing minutes.

IX MINUTES OF GROUP DECISION MEETINGS

Minutes must be (1) accurate (2) clear and unambiguous (3) brief, (4) self-explanatory. They should be in past tense reported speech (see Appendix II). It is recommended that each minute be numbered and, preferably, supplied with a title.

Although probably all who have experience in drafting minutes would agree with all these points, there is wide disagreement as to their precise interpretation, and minutes vary considerably from organisation to organisation and from secretary to secretary.

The most noticeable variation is in finding a point of balance between two requirements – to be brief but to ensure that the minute is self-explanatory. At one extreme, some secretaries maintain that only the decision itself need be minuted, and with a successful motion for instance will confine themselves to its wording, preceded by 'It was resolved' or 'Resolved'. At the other extreme, some – especially secretaries of social and recreational groups – will include not only such details as the names of the proposer and seconder (which is reasonable enough) but also details of the voting and a summary of the principal arguments put forward by speakers in the discussion. Legitimate versions of these extremes are exemplified by the following two methods of minuting a discussion, by an executive committee, leading to the selection of a suitable venue for an annual conference.

METHOD I
Annual Conference Venue

It was resolved :

1. *That the Royal Pavilion be adopted as conference centre for 19..*
2. *That fifteen-minute adjournments for refreshments morning and afternoon be provided for in the conference programme.*

METHOD 2
Venue of annual conference

A further detailed discussion of the relative merits of the Royal Pavilion and the Palace Ballroom took place. It was generally agreed that the Royal Pavilion had better acoustics but that its refreshment facilities were inadequate. There was some disagreement over the suitability of seating accommodation provided for delegates at the Royal Pavilion. Mr Carter proposed and Miss Branson seconded 'That the Royal Pavilion be adopted as conference venue for 19.., the refreshment difficulty being met by a fifteen-minute adjournment morning and afternoon'. The proposal was carried unanimously.

Both are sound minutes. It is a question of what the purpose of the minute is. In business, minutes serve only to provide a legally binding record of decisions for future action. The first form of minute serves this purpose. With clubs and societies, the aim often seems to be to provide through the minutes an outline history of the organisation, and a record of what took place for the benefit of future officers or members who missed a meeting. The second minute would fulfil this purpose.

Both minutes are, however, certainly on the extreme margins of what could be considered sound. Any attempt to compress the first further would make it less than self-explanatory. The second is rather wordy, in a style more appropriate to a report, and if a less summary treatment of the arguments leading to the resolution had been attempted would have laid the secretary open to possible attack on the grounds of misrepresentation of a member's viewpoint.

The most satisfactory minutes lie between these extremes. They consist of two parts:

1 A PREAMBLE. This makes clear the stimulus – motion, report, letter – and sometimes gives a broad indication of the principal argument leading to the resolution.

2 THE RESOLUTION. This makes clear for future action or reference what has been decided.

Various styles are used for drafting minutes on these lines. For example:

(a) On a motion by Mr —.
   It was resolved : or *Resolved* :
   That etc.
(b) Mr — proposed, Mr — seconded and *it was resolved* :
   That etc.
(c) Mr — proposed and Mr — seconded : 'That etc.' *The proposal was carried.*

Where the stimulus is not a motion but a letter or report, the preamble has to be more explanatory. For example, the following is not a satisfactory minute:

> *Shannon Gutters*
> On a report by the Borough Engineer.
> Resolved : That the action referred to be adopted.

What is required if the minute is to be self-explanatory is something like this:

> *Shannon Gutters*
> The Borough Engineer reported that Shannon Ltd had completed the first contract, for relining gutters of 100 dwellings; that they had submitted quotations (at the same rates as hitherto) for a further 100 dwellings; and that in order to provide continuity of work he recommended acceptance of this quotation.
> *Resolved* : That the quotation referred to be accepted.

The wording of the preamble of the second version also avoids the curious non-sentence: *On a report by the Borough Engineer* – a form common in minutes but with nothing to be said in its favour.

The word *recommended* is sometimes substituted for *resolved* where the minute is that of a committee which on this matter can make only a recommendation to its parent body.

Not every item in minutes can be shown as a resolution or recommendation. Date and place of meeting are frequently incorporated in the heading:

> *Minutes of the Annual General Meeting of the Bromhill Drama Group held on 19th August 19.. at the Assembly Rooms, High Street, Bromhill.*

The next item in minutes is to show those present.

They are shown by name, in a small meeting:

> *Present: J. Fitchins (in the Chair); Mesdames: Lavington; Miller; Thomas; Messrs: Adams; Freeman; James*

or number, in a large meeting:

> *Two hundred and forty members were present. Mr. J. Fitchins was in the Chair.*

It is not necessary to minute apologies for absence, unless these are the subject of a resolution (for example, to send condolences). The numbered items of the minutes start with the reading and signing of the previous minutes.

These may be minuted either descriptively:

> *Minutes of previous meeting*
> *The Secretary read the minutes of the meeting held on ... and these were thereupon signed by the Chairman*

or as a resolution:

> *Minutes of previous meeting*
> *Resolved: That the minutes of the meeting on ... be signed as a correct record.*

From this point onwards, items should be numbered in the order in which they occurred. The secretary should attempt to show as many items as possible as decisions. Even expressions of thanks, regret, congratulations etc can be shown as resolutions:

Resolved : That the committee's regrets at the absence of Mr – owing to illness be conveyed to Mr —— by the Secretary with the Committee's wishes for his speedy recovery.

Where reports, letters etc are read out but it is decided to take no action (i.e. there is no resolution) they are minuted as 'received':

Proposed joint production
A letter from the Bromhill Barnstormers proposing a joint production for 19.. was received.

If it was intended to do something about this proposal, the minute would read:

Proposed joint production
The Secretary read a letter from the Bomhill Barnstormers proposing a joint production for 19...
Resolved : That the Secretary write to the Secretary of the Bromhill Barnstormers proposing the formation of a joint committee of four (two members from each society) to prepare detailed proposals.

In the attempt to reduce wording many secretaries write their minutes in semi-note style. Specifically they omit *the, and, a* etc. Thus:

Treasurer reported increased number of members had paid subscriptions in advance

when the full form would read:

The Treasurer reported that an increased number of members had paid their subscriptions in advance.

The improved readability of the full form would seem a greater advantage than the small saving of space resulting from semi-note style. Where minutes are of considerable bulk, however, and have to be printed (as local authority minutes) it is possible that this saving is worth while.

X TAKING NOTES AT MEETINGS

Undoubtedly the best way of taking notes at a meeting is by shorthand. A verbatim note of the entire meeting is then possible, although rarely required; the note taken even by a skilled shorthand writer will usually be selective. Where it is necessary for an extensive note of proceedings to be taken at important meetings, a shorthand writer or shorthand-typist should be present to supply the secretary with a note.

Individuals present at the meeting and requiring notes normally have to take their own, and these will need to be highly selective if shorthand is not used. What is usually required is a note that will give the gist of what was said on matters having future reference. The note is to remind only. How much detail is required for the note to be an adequate reminder varies greatly with the individual. Many write very full notes, the composition of which prevents the writer from contributing fully to the meeting while he is there, and which are laborious to read through afterwards. Others scribble down cryptic one-word mnemonics that are of no help at all when the notebook is consulted later. What is right for the individual between these two unsatisfactory extremes will be found only by trial and error; but the aim should always be to take the minimum note that will serve the purpose.

Notes should be selective and systematic, material being broken down into logical subdivisions. In selecting and compressing material for notes, precisely the same skills are employed as in précis; practice at the one activity will improve performance in the other.

Appendix IV (page 344) provides basic information on note-making and should be consulted.

XI EXERCISES

Exercise A (Committee practice work with films)

Films of short committee meetings (lasting about twenty minutes) are available from the Commercial Educational Department of the London Chamber of Commerce. Originally intended as examinations in Meetings, for the Private Secretaries' Diploma Examination, they can be used to provide practice in note-taking, minuting, or reporting. If the examination papers for the year of the film hired (the films are classified by year) are also obtained these will provide a memorandum and instructions for a secretarial task to be carried out for that particular filmed meeting. Instructions are intended for shorthand-typists but can be readily adapted for use with longhand.

Exercise B (Committee practice work without films)

Committee work can be simulated in class:

1 by choosing a topic of general current interest to discuss and attempting a group decision

2 by selecting an agenda of debatable topics within the college (e.g. staggering of breaks, increasing number of books on loan to students from the library at one time). Motions can be prepared in advance or formulated during discussion.

For both the above methods at least one student should be allocated the task of minuting the meeting.

It may be necessary for the class tutor to act as chairman initially, but this role should be taken over by students, in turn, as soon as possible.

Correct meeting discipline must be maintained and all remarks addressed to the Chair.

Exercise C (Command meeting practice work)

This can be simulated by role-playing, one member of a group being selected as convening manager and the others taking roles as his immediate command. For example, the convening manager may be the Managing Director, and his subordinates the Office Manager, Chief Accountant, Personnel Manager, Sales Manager, Research and Development Manager, Chief Engineer etc. Or the meeting may be at a lower managerial level – e.g. between one of these departmental managers (for example the Chief Accountant) and his immediate command. Topics, or one topic, appropriate to the level of managerial decision selected are chosen, within the limits of the knowledge of the group (some reading-up for the occasion will be necessary) and information and recommendations made to the convening manager who then makes his decision based on this. Either the convening manager or one of the group selected as his secretary should keep minutes of decisions reached.

Exercise D (Consideration of actual minutes)

The group obtains copies of current minutes of the local authority (probably the most accessible of professionally competent minutes). Selected minutes are then discussed from the following viewpoints:

1 Is it self-explanatory?
2 Is it unambiguous?
3 Is there a preamble? If not, why not?
4 What kind of language is used (tone, clarity etc)?
5 Is it in semi-note style?

Exercise E

1 As P. F. Sellars of 13 Granville Street, Bromhill, Kent, BRO45 7AL, write to the Borough Engineer requesting renumbering of your house to 12A Granville Street.

2 This letter is put before the Highways Committee which agrees to the request. Write the relevant minute (including a title).

Exercise F

Imagine you are the secretary of a college club or other similar social or recreational group. The organisation can be real or fictitious, but choose an activity of which you have some knowledge. The annual general meeting is about to take place.

Draft (1) The notice of meeting to be sent to members
     (2) The agenda
     (3) The minutes
     (4) A short report of the meeting for the Press.

You should include one motion of which prior notice has been given; one letter which leads to a resolution at the meeting; one letter about which no action is to be taken.

Part IV

Chapter 15

Non-verbal communication

1 BODY LANGUAGE

Although *language* should by derivation refer only to that which involves the tongue, i.e. spoken words (and their written equivalent), it is common practice to employ the word with reference to other communication systems. *Body language* is a convenient generic term for communication by the use of parts of the body other than the tongue – by hand gestures, facial expression, mime, touch, posture.

Gesture seems likely to have been man's earliest communication system, long preceding speech. In fact there are those who believe that speech originated in attempts to make gestures with the tongue while the hands were occupied – in carrying a load, for example. Gesture can be very useful in noisy environments or in a foreign country where one does not speak the language. In many countries extensive use is also made of gesture to supplement and intensify speech. This is not very noticeable in England and it would seem that in the northern hemisphere there is increased use of gesture the further south the country of the speaker's origin.

Facial expression communicates mostly emotion and attitudes – friendliness, affection, dislike, suspicion, anger, contempt, bewilderment, anxiety etc. There is a remarkable universality of facial expression symbols as has been shown by secretly filming people of many countries in similar communication situations; they reveal very similar facial expressions. This seems something basic to human beings. It is not part of our animal heritage. When we expose our teeth and lift the corners of our mouth slightly the meaning is 'I like what you are doing' or 'I feel friendly towards you'. If a monkey does this it means something like 'I have very large teeth and shall bite you if you carry on like this'.

Mime and touch have very little relevance to business communication but posture can, often unconsciously, communicate much in a business situation. How a man stands before the person giving him orders, how he sits in a committee, what he looks like when viewed across his desk – these can give important indications of his attitude (to the person he is communicating with, to authority, to his job, to the specific proposal now being put to him etc).

Facial expression and posture (and physical behaviour generally) provide good feedback in face-to-face communication and should always be examined closely (but not obviously) by the alert Tx. A puzzled look can show the Tx he is not making his point. The consumption of surplus energy by rolling a pencil up and down the desk shows the Rx's interest not fully engaged. A stiffness in the shoulders can reveal a growing dislike of what the Tx is proposing.

The Tx should also remember to line up his body language with what he says. Facial expression or posture may easily run counter to his carefully chosen words, revealing uncertainty or duplicity in his message. When you are the Rx it is worth remembering that the message that comes from body language (if different from the message of the words spoken) is the one to believe, as it is usually being communicated unconsciously.

II DRESS AND GROOMING

Closely allied to body language is the way we clothe and decorate our bodies in order to send messages about ourselves to all we meet. A young man's 'interview suit', a girl's supertight jeans, the school of art lecturer's handwoven mustard-yellow tie – these are communication devices of just the same kind as the primitive tribesman's war paint and necklet of animal teeth. On special occasions we dress to suit the occasion. At all times we dress to indicate the kind of person we wish to be thought to be and the sort of role we wish to play in life.

Difficulties and misunderstandings arise at work because the messages we are trying to send about ourselves as private persons often differ considerably from those we are expected to send in our business role. Since we cannot keep changing our clothes, hair-style etc during the working day, we have to decide which takes priority, our private aims or our business role. Most people realise, perhaps a little sadly, that it must be the latter; and that means learning to dress and groom to suit the job.

It is quite impossible to give rules about this as fashion is involved and consequently the situation is always changing. We are at the time of writing a very long way from the days when every potential (male) manager knew he must have his hair cut 'short back and sides', and wear a dark suit without much pattern, a white shirt, a quiet tie, and highly polished black lace-up shoes, to show he was a sound establishment figure, suitable for promotion. But the more casual attitude towards dress and grooming these days poses special problems. In communication terms it means that there are more symbols available to choose from, and there is no real agreement about what the symbols mean. Thus the distortion that occurs when the Rx decodes the message can be considerable. As with any other communication system it is up to the Tx to work out what interpretation is likely to be put upon his symbols. Once we have dressed for the working day we are probably going to meet a large number of different Rxs; it is necessary therefore to decide what are the typical characteristics of the kind of Rx who matters most to us in our work and to try to assess such a person's likely interpretation of our dress and grooming signals.

Girls are usually pretty well aware how much their personal style of dress and grooming sends out a message. Young men are a little naïve about this and seem to expect that people will mysteriously divine what they are really like (or want to be thought to be like) and will take no notice of the messages sent by dress and grooming. But when a knowledgeable person meets somebody for the first time (in private life as well as in business) he/she tends to read off indicators from the other's appearance which he/she decodes according to his/her previous experience (and perhaps prejudices) to form an impression of the other's personality, attitudes, and potential reliability. An older man may look at a younger, for example, and give attention to such points as the following:

How long is his hair?

Has he beard, moustache, sideburns?

If clean-shaven, how closely, how recently?

Does he, rather obviously, use after-shave lotion? (An unfavourable indication to most men but – according to the author's informal investigations – a favourable one to most girls.)

Is he wearing a suit? Any sort of jacket? A tie?

What sort of shoes is he wearing? Lace-up or pull-on? Black or brown? If brown, suede or polished? If suede, light or dark? Are they clean? etc, etc.

It is not only older people who make such assessments. When a young man or girl sums up another on first meeting as 'arty type' or 'hard man' or 'smoothie' the impression thus formed will have been largely based upon the other's dress and grooming signals. It is, however, probably true to say that as you get older you read such signals more consciously and are more aware of what interpretations you give to them.

Communication by dress and grooming is as subject to misunderstandings as is verbal communication and in the same fundamental way: distortion at the coding stage followed by further distortion at the decoding stage (cf Figure 6 page 31). In fact since there is no dictionary to turn to in which to check the agreed meaning of the symbols used misunderstanding is likely to be more likely than when using words. The author recalls particularly one occasion on which he was serving on a panel interviewing an applicant for a first teaching post at a technical college. The young man, who had hair down over his shoulders, was wearing jeans, an ultramarine sweater the elbows of which were worn through, and rather grubby sneakers. The applicant probably saw these signals as transmitting a message something like this: *I am an independent type. I don't care what other people think about me. I don't go much for outward appearances. I am me – take it or leave it.* The members of the panel made it clear in discussing him that they all interpreted these signals as: *I am slack and careless. I am against authority and convention. You will have a hard time trying to make me toe the line.* He did not get the job. To the author fell the task of telling him he had not been appointed. The young man's comment was 'It's the same every time I get an interview. They always turn me down. I can't understand it.'

It is not suggested that the young man should have had his hair cut short for the occasion and donned shiny black shoes and what was referred to by multiple tailors in the 1930s as a 'gent's natty business suit'. That would have meant sending false signals, transmitting lies about himself. If, however, we consider this episode in terms of the communication fundamentals discussed in Part I we are able to see what went wrong. It is basic to communication that we communicate to produce a desired response – in this case to secure an appointment by successful interview. To begin with, the applicant picked the wrong message. He must have had personality characteristics more relevant to the post applied for than those that the author estimated that he was endeavouring to transmit. But even those he failed to convey to most of the panel. That was because he did not observe the fundamental communication rule that you should think of your Rx, not yourself. As a result he selected dress and grooming signals that he must have realised were liable to be misinterpreted to his disadvantage by at least some of the panel.

Women are reputed to be much more perceptive than men in noting and interpreting dress and grooming indicators (especially those of other women). Whether this is true or not they certainly seem much more aware that such scrutiny takes place and prepare themselves for it carefully when, for example, attending an interview.

It is certainly worth while becoming aware that you are frequently going to be subjected to such assessment even if you do not intend to do any assessing of this kind yourself. You can then, at least on important occasions, try to make sure that your dress and grooming transmit the message about yourself that you want them to transmit. As time goes on you might also like to experiment, very cautiously at first, with trying to learn more about those you meet by interpreting such indicators yourself.

III NUMBERS

Mathematics is a medium of communication by which mathematicians can exchange information by means of a specialised system of symbols, sometimes without the use of any words at all, although a few are usually incorporated. It is a language increasingly employed for the communication of technical information. It is internationally understood and has the further advantages of precision and freedom from ambiguity. On the other hand it has the serious disadvantage that it is incomprehensible to many people who hold key positions in industry and commerce. Mathematical presentations should be avoided, therefore, whenever the subject matter permits. The number of Rxs capable of interpreting a mathematical presentation is limited and may not include those you most wish to influence in your project or memorandum.

Similarly, but to a more limited degree, those with a knowledge of accountancy can communicate between themselves, largely non-verbally and to the virtual exclusion of outsiders. The information conveyed by balance sheets, profit and loss accounts, summaries of net tangible assets etc is not easily uncovered by those unused to this particular coding.

Much other information of vital importance to the businessman (woman) – market reports, stock prices, international currency quotations, interest rates etc – is conveyed by the numerical medium. Numbers are also the basis of the various invented languages by which inputs and instructions are fed to computers, thus providing media of communication between man and computer, as well as between computer and computer.

Finally numbers are the essence of all statistical information. Statistics constitute in themselves a major communication device in business, one combining several media: numbers and words always, but usually nowadays some element of visual presentation as well. This last may consist in no more than tabulation but graphical presentations have of recent years become so sophisticated as to merit being treated as a communication medium in their own right, as they are in Section IV B.

IV PICTURES

A *Pictures versus words*

Pictures must have come very early in man's attempts to communicate. It is difficult to imagine how he did his thinking before he had language but presumably he thought in pictures; first attempts at communicating with others must certainly have included trying to portray the pictures inside his head in a way others could see. Paintings by primitive man (of animals and hunting scenes mostly) that have been preserved on the walls of dry caves in France are thought to date back as far as 30 000 BC, but simple drawings scratched in the earth with a stick must have long preceded these.

The arrival of language would have weakened the importance of the picture considerably but it was still the only way to preserve ideas and knowledge for the future. Not until the invention of writing (about 6000 years ago) would pictures start to become subordinate to words. Even then, for thousands of years to come, pictures were going to remain of great importance; few could read, and writing was a specialised skill, for the most part practised only by the professional scribes. Distribution of written material was slow and laborious as all writing had to be hand copied; it could take a copyist several years to produce one book. The really big change does not come (in Europe) until the fifteenth century when Gütenberg's invention of printing from movable type suddenly made possible rapid accurate reproduction of written material. For five hundred years to come the printed word was to dominate the western world (at least as far as the educated minority was concerned; it was not until the nineteenth century that the majority of people could read in the UK, and the rest of Europe lagged behind the UK).

In our own period we are seeing that dominance at last starting to weaken, with a resurgence of the picture as a medium of mass communication. The invention that led to this revolution was the camera which, towards the end of the nineteenth century, began to make possible exact pictures of the material world that could be reproduced in quantity and did not depend upon the expensive employment of a highly skilled artist/craftsman. Previously illustrations for books, pamphlets, and posters had to be printed from steel engravings, wood blocks, or etchings, produced by such a specialist.

At the turn of the century the moving picture arrived. It rapidly demonstrated its extraordinary capacity to compel the attention and control the eyes and thoughts of the audience sitting half-hypnotised before the huge bright screen in the darkened cinema. That here was a new medium not only of entertainment but also of mass communication was quickly grasped. Educationists and employers recognised film as a potential new aid in instruction. Private advertisers and governments seized on its possibilities for selling and propaganda.

Today television brings moving pictures right into our homes and it has been doing so on a substantial scale since the mid 1950s. As a result a large part of the population has become acclimatised to responding to pictures again and is losing its capacity to respond to written or printed words. In the Middle Ages the mass of the people learned the Bible stories from the stained glass windows and wall paintings in the village church because they could not read; today they learn about world events from moving pictures in their own homes and do not need to read.

The effect of this change is steadily cumulative. Skilled professional communicators outside film and television working on newspapers or magazines, for example, or preparing advertising campaigns for these channels, or devising public signs for an authority, or designing labels and packages, are well aware that they have to compete with the compulsion of the moving picture and that people are beginning to find reading slow and troublesome. They have therefore sought every opportunity to replace words with pictures, to supplement words with pictures, and, sometimes, to put in a picture even if it has very little to do with the message, just to make the potential Rx take some notice of them.

In many ways the resultant changes have been highly desirable. The signs

which we are now so used to, have not only saved many foreign visitors from embarrassing mistakes but spared some local councils the agony of choice between

	WOMEN	MEN
or	LADIES	GENTLEMEN
or	LADIES	MEN

(the last of these having been at one time surprisingly popular with local councils, especially in the Midlands and North).

Such *pictograms* have become very familiar in recent years, particularly in connection with travel (where their freedom from language restriction is so valuable). One thinks immediately of road signs; of the symbols on motorways that indicate food, petrol, conveniences available; of railway station and airport signs for telephones, left luggage, refreshments etc. The pictograms used on freight packages (especially on those going overseas) communicate admirably.

THIS WAY UP

may not be understood by every dock worker in every port (some may not be able to read at all). An arrow device on the top edge of side and end of the crate may succeed better. The British Standards Institution's version of such arrows looks like this

to be stencilled on the package in black. Stencilled pictograms of this sort are being increasingly used. They are frequently devised within a firm's despatch department, accurately drawn out, and sent off to a specialist

Use no hooks

Fragile. Handle with care

Keep away from heat

Keep dry

Figure 12 Pictograms for goods in transit

firm to be converted into plastic stencils. The British Standards Institution has recommended eight (four of which are shown in Figure 12) a tiny but invaluable 'vocabulary' of agreed symbols.

Consideration of pictograms quickly draws attention to the major advantages of all pictorial communication.

PICTURES are: 1 International
2 Instantaneous in their impact
3 Comprehensible to the illiterate
4 Easily remembered
5 Non-linear.

That it is non-linear is a very important advantage of visual presentation of fairly complicated material (such as statistics). It means that all the information is available at once for the Rx to tackle in an order of his own choosing. With words the Rx has to accept the order prescribed by the Tx. Pictorial devices used to communicate in business include photographs, sketches, posters, maps, plans, block diagrams, flow charts, and various methods of presenting statistical information, the most important of which are outlined in the following section.

Where it is a question of:

1 what something looks like
2 where something is
3 how something moves

such devices score heavily over words.

Pictures (or, to be more exact, pictures supported by a minimum of words, as in good posters) can be very effective for publicity, attitude changing, 'education' etc. Thus a campaign for safety in works, economy with energy sources, increased use of the suggestion box, even increased productivity, is much more likely to succeed if it relies principally on a series of large boldly coloured and witty pictures supported by easily remembered slogans only a few words long. A series of meetings featuring talks by leading figures in the firm would be much less successful even if very well done. A series of carefully prepared typewritten or printed statements posted upon noticeboards (even if incorporating all the communication suggestions made in the early part of this book!) would be, in turn, less successful than the talks.

Visual methods are not suitable for such material as reasoned arguments; detailed instructions; exact information; definitions; records of discussions; legal matters (rules, regulations etc). In short, only rather simple material lends itself to pictorial communication outside the three areas listed above. Pictures are thus limited in their communication potentialities, although to be preferred to words for certain communication tasks. It is regrettable therefore that, as a result of the resurgence of the picture, the majority of people in the UK have become less capable of understanding what they read than previously and less proficient in writing to communicate.

B *Pictorial presentation of statistical data*

1 INTRODUCTION. Pictorial presentation of statistics has become familiar to all in recent years through newspapers, TV current affairs programmes, and financial advertising. This section is intended to provide those who are not studying statistics as part of their business or technicians' course with a brief introduction to the most commonly employed methods.

A few points common to all methods may be made before examining specific techniques.

The advantages of pictorial presentation of statistical data are as follows.

1 A quick impression of the overall tendencies indicated by the figures is obtained.

2 The relationship between figures can be appreciated more easily than from tables.

3 Differences stand out.

The following words of warning are appropriate.

1 There is no point in using a pictorial presentation if it does not produce advantages of this kind.

2 Misleading presentations of figures are easy to produce, both through lack of skill and through intention to deceive.

3 All presentations must be titled and labelled to indicate what is being represented.

4 The scale must be clearly indicated.

5 The date of the information must be shown.

For presentations drawn up within a firm or organisation it is usual to include the name of the person preparing the presentation and the date of presentation.

2 STRAIGHT LINE GRAPHS. Most people using this book will already be familiar with graphs from mathematics and science classes in school.

They are essentially a matter of plotting, using squared paper, a dependent variable on the vertical (y) axis against an independent variable on the horizontal (x) axis. They are thus very suitable for such business applications as showing variables like sales, or production, or consumption of raw materials (y) against days, months, or years (x). There is, however, an important difference between graphs of scientific readings (or of mathematical functions) and those based upon statistics. The former are normally continuously varying (on the y axis) while with statistics we have a series of discrete figures. Thus the former come out as straight lines or curves from which approximate additional figures can be read off between the points at which actual readings have been taken but there is no equivalent to this with graphs of statistical data – the figures plotted on the y axis are the only figures. For this reason the points plotted must be connected by straight lines, not smoothed out into a curve as with a continuous series. Such graphs are usually called 'straight line graphs' (which can cause some confusion to those with a school science background as their minds tend to leap back to that particular type of straight line graph that indicates a direct correlation between x and y when a continuous series is plotted). Diagram (a) of Exercise H (on page 294) is a typical straight line graph.

Graphs of a time series (i.e. with years, months etc as the x axis) are sometimes called *histiograms*.[1]

3 TREND GRAPHS. Histiograms often leap up and down a good deal as a result of short term fluctuations and seasonal variation (the way ice-cream sales drop in winter, central heating installations rise in the late summer, for example). This can make it quite difficult for the Rx to distinguish the underlying trend of the figures (which is what you are usually wanting to communicate when you graph statistics).

To overcome this a 'trend' or 'moving average' graph may be plotted, usually alongside the basic graph. To calculate, for example, an *annual* moving average you take one year's total figure, divide it by twelve, and plot this at the midpoint of the year on the x axis scale. At an interval of (say) one month later on the x axis you plot that month's figure plus the previously obtained annual figure minus the figure for the corresponding month of the previous year (all divided by twelve). This is repeated for

[1] Not to be confused with *histograms*, which are used to show frequency distribution. A histogram looks very like a vertical bar chart (cf pp. 278–82) but the *area* of the bars (not just their height) is proportional to the frequencies represented.

every month. The resultant histogram will be largely free of short-term fluctuations and seasonal variations. Shorter periods than a year are also used, for example quarters or half-years. The shortest period that does the job is what is needed, as trend graphs tend to iron out all variations if you overdo the process.

Figure 13 shows a histogram with a trend graph based on a quarterly moving average. For this the following (simulated) statistics were used.

Total Monthly sales, Maddison typewriters, 1000s

	Jan.	Feb.	Mar.	Ap.	May	June
1976	132	105	153	173	190	225
1977	180	135	190	220	240	285

	July	Aug.	Sept.	Oct.	Nov.	Dec.
1976	180	140	210	240	260	315
1977	245	220	270	310	330	280

There is a simple formula for the calculation of moving averages. For a quarterly moving average, for example, if the monthly figures are symbolised as n_1 n_2 n_3 etc and the averages (or 'means') by m_1 m_2 m_3 then

$$m_1 = \frac{n_1 + n_2 + n_3}{3}$$

$$m_2 = m_1 + \frac{n_4 - n_1}{3}$$

$$m_3 = m_2 + \frac{n_5 - n_2}{3} \text{ etc.}$$

Thus in our example the first means (to be shown on the trend graph midway through the quarter, i.e. mid-February) will be

$$\frac{132 + 105 + 153}{3} = 130$$

The second (to be shown mid-March) will be

$$130 + \frac{173 - 132}{3} = 144 \text{ (rounded up)}$$

The third will be

$$144 + \frac{190 - 105}{3} = 172 \text{ and so on.}$$

Total monthly sales, Maddison typewriters Jan. 1976–Dec. 1977

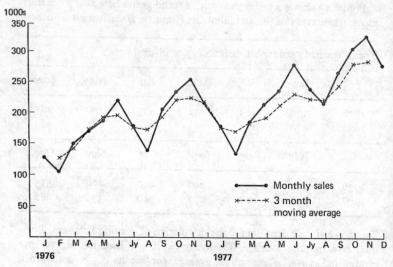

Figure 13 Histiogram with trend graph

4 FALSE ZERO. When high figures without much variation between them are plotted there is a large amount of space between the zero and the plot 'wasted'. If – to save this space – the bottom part of the graph is cut away it must be made clear that the y axis does not now start at zero. Those wishing to make comparatively small variations in large figures look more interesting sometimes not only cut away the lower part of the graph but also draw an x axis across at a figure only slightly below the lowest value to appear on the graph. This trick (known as 'false zero') in itself brings in an element of distortion but if the constructor of the graph now also uses a different scale so as to make the comparatively small variation between figures look large (as he can easily do once he has adopted a false zero) he can completely mislead an Rx who is not aware of the necessity to check on such points when reading a graph (of share performance, for example).

5 BAR CHARTS. Bar charts are increasingly favoured to provide quick

comparisons of quantities (for example, coal production in various countries) or sums of money (for example, company profits over a number of years). Elongated oblongs or bars are constructed (of a uniform width) the length of which is proportional to the quantity or sum represented. They may be drawn horizontally against a horizontal scale or vertically against a vertical scale. They may be drawn touching each other or separated by a short space, according to individual taste.

Diagram (b) of Exercise H on page 295 is an example of a bar chart. This one is not the simplest kind as two pieces of information are supplied by each bar, the 1960–64 figures and the 1970–74 figures. It is intended in this example to indicate that the whole bar represents the figures for 1970–74 and the shaded part those for 1960–64. This way of representing two sets of figures is not entirely satisfactory as *composite bar charts* are also commonly employed where the various shaded or non-shaded sections represent *the parts that make up the total*. Thus Figure 14 represents variation in the number of students at the imaginary

Enrolments, Pidderminster Technical College, 1971–7 inclusive

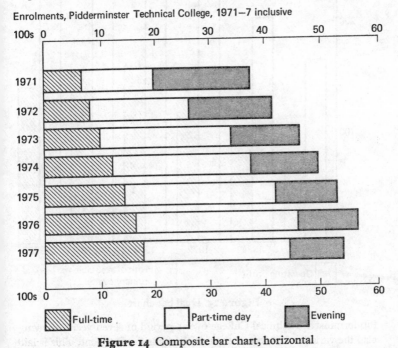

Figure 14 Composite bar chart, horizontal

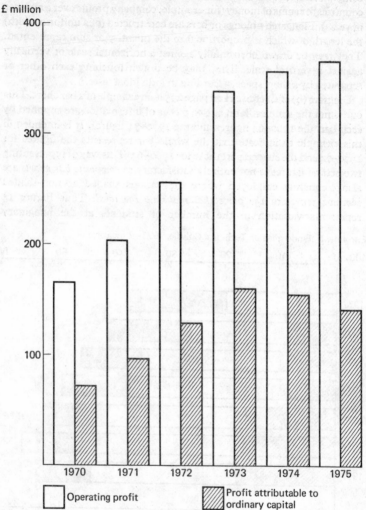

Operating profit and profit attributable, Unilever Ltd.

£ million

Operating profit

Profit attributable to ordinary capital

Figure 15 Dual bar chart

Pidderminster Technical College over a period of seven years, showing also the variation between the various categories of student. This is laid out as a horizontal bar chart. Students should satisfy themselves that they understand the difference in interpretation between the unshaded part of the bars in this chart and the unshaded part of the bars in diagram (b) of Exercise H.

The type of statistical information represented in Exercise H by having one bar imposed on the other is much more satisfactorily portrayed by a dual bar chart.

Figure 15 makes a double comparison – between Unilever Ltd profits in various years and between total profits and the amount of this attributable (i.e. available for distribution as dividends to shareholders) each year. The two bars for each year are placed next to each other, not imposed on each other, and this removes all possibility of confusion with a composite bar. Professionally produced (printed) dual bar charts sometimes show the shaded bar imposed over the unshaded one but offset a little to the right so that the whole of the lefthand side of the unshaded area is visible – a neat solution but one at present not normally used for handdrawn charts.

Another variation on the bar chart is the *percentage bar chart*. Figure 16

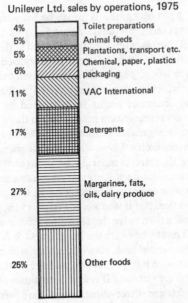

Unilever Ltd. sales by operations, 1975

4%	Toilet preparations
5%	Animal feeds
5%	Plantations, transport etc.
6%	Chemical, paper, plastics packaging
11%	VAC International
17%	Detergents
27%	Margarines, fats, oils, dairy produce
25%	Other foods

Figure 16 Percentage bar chart

illustrates a chart of this kind, for a single year, also based upon Unilever figures. Of course several such bars can be drawn together to add comparison between various years (for example). With the percentage bar chart the bar represents the total figures and the shaded sections the percentage of that total made up by the various contributory elements. Where several such bars are drawn together they will, of course, all be the same height.

Printed bar charts employ shading medium to improve the appearance of the bars. For handdrawn charts neat pencil or pen shading or colouring with crayons is necessary. Professional charts sometimes feature tiny pictograms in place of shading (more effective with horizontal bar charts than vertical). Thus a row of tiny black sacks could indicate coal production. For popular presentations these serve to act as jam on the pill of information, but within a firm they are a waste of energy, and usually beyond the amateur constructor's skill. Pictograms also reduce accuracy as a half unit is probably the smallest division that can be successfully drawn.

6 COMPARISON PICTOGRAMS. It must be admitted that the term *pictogram* is overworked these days. Apart from its use in what some people call 'symbol charts' as referred to at the end of the previous section we have already met it as a name for the bold stylised pictures that are employed as signs or labels (page 272). It is also used to refer to simplified scaled drawings which represent compared statistics. Thus coal production in two countries might be compared by means of scaled drawings of two sacks representing production in those countries.

Such a device certainly makes the material look more interesting to the Rx, but it is very treacherous. Those who use pictograms in this way seem uncertain whether they are comparing heights (as with a vertical bar chart) or areas, or even volumes. Suppose we are comparing an output of 1·2 million tonnes with one of 2·4 million tonnes. One is twice the other – nothing could be easier. But if we look at Figure 17 the 2·4 million tonne sack looks much more than twice the 1·2 million tonne one. If we think of height only sack B has to be twice the height of sack A (as it *is* in Figure 17). But such a sack would look very odd unless widened in proportion also. But when we widen it in proportion we have doubled dimensions in *both* directions; the area of sack B is now four times the area of sack A. Furthermore, sacks are three-dimensional (are often drawn three dimensionally in pictograms, as in our example). Thus they are thought of by the Tx as having volume. By volume sack B is eight times the size of sack A.

Comparison pictograms, therefore, can make differences between figures look bigger than they are (especially if the actual figures are very unobtrusively quoted), and unscrupulous advertisers have used them in this way. On the other hand, because of the points already mentioned, correctly scaled pictograms fail to bring home to the Rx the full extent of difference between figures thus compared. (It is in fact impossible to devise a completely satisfactory comparison pictogram because of the Rx's tendency to think of it as representing a three-dimensional object.) It would seem therefore that the comparison pictogram is unlikely to be employed except where there is some intention to present the figures in a way deceptively favourable to the Tx's viewpoint.

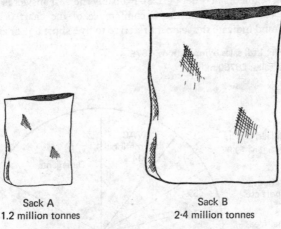

Sack A
1.2 million tonnes

Sack B
2·4 million tonnes

Figure 17 Deceptive comparison pictograms

7 PIE CHARTS. Pie charts (sometimes referred to as *pie diagrams* or *circle diagrams*) are so-called because they look like a plate pie divided into slices (see Figure 18). They are useful for showing how a total is made up and to give an approximate idea of the relative importance of the parts making up the whole. Before a pie chart can be devised 'slices' of convenient size and logical nature have to be selected, using the principles of classification and analysis described in Chapter 2 (pp. 19–21). Percentages have then to be worked out and multiplied by 3·6 to decide the angles of the various segments. These are then drawn with a protractor on a circle of

convenient size and labelled clearly. The area of each slice is then the same percentage of the area of the circle as the item illustrated was of the total. It is desirable to include the percentage with the labelling as it is difficult to detect small differences of percentage on a pie chart. For the same reason it is sound practice to arrange the segments in order of size to aid comparison. The appearance of a handdrawn pie chart may be improved by shading or colouring the segments to increase contrast.

Labelling presents some problems. Writing in the labels like spokes of a wheel makes them impossible to read without turning the chart round. Horizontal labelling is difficult to fit into the smaller segments except where they are almost horizontal. Sometimes the chart can be so arrranged that the large segments lie top and bottom, thus keeping the narrow segments horizontal (but this runs counter to the principle of arranging segments in order of size). Probably the best answer is to write some of the titles outside the circumference of the chart (as in our example) and indicate the segment referred to by a short line or arrow.

Unilever Ltd. sales by operations, 1975
(Total sales: £6760 million)

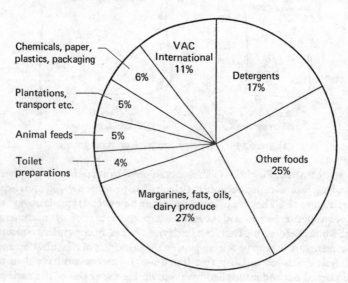

Figure 18 Pie chart

The advantages of pie charts are that the Rx can grasp the information provided quickly and can readily understand the relationships between the component parts. Their disadvantages are that they are rather time-consuming to draw and cannot be more than approximate. Bar charts can give similar information more accurately but less interestingly.

The pie chart in our example uses the same figures as were used in Figure 16 (the percentage bar chart). Thus students can compare the two methods for themselves and decide which they consider communicates the information more effectively.

V COLOUR

The use of colour as a medium of communication is increasing. As a medium it enjoys the two major advantages of pictorial communication (speed of impact and freedom from linguistic boundaries) without the need to design and reproduce the picture. It also offers particular advantages in labelling very small objects (e.g. colour coding of resistors) or very large ones (such as pipelines). It has the disadvantage of providing only a limited number of potential symbols, some of which are unserviceable because they cannot be distinguished by the partially colour blind.

Black for death, white for purity are very ancient colour symbols. Also very old is the concept of gold for first, silver for second, bronze for third (although the metals themselves rather than their colours formed the original basis of this distinction). Red (the colour of blood and fire) for danger, green (the commonest colour in nature) for safety became widely established before it was realised that these two colours were impossible to distinguish for those suffering from one not uncommon form of colour blindness.

Today there is a strong move to make yellow the colour for danger (while retaining green for safety). Red and yellow together or black and yellow together (in stripes) are commonly used to communicate danger. The first of these combinations is familiar to all from long-load lorries.

A familiar example of communication by colour is the coding of the insulation on the wires of a three-core electric cable:

Brown	*live*
Blue	*neutral*
Green and yellow stripes	*earth*

A less familiar but striking example of communication by colour is the coding of medical gas canisters (British Standards Institution recommendation), which is as follows:

Cylinder body	Valve end	Gas
violet	violet	*ethylene*
orange	orange	*cyclopropane*
blue	blue	*nitrous oxide*
brown	brown	*helium*
grey	grey	*carbon dioxide*
grey	black	*nitrogen*
black	black	*oxygen*
black	grey and white	*oxygen and carbon dioxide mixture*
black	brown and white	*oxygen and helium mixture*
grey	black and white	*air*

Another interesting example of the increasing use of colour as a labelling device is the British Standards system for pipelines. It is desirable that all senior staff working in an industrial environment are familiar with this coding.

Colour pipeline is painted or banded	Contents
green	*water*
silver-grey	*steam*
brown	*oils, combustible liquids*
yellow ochre	*gases (gaseous or liquid) other than air*
violet	*acids, alkalis*
black	*other fluids*
light blue	*air*
orange	*electrical services*

Additional colour communications associated with pipelines are:

red	*fire fighting*
yellow and black diagonals	*danger*
yellow with black trefoil	*ionising radiation*
bright blue ('auxiliary blue') used as a band over green	*fresh water (not necessarily potable)*

These examples will suffice to indicate the labelling applications of colour. Market research has indicated that colour communicates in other ways. Vance Packard in *The Hidden Persuaders* illustrates this by reference to the firm seeking advice on packaging its washing powder from the Color Research Institute (in America). Customer reaction to a yellow pack indicated fear that the powder would be so vicious in its action that laundry could be damaged. Reaction to a blue pack was almost opposite: that the powder would be ineffective, leaving laundry still dirty. It was the same powder in both packs. As a result of these findings a further testing was arranged by the Institute using the same powder again but in a blue package flecked with splashes of yellow. Customer reaction was now wholly favourable towards the product.

This is an area in which investigation is still at an early stage; but it seems certain that managers of the future will be giving much more attention to the communication element when choosing a colour for the firm's letter head, the print on its publicity leaflets, the cover of its user handbook, than is customary at the moment.

VI EXERCISES

Exercise A

	Perceived standards of living	Deserved standards of living	Increases
Company directors	9·1	8·4	−0·7
Doctors, etc	8·9	9·3	0·4
Shareholders, investors	8·7	7·5	−1·2
Civil servants	7·4	7·8	0·4
Skilled workers	7·2	8·4	1·2
Shopkeepers	6·9	8·0	1·1
Teachers	6·6	8·1	1·5
Policemen	6·4	8·3	1·9

	Perceived standards of living	Deserved standards of living	Increases
Office clerks	6·2	7·4	1·2
Shop assistants	5·4	7·3	1·9
Coloured people	5·3	6·5	1·2
Unskilled labourers	5·3	7·0	1·8
Students	5·0	6·3	1·3
People on social security	4·6	5·6	1·0
Pensioners (old age)	3·8	7·4	3·6

The above table shows the results of a survey carried out in 1975 which asked those interviewed (1) to place the standard of living they associated with various occupational groups on a scale from 0 to 10 (2) to indicate what standard they thought each occupational group *should* enjoy in an ideal society.

In about 150 words indicate the general tendencies of the answers obtained in this survey, stressing points that you find of particular interest.

Exercise B

Continental areas	Population millions	Teachers millions	Teachers per cent of population	Teacher shortage from 0·86 per cent norm millions
Africa	288	0·69	0·24	1·79
N. and C. America	291	2·94	1·01	−0·44
S. America	165	0·98	0·59	0·44
Asia (less USSR)	1742	4·48	0·26	10·52
Europe (less USSR)	442	2·95	0·67	0·85
USSR	231	1·90	0·82	0·09
Australasia	14	0·13	0·93	−0·01
	3173	14·07	0·44	13·69
				−0·45
				13·24

Country	Population millions	Teachers millions	Teachers per cent of population
Sweden	7·7	0·075	0·98
France	50	0·460	0·92
Canada	20	0·239	1·19
UK	54	0·464	0·86
USA	195	2·393	1·23

Statistics derived from figures published by the Bureau International d'Education (Geneva).

Reprinted from *Journal of the Royal Society of Arts.*

The above table shows the ratio of teachers to population throughout the world as divided into seven continental areas. It also shows the ratios in five countries (including the UK) where educational standards are generally recognised to be high.

1 0·86 per cent is shown as the 'norm'.
   (*a*) What does *norm* mean?
   (*b*) By what standard is 0·86 per cent the norm?
   (*c*) Express 0·86 *per cent of population* in another way
2 What is the significance of the negative percentages shown in the last column?
3 What deduction/s can you make as a result of comparing the figures for Canada and USA with those for North and Central America?
4 Write an article of about 180 words entitled 'World Education'. You should pay particular attention to (*a*) the overall teaching situation, (*b*) comparison between the various continental areas, (*c*) the UK position relative to (i) the rest of the world (ii) Europe outside the USSR (iii) the USSR.

Exercise C

The pictograms below are those recommended in *Dangerous chemical substances and proposals concerning their labelling* (better known as the *Yellow Book*) published by the Council for Europe. This divides dangerous chemical substances into the following categories:

I Explosive
II Oxidising[1]
III Flammable
IV *(a)* Toxic *(b)* Harmful
V *(a)* Corrosive *(b)* Irritant
VI Radioactive

1 Define *exothermic*.
2 Distinguish between *(a) toxic* and *harmful (b) corrosive* and *irritant*.
3 One of the pictograms above is used for two categories. Remembering this, indicate the pictogram for each category.

[1] Producing a highly exothermic reaction when in contact with other substances. Examples of oxidising substances include potassium chlorate and fuming nitric acid.

Comparative rates of inflation
% increases in consumer prices over a year earlier

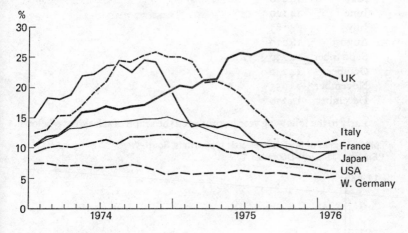

Source: OECD *Main Economic Indicators*

Exercise D

1 How much higher were prices in the UK in January 1976 than they had been in January 1975?
2 Were prices higher in Italy in February 1976 than in February 1975 or lower? By how much?
3 Identify the months in which the inflation rate in Japan and France was the same.
4 Write a paragraph of about 150 words about inflation in the UK compared with that in other European countries during the period illustrated.

Exercise E

Harry Flashman was appointed by Maddison Typewriters Ltd Area Sales Manager for South-West England 1st February 19... In the previous year monthly sales of electric typewriters in the area had averaged 13265. The January sales were 13850. Sales after Harry's appointment were as follows:

| February | 13 830 |
| March | 13 945 |

April	14 005
May	14 090
June	14 140
July	14 185
August	14 210
September	14 220
October	14 240
November	14 255
December	14 270

Early in the following year he produced the graph of sales shown below.

Monthly sales of Maddison electric typewriters, South-West
England, January–December 19..

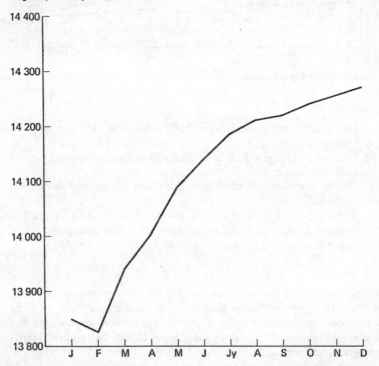

1 Comment on Harry's graph
2 Draw a graph which in your opinion more accurately indicates the

effect on sales of Harry's appointment. In case you think you can provide a more useful graph by incorporating monthly sales of the previous year these are shown below:

January	13 090
February	13 060
March	13 080
April	13 085
May	13 095
June	13 105
July	13 115
August	13 150
September	13 310
October	13 680
November	13 790
December	13 820

Exercise F

Reproduced below is part of an electioneering leaflet distributed in Mudcastle by the group that has been in control for just over a year. The numbers of council houses built in the two years referred to was respectively 3200 and 4000. The pictograms seem to make the present council's advance on the previous one's municipal housing performance greater than these figures indicate.

1 How has this effect been achieved?
2 Redraw the pictograms to present the situation more fairly.
3 Devise a different method for comparing the two figures; your method should be both fair and effective.

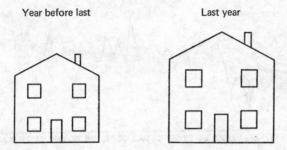

New council houses built
for you in Mudcastle

Year before last   Last year

Exercise G

In 1976 it was estimated that production of beer in the UK was divided between the seven major groups and 80+ independent brewers approximately as follows:

	percentage
Allied	16
Bass Charrington	20
Courage	8
Grand Metropolitan (Watneys etc)	14
Guiness (including Harp)	9
Scottish and Newcastle	10
Whitbread	12
Independent brewers	11

Draw a pie chart to illustrate the position.

Exercise H

1 What is meant by *1970 prices, seasonably adjusted* on chart (a)?
2 The personal savings ratio measures the proportion of total personal disposable income which is not spent by the consumer. From information supplied by the two charts, compile an 130 word account of

(a) UK personal savings ratio
   1970 prices, seasonally adjusted

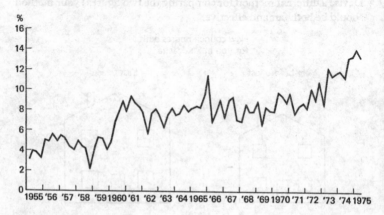

(b) Personal savings ratios in some industrial countries

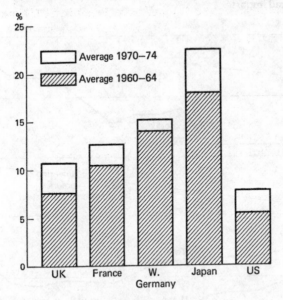

Source: *Treasury Economic Progress Report No. 68*

the tendencies shown by the UK personal savings ratio over the period 1960–75 and make a comparison with other major industrial countries. Include your own, brief, explanation of what you have observed. You should assume your typical Rx to be in the 18–25 age group, without formal training in economics, and without access to the charts you are using.

Exercise I

In about 150 words attempt a verbal interpretation of the information about engineering orders in the UK in 1968 represented graphically on page 296. You should make specific reference to:

1 Comparison between 1968 and 1958 performance
2 The general pattern of total and home orders during 1968
3 Differences between this and the trend of export orders – remember 1968 was an early example of the many recent years in which the UK

has been struggling to reduce an unfavourable trade gap between exports and imports.

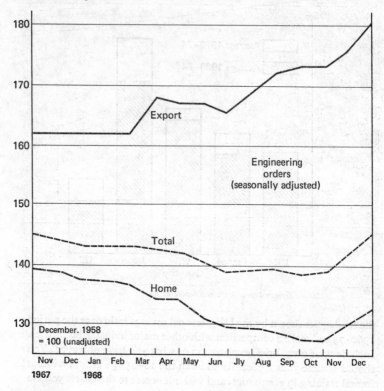

Exercise J

The two plans on page 298 show the development in the Lovat Lane area proposed by the Corporation of the City of London in 1976. It should be noted that the area left white on the 'existing situation' plan represents old rundown buildings of no architectural interest, such as those revealed in the photograph of Lovat Lane in 1976 reproduced on page 297.

In an article of about 250 words, intended for use in a public relations news-sheet published by the City of London, describe the changes envisaged and indicate the advantages of carrying these out. You should not assume that the readership will have seen either Lovat Lane or the plans and photograph reproduced here.

Lovat Lane area
Existing situation

St. Mary-at-Hill

St. Mary at Hill Church

Eastcheap

Lovat Lane

Botolph Alley

Botolph Lane

Lwr. Thames Street

Monument Street

Open space
Post war buildings
Listed buildings
Pedestrian way

0 ⟶ 50
Yards

Planning proposals

St. Mary at Hill Church

Lovat Lane

Botolph Alley

Open space
Refurbish
⟷ Pedestrian access

Listed buildings
New buildings
ıııııı Study area boundary

Retain

Part V

Passages for Comprehension and Discussion

Passage 1

In the following extract *pile* refers to an atomic pile. The part of the book it comes from deals with one of the first attempts to build one of these (in 1943). Read the passage carefully and select from the suggested answers for each question the one that seems to you the best.

Those in the secret did not talk easily with each other, and as the months passed and Luke's 'pile' went up, it was hard to judge how many believed in him. In committee heads were shaken, not much was said, yet feelings ran high. Luke was one of those figures who have the knack, often surprising to themselves, of stirring up 5 controversy; people who did not know him, who had no conception of his exuberant, often simple-hearted character, grew excited about him, as someone who would benefit the country or as a scandalous trifler with public money, almost as a crook.

Of his supporters, the most highly placed of all was lost in the 10 April of 1943, when Bevill was at last told that his job was wanted for another.

Now that his suspense had ended, I was astonished by the old man's resilience. He moved his papers from Whitehall the same day. Briskly he said goodbye to his staff and made a speech with a 15 remarkable, indeed an excessive, lack of sentimentality. He was not thinking of his years in the old office; he was thinking of nothing but the future. Without any procrastination at all he refused a peerage. If he accepted it, he was accepting the fact that he was out of politics for good: at the age of seventy-four he was, with the occupational 20 hope of politicians, as difficult to kill as the hope of a consumptive, reckoning his chances of getting back again.

As soon as he left, my own personal influence diminished; I could intervene no more than other civil servants of my rank (in his last month of office, Bevill had got me promoted again, which Rose 25 thought excessive). All I did had to go through Rose, and we were more than ever uneasy with each other.

C. P. Snow, *The New Men*, 1954

1 The word *pile* in line 2 is placed in inverted commas
   (a) because it was a word actually spoken by somebody
   (b) because it was at that time a slang word only used by the scientists concerned
   (c) because it was only an imitation pile
   (d) to emphasise it.

2 All the following comments about the committee are true *except*
   (a) they did not say much
   (b) they became very emotional
   (c) they turned every proposal down
   (d) they had doubts of the success of the pile.

3 If Luke has the knack of stirring up controversy, he
   (a) likes causing trouble
   (b) makes people disagree with each other about him
   (c) makes people excited about him
   (d) disagrees with other people frequently.

4 People who did not know Luke's character thought him all the following *except*
   (a) simple-hearted
   (b) almost a crook
   (c) the kind of man who would do good to his country
   (d) a man who would waste public money.

5 In line 14 *resilience* is nearest in meaning to
   (a) toughness
   (b) stupidity
   (c) relief
   (d) briskness.

6 Bevill's parting speech to his staff would be most accurately described as
   (a) remarkable
   (b) highly emotional
   (c) not highly emotional
   (d) too unemotional.

7 In line 18 *procrastination* means
   (a) delay
   (b) deception

     (c) argument
     (d) reason
8 Bevill refused a peerage because
     (a) he did not think he deserved it
     (b) he wanted another political job
     (c) he was a consumptive
     (d) he wanted to leave politics.
9 Which ONE of the following is true of Luke?
     (a) he easily grew excited
     (b) he was resilient
     (c) he was a crook
     (d) he was very high-spirited.
10 Rose thought that Bevill's action in promoting the narrator in his last
month of office
     (a) was more than the narrator deserved
     (b) was carried out too late in Bevill's career
     (c) was carried out very quickly
     (d) was going too far.

Passage 2

I have never enjoyed making a fuss about defective goods or poor
service. I loathed it when I lived in the safe anonymity of a large
city, but living as I do now in a small rural community I hesitate
before taking action. It is so easy to be noticed here and word travels
around the neighbourhood if you do anything untoward. I soon   5
became labelled 'anti-bomb', and to this was added 'anti-fox-
hunting' after an unlooked-for fracas with the local hunt. So it was
with a good deal of diffidence that I became involved in yet another
field and thus risked becoming known as 'anti-everything'!

However, so many of my purchases have developed defects   10
recently and I have had so many examples of poor and uninterested
service from a variety of sources that it has been necessary to waste
a good deal of time attempting to have matters put right. I wonder if
I have been unusually unlucky or whether the following
experiences are common.   15

The first issue on which I really took a stand was over a minor
repair to my typewriter. It needed a small roller replacing on the
back so I sent it off to a firm specialising in typewriter repairs to
have it replaced, expecting to have the machine back within a few

days. It was away for six weeks. I was nearly frantic as I cannot 20
write easily without it, but eventually it was returned with a new
small roller – and a bill for £8·90.[1] Utterly amazed, I queried this
and asked for details of how such a sum could be justified but I did
not receive any satisfactory answer. During the next few weeks I
made several further attempts, all to no avail; so, after talking it 25
over with my husband, I refused to pay the bill.

The matter was then put into the hands of the firm's solicitors
and eventually a bailiff arrived at my door to serve me with a
summons. By this time I had cold feet but my husband filled in the
'defence' section of the summons form with a statement to the effect 30
that we would ask the court how they thought the replacement of a
small rubber roller could cost £8·90, and then see what happened.
By return of post we had a letter from the solicitors of the firm
concerned asking us what price we would be prepared to pay for the
job. We sent a cheque for the amount we thought sufficient and 35
heard no more of the matter.

The two other most flagrant examples concerned a new
refrigerator and a new vacuum cleaner. The refrigerator was a
major buy embarked on because shopping is so difficult. Within
three months the inside lining of the door (which holds butter, milk 40
bottles, etc) had begun to break away from the door itself. I
went along to the local showroom of the nationalised industry from
which I had purchased the fridge and asked them to do something
about it. To my astonishment I was told that nothing could be
done; in effect, it was my bad luck. As I was buying on a hire- 45
purchase agreement I refused to pay any more payments until the
matter was put right. The day after I had written explaining what I
intended to do a man arrived with a new lining which he fixed inside
the door for me, but he seemed to think that I had 'got one over' the
supplier in some crafty way. 'Other people with this trouble,' he 50
said, 'have paid for a new lining themselves.'

Shortly after this a representative from the firm who made the
refrigerator came to see me and told me that the lining should have
been replaced at once. But he also added the astonishing
information that my fridge was one of a batch which had been sent 55
out with the wrong sort of plastic used in the door. This plastic was
found to crack at low temperatures but he offered no explanation as

[1] Original figure adjusted to 1977 equivalent.

to why the plastic had not been tested before being used in such a
way. I was left to ruminate on those people who had paid for their
own replacements.   60

When the new vacuum cleaner packed up when we were in the
midst of a building job which caused a great deal of dirt I began to
think there really were such things as gremlins. Once more I
repaired to the same local showroom from which I had been
misguided enough to purchase my vacuum cleaner and implored   65
them to send up a mechanic as soon as possible to see what was the
matter. Nothing happened. Ten days later I asked again, to be told
that they had passed on my message to the representative of the firm
which made the cleaner who had 'given the impression' he might be
up soon.   70

Another week passed. Again I asked what was happening but by
this time no one had any record of any complaint; but nevertheless,
I was promised action shortly. A week later I rang in fury to be told
that there was no trace of any complaint made by me but that they
would see that a mechanic came up before the weekend. On the   75
Wednesday of the following week I spoke to the manager
explaining the whole story. He told me not to be 'hasty' and
promised that someone would come and put the matter right the
following morning. I told him civilly that if I was let down again I
would ring the head office of the firm in Middlesex which made the   80
cleaner and also his own area manager to inform them of how I felt.
I waited in throughout most of the next day but when it became
obvious that nothing was going to happen I did what I had
threatened to do and made my telephone calls. Then, of course,
there was action. First the manager of the local showroom rang me   85
up and told me through clenched teeth that someone would be up
directly, and during the following day we received a slow stream of
mechanics and representatives of the vacuum cleaner firm. Again I
wonder what happens to people less persistent than I am.

There are countless other smaller examples such as the parcel   90
dispatched per British Road Services from Exeter (a distance of
180 km) which took eleven days to get here, and the wood sent from
London by the same quaint method of transport which, after eight
days, has still not arrived. It could hardly have taken longer by ox
wagon in the Middle Ages.   95

Goodness knows what the answer is. The Consumer's Association and the various local consumer groups help the customer, but

the fault lies deeper than this. How can a man making, say, a
vacuum cleaner in a huge concern, who spends every hour of every
day of his working week doing a simple, repetitive task in the course   100
of the mass production of the article, feel anything at all for the
customer who will receive it? He probably does not even see the
finished product and is only interested – and who can blame him? –
in getting home to his family at the end of the day and the amount in
his pay packet.   105

Employees in branches of large concerns, either private or
nationalised, rarely feel the interest in the customer that a small
family business would have. If my vacuum cleaner goes wrong
within weeks of its being purchased it does not really matter much
to them whether or not I am satisfied as there will be no lack of   110
customers if I never cross the threshold again.

It seems to be assumed that in this affluent society we are all so
rich that we can afford to buy expensive pieces of household
equipment without caring how long they will last, be prepared to do
without them for weeks if they show a defect, and be happy to throw   115
them away within a year or two for a later model.

I have little energy to spare and feel that there are bigger issues to
fight than whether or not my refrigerator falls to pieces, but as a
housewife on a very limited budget I cannot afford to pay for other
people's mistakes. Am I taking it all too seriously?   120

Judith Cook in the *Guardian*, 28 October 1963
(*decimalised and metricated version*)

1 (*a*) What is the meaning of 'safe anonymity' in the second sentence? (*b*)
Can you detect an ambiguity in this sentence?

2 What is the precise force of (*a*) *fracas* (l. 7), (*b*) *quaint* (l. 93)?

3 Comment on the following expressions (*a*) *cold feet* (l. 29), (*b*) *major buy*
(l. 39), (*c*) *fridge* (l. 43), (*d*) *packed up* (l. 61).
Do you consider these appropriate in register? What do you assume to be
the author's motive in using them?

4 Why does the author write *its being purchased* (l. 109) and not *it being
purchased* (which is what most people would certainly *say*)?

5 Which of the following statements seems to you closest to the truth?
   (*a*) Since this passage was written the situation described has got
       worse.
   (*b*) Since this passage was written the situation described has got
       better.

(c) Since this passage was written the situation described has stayed much the same.

(d) People still make complaints of this sort but they have little substance; this writer's complaints seem also to have little substance.

6 Do you consider that in any of these episodes the author would have been treated differently if she had been a man?

7 Do you detect any points in these episodes where communication failure may have (a) caused the unsatisfactory service (b) aggravated the situation?

8 What impression of the writer have you formed after reading this article?

9 What answer would you give to the rhetorical question she asks in her last sentence?

10 In lines 96–116 she attempts a common fundamental explanation for all her experiences. Do you consider (a) that such a common explanation is probable or (b) that each experience requires its own separate explanation?

f (a) do you consider hers a fully satisfactory explanation? Discuss.

If (b) what explanation would you offer for each episode?

Passage 3

In considering the art of teaching, the first point is the actual teaching process, the skill of passing on to the student the benefit of the teacher's own experience. As a definition this is too simple. The teaching process is a two-way one which involves the student as a learner, as well as the teacher as a teacher. The teacher's function is   5
to guide the student's learning along effective and economic lines and to teach the student how to learn a subject rather than to teach the subject itself. One of the objects of technical teacher training is to make the teacher aware that effective teaching does not just happen; it is the consequence of careful preparation along specific   10
lines.

The teacher must appreciate that education and instruction are not synonymous. A study of effective learning in classroom and other situations, treated in a practical and realistic way, must therefore be given some degree of priority in a training scheme. The   15
function of technical education is, however, education and not simply instruction, and more subtle factors are therefore involved.

It is essential that a teacher should develop an inquiring attitude of mind and a wide outlook to enable him to make use of every opportunity, however it may arise, to widen the educational horizons and develop the understanding of his students. Such an attitude of mind, if not already in existence, must be encouraged and nurtured during training. Discussions and seminars yield good results in this field.

All too frequently the teacher considers himself as a passer-on of information, a middleman between the recognised authorities and the student. His teaching is too often no more than the provision of pre-digested textbook material for his class. This is at once not enough and too much. The student only learns by active participation. To sit and listen to a lecturer while taking an occasional note does not constitute efficient learning. The most important function of the teacher is to make the student think. The teacher who, in an effort to save the student's time, does his thinking for him, is doing the student a grave disservice.

The teacher must therefore be shown how best to prepare and present his lessons so that the student shall most effectively learn. He must be made aware of the many teaching aids now available in addition to the blackboard, whether they be the simple home-made ones or the more sophisticated commercial products. He must learn to recognise their value in raising teaching efficiency by involving more than one sensory experience.

He must also be aware that he is doing more than producing technicians, technologists or craftsmen. He must have a sufficiently wide outlook to see his subject in the broader perspective of the course generally and of the culture in which we live. The specialist teacher has a tendency to consider his own subject as the most important in the curriculum and any course of teacher training should lead him to see his subject as part of a whole. To this end the history of education and allied subjects should be studied during the training as an aid to the creation of a sense of social purpose and as a means of obtaining a deeper understanding on the part of the students.

Assuming the teacher has learnt how to prepare and present his lessons and make full use of all suitable aids, he must also be made aware of his own personal influence on the teaching process. He must be shown that even good teaching methods can be enhanced if presented with interest and developed with enthusiasm, and if the subject can be suitably related to current practice via the teacher's familiarity with industry. The effect of the teacher's attitude to his work cannot be over-emphasised. Too many teachers tend to base their teaching on their memories of being taught at the final stages of their own courses.

A further function of teacher training is to enable the teacher to develop the student's ability for rational thinking. This can be achieved by means of feedback from his students. The teacher must therefore be shown how to adapt his presentation in such a way as to involve the students actively. The teacher then functions as a guide rather than a dictator. His leadership of the class is more acceptable and disciplinary problems are minimised. He must be made to appreciate that his job is to teach and that in order to do this he must make his teaching acceptable. To say that a class is bored or will not work is in reality a reflection on the teacher rather than the class. It is the teacher's duty to present his material in such a way that the class will be interested and consequently learn. He must set an example of logical clear thinking and of neat orderly presentation which the class can emulate.

It may seem superfluous to suggest that a teacher should be able to express himself clearly and logically. This unfortunately is not so. A new entrant to the profession may never have addressed more than two or three people at a time; he may be unaware of the different techniques required to speak to a group of 20 or 30 people. Too many teachers unconsciously involve themselves in nervous mannerisms or make use of stereotyped phrases and dreary monotones. A tape recorder to enable the teacher trainee to hear himself as his classes will hear him, often has a salutary effect. A further failing, particularly with the specialist teacher, is to indulge in the 'jargon' of his subject on the assumption, frequently incorrect, that his students know the language. Training can help to eradicate these undesirable tendencies.

Technical Teacher Training,
The Association of Teachers in
Technical Institutions, 1963

1 What is the meaning of the following words as used in the passage: *economic* (l. 6) *specific* (l. 10) *factors* (l. 17) *nurtured* (l. 23) *seminars* (l. 23) *sophisticated* (l. 39) *curriculum* (l. 47) *enhanced* (l. 56) *rational* (l. 64) *emulate* (l. 76) *stereotyped* (l. 83) *eradicate* (l. 89)?

2 Do you consider this policy statement justified in referring to teaching as an 'art' in l. 1 ?

3 (a) In what ways is the gloss of the words *actual teaching process* in the first sentence too simple for a definition?

   (b) Does the word *actual* serve any purpose in this phrase?

4 In what ways are *education* and *instruction* not synonymous? (l. 12)

5 In what ways is *the provision of pre-digested textbook material* an inadequate conception of teaching? (ll. 27–8)

6 What types of *sensory experience* can be provided during a class? (l. 41)

7 In what ways can there be feedback from a class? (l. 65)

8 What differences of technique are required for addressing 20 or 30 people as distinct from two or three?

9 List, in note form, all the functions of a teacher mentioned in the passage.

Passage 4

Under some conditions, people will hold money, not simply for early use, but as a convenient way of storing wealth for future needs. In some of its forms, money provides a store of wealth which is easily protected against theft or destruction – while remaining 'liquid', that is usable at any moment. The liquidity is something   5
valuable, and can itself be 'sold'; in most societies, a man who gives up control over a stock of money for a period (by lending it to someone else) will expect to be repaid 'with interest', that is to say, with a percentage added. The interest is not only a recompense for running a risk, for it is still paid when the risk is negligible; it is a   10
recompense for the disadvantage of giving up liquidity. The existence of an organised system of money loans is itself a great convenience to a complex community; it makes it possible (for instance) for a man who has a good use for money (say, to build a new factory) to get ahead without waiting for the tedious process of   15
saving up the money from his own income.

But, after all this, what is money? There have been so many different forms of money that it is not easy to find a consistent definition; but I shall here define money as anything which is widely accepted in payment for goods and services, or in discharge   20
of other business obligations. Some kinds of money not only *are*, but by law, *must be*, accepted for payment. Such money is called *legal tender*, but for my definition acceptance in fact will suffice, whether or not the acceptance is required by law.

Some kinds of money have a value apart from their value in use as   25
money. For instance, the old gold sovereign was valuable as gold;
you could melt it down, and still have something which men prized
highly. The paper of a bank-note, on the other hand, is useless, and
the note acquires its value simply from what is printed on it. The
various coins which we use in Britain are the metal equivalents of   30
bank-notes. The value of their metal content is much below their
face value, and so they retain their face value simply because a
Government has said 'It shall be so', and the people have agreed to
accept the coins so certified.

It can be seen from this that it is a very important function of the   35
State – and one which must be carefully protected against the
imitations of coiners and forgers – to issue and certify money. It is
convenient to have a single trustworthy central authority,
producing money in forms appropriate for the carrying out of
everyday transactions. Nevertheless, it sometimes happens that   40
people accept, and even prefer, money which is actually or
apparently certified by some authority other than the State.
Throughout Ireland, British and Irish notes and coins circulate
side by side; and the gold sovereign, dropped from our currency a
generation ago, still circulates in some areas abroad.   45

The state-certified notes and coin are, however, really only small
change. In Britain and the United States, much the largest part of
the stock of money is bank money, whose visible evidence is the
figures in the account books of banks of amounts standing to the
credit of depositors. About £2500 million of notes and coin are   50
outstanding in the United Kingdom, including £185 million of
coins; the notes and coin actually in circulation with the public
amount to £2000 million. But bank deposits are of the order of
£7000 million. It is true that a bank cheque is not universally
accepted as money; a great many shopkeepers would refuse a   55
cheque, on the grounds that they have no assurance that there is
money to meet it in the bank. But cheques are nevertheless so
widely accepted (especially for the larger transactions) that they
have a dominant position in the total of money transactions.

The room for manoeuvre in making purchases, which is given by   60
the existence of money, can be expressed another way. Money
breaks the link between income and spending; it makes it possible
to spend in a year less than a year's income (holding back the rest as
a money stock) or to spend more than a year's income (running

down a money stock). But this is potentially dangerous; for if it is   65
possible to create or destroy money, adding or subtracting it from
people's store of wealth, it is possible to create inconvenient
fluctuations in demand (and therefore in prices). Thus it has come
to be regarded as necessary for a strong central authority, not
merely to issue and certify the small change, but to control the size   70
of the whole stock of money.

C. F. Carter, The Science of Wealth, 1960

1 What is the meaning of the following words as used in the passage:
negligible (l. 10)   *complex* (l. 13)   *obligations* (l. 21)   *dominant* (l. 59)
manoeuvre (l.60)?

2 How does the author establish the meaning his Rx is to assign to (*a*)
liquidity (*b*) *money*?

3 What is meant by *Some kinds of money have a value apart from their
value in use as money* (ll. 25–26)? Have the two uses of (*a*) *value* and (*b*)
money the same area of meaning?

4 What is the force of *actually or apparently* in *money which is actually or
apparently certified by some authority other than the State* (ll. 41–42)?

5 In what sense are state-certified notes and coin 'small change'?

6 What is meant by *Money breaks the link between income and spending* (ll.
61–2)?

7 Write notes on this passage, paying special attention to headings and
subheadings.

Passage 5

Money began in nonliterate cultures as a commodity, such as
whales' teeth on Fiji; or rats on Easter Island, which were
considered a delicacy, were valued as a luxury, and thus became a
means of mediation or barter. When the Spaniards were besieging
Leyden in 1574, leather money was issued, but as hardship   5
increased the population boiled and ate the new currency.

    In literate cultures, circumstances may reintroduce commodity
money. The Dutch, after the German occupation of World War II,
were avid for tobacco. Since the supply was small, objects of high
value such as jewels, precision instruments, and even houses were   10
sold for small quantities of cigarettes. *The Reader's Digest* recorded
an episode from the early occupation of Europe in 1945, describing
how an unopened pack of cigarettes served as currency, passing

from hand to hand, translating the skill of one worker into the skill
of another as long as no one broke the seal.   15

Money always retains something of its commodity and community character. In the beginning, its function of extending the
grasp of men from their nearest staples and commodities to more
distant ones is very slight. Increased mobility of grasp and trading
is small at first. So it is with the emergence of language in the child.   20
In the first months grasping is reflexive, and the power to make
voluntary release comes only toward the end of the first year.
Speech comes with the development of the power to let go of
objects. It gives the power of detachment from the environment
that is also the power of great mobility in knowledge of the   25
environment. So it is with the growth of the idea of money as
currency rather than commodity. Currency is a way of letting go of
the immediate staples and commodities that at first serve as money,
in order to extend trading to the whole social complex. Trading by
currency is based on the principle of grasping and letting go in an   30
oscillating cycle. The one hand retains the article with which it
tempts the other party. The other hand is extended in demand
toward the object which is desired in exchange. The first hand lets
go as soon as the second object is touched, somewhat in the manner
of a trapeze artist exchanging one bar for another. In fact, Elias   35
Canetti in *Crowds and Power* argues that the trader is involved in
one of the most ancient of all pastimes, namely that of climbing
trees and swinging from limb to limb. The primitive grasping,
calculating, and timing of the greater arboreal apes he sees as a
translation into financial terms of one of the oldest movement   40
patterns. Just as the hand among the branches of the trees learned a
pattern of grasping that was quite removed from the moving of food
to mouth, so the trader and the financier have developed enthralling
abstract activities that are extensions of the avid climbing and
mobility of the greater apes.   45

Like any other medium, it is a staple, a natural resource. As an
outward and visible form of the urge to change and to exchange, it is
a corporate image, depending on society for its institutional status.
Apart from communal participation, money is meaningless, as
Robinson Crusoe discovered when he found the coins in the   50
wrecked ship.

Marshall McLuhan, *Understanding Media*, 1964

1 What is the meaning of the following words as used in the passage: *mediation* (l. 4) *avid* (ll. 9 and 44) *staples* (ll. 18, 28, and 46) *mobility* (l. 19) *reflexive* (l. 21)   *environment* (l. 24)   *arboreal* (l. 39)   *enthralling* (l. 43) *status* (l. 48)?

2 What is the difference between a *literate culture* (l. 7) and a nonliterate one?

3 How is the 'pack of cigarettes' in l.13 acting as currency until the seal is broken? In what sense does it translate the skill of one worker into the skill of another at each transaction?

4 Substitute your own words for:

(a) the sentence (l. 24) that starts: *It gives the power of detachment* ...

(b) the sentence (l. 29) that starts: *Trading by currency is based* ...

5 In what way can trading be likened to swinging from limb to limb of a tree (l. 38)?

6 Show how the trader and financier have developed 'abstract activities' from commodity trading (l. 44).

7 How is money meaningless 'apart from communal participation' (l. 49)? How is it a 'corporate image' (l. 48)?

8 What is the essential difference between commodity money and modern money?

9 Make a précis of the passage in approximately 140 words (one-quarter) and supply a title.

10 In about 200 words outline the differences in attitude towards money shown by the authors of passages 4 and 5.

Passage 6

G.16 Subject to Regulation G.17, bare or lightly-insulated conductors of copper or nickel, having a cross-sectional area of not less than 0.3959 mm^2 ($1/0.71$ mm), may be used for series connections in circuits operating at a voltage exceeding low voltage, e.g. for window signs, provided that either—

(i) the conductor does not exceed 1 m in length, is supported at intervals not greater than 500 mm, is not exposed to the likelihood of mechanical damage, and is completely protected by non-combustible, non-hygroscopic insulating material which, if in the form of glass tubing, has a wall thickness not less than 1 mm, an overall diameter not less than 5 mm, and is so arranged as to be reasonably secure against any displacement which would expose any part of the live metal, or

(ii) the conductor is in an enclosure to the interior of which only
authorized persons can have access.

G.17 For shop-front fascia installations, bare or lightly-insulated
conductors shall be used only for connections housed within an
earthed metal enclosure or for connections between the terminals of
electrode housings. For all other connections behind or through
fascia panels, including series connections, armoured or metal-
sheathed or metal-braided cable shall be used. In all instances the
wiring shall comply with the requirements of B.S.5055.

Regulations for the Electrical Equipment of Buildings,
Institute of Electrical Engineers, 1976

List all the essential conditions which must be observed if bare
conductors (of copper or nickel) are to be used for high voltage series
connections. If any of these conditions are alternatives to each other
indicate clearly which these are.

Passage 7

The fundamental questions about buying are what, why, who and
where. What and why are, of course, interlinked. Goods may be
divided into durables and non-durables or into essential and non-
essentials, but the boundaries in both cases are blurred. For
example, different people have different views about what is   5
essential; so may the same person at different times. Food is
essential, but few people in this country would now regard as
essential only those ingredients necessary for adequate nutrition,
though they might have been more prepared to do so 30 years ago.
'Essential' needs change, and the desire to stay alive and fit has been   10
augmented by a need for variety and stimulation. Food advertisers
recognise this, and try to convince us that a product is both good for
us (essential) and a treat (non-essential), thus providing both
rational and emotional incentives to buy it.

Those who try to influence what we buy have been forced to   15
change their techniques over the last 20 years. Once they tried to
persuade us to buy a particular product or brand, but the great
mushrooming of products which accompanied growing economic
prosperity has forced them to adopt more subtle approaches.
Minority tastes are now accepted and partial brand loyalty   20
tolerated. We are allowed to flirt with rival products, especially if

they are new. So long as we return to the old faithful after these
bouts of promiscuity, the admen are content. But the recession of
the last few years has seen an interesting return to older methods,
with more sophisticated attempts to re-establish brand loyalty.   25
Only Persil mums are caring mums, and we can all recognise the
chap who drinks Guinness: he's the calm, relaxed one in the corner,
content to wait until the head on his beer subsides.

Who buys what? The old demographic classification of buyers
has been abandoned as it became clear that the buying habits of,   30
say, a single 24 year old woman were different from those of a
married lady of the same age: they may both covet the same
perfume, but the latter may have to temper her enthusiasm with the
recollection of a mortgage. The analysis of buying behaviour has
become finer-grained, with attention being directed towards   35
factors with heavy psychological labels like self-image; position in
the life cycle; and peer and reference group (which may be identical
– a 15 year old boy uses Brut because all 15 year old boys do so; or
different – 15 year old boys used to apply Brylcreem because Denis
Compton did so). Two-brand smokers buy cheap cigarettes to   40
smoke at work and a more expensive variety for an evening out.
Self-image has been exploited with legendary success by Embassy
cigarettes, which rose from nothing to being the leading brand on
the back of an advertising campaign which implied that anyone
could smoke an Embassy anywhere.   45

The increased sophistication of advertising and marketing
techniques is probably more than matched by the rise of the
consumer movement. Studies show that active pursuit of the best
value is equally common at all levels of socio-economic status,
though its motivation may differ: bargain-hunting may either be   50
fun or reflect the *need* to be economical. There is also evidence that
price consciousness is possessed by some people more than others,
regardless of economic circumstances or any other factors. But the
buyers have not had it all their own way. Sellers have fought back
with a series of marketing manoeuvres designed to bamboozle all   55
but the canniest shopper. The banning of retail price maintenance
has encouraged the use of trading stamps, banded offers, 'special'
offers (6p off: but off what?) and the introduction of special-offer
coupons. A number of market research firms have tried to evaluate
the effectiveness of these different techniques for persuading us to   60
part with our money. It looks as though in Britain we are most

attracted by the prospect of actually having cash handed back to us
when we have bought something.

John Nicholson in *New Society*, 20 May 1976

1 What is the meaning of the following words as used in the passage:
fundamental (l. 1)   *durables* (l. 3)   *promiscuity* (l. 23)   *recession* (l. 23)
covet (l. 32) *factors* (l. 36) *sophistication* (l. 46) *canniest* (l. 56)

2 Express in other words:
augmented by a need for variety and stimulation (l. 11)
partial brand loyalty tolerated (l. 20–1)
The analysis of buying behaviour has become finer-grained (ll. 34–5)
heavy psychological labels (l. 36)

3 How would you rephrase the third sentence to avoid the use of *case* (see
page 88)? Do you consider your sentence superior to the original, and if
so in what way?

4 What is the effect of the inverted commas round *Essential* in line 10?

5 (a) To what is the author indirectly comparing brand loyalty by his
choice of word on three occasions (b) Identify these three occasions.

6 (a) Distinguish between rational and emotional incentives to buy
(b) How do advertisers attempt to appeal to both at once in selling food?

7 (a) What must a 'demographic classification of buyers' have been?
(Use a dictionary if necessary.) (b) Why has it been abandoned, according
to the author?

8 What illustrations of the effect on buying of 'position in the life-cycle'
are supplied in this passage?

9 Distinguish between a 'peer group' and a 'reference group'.

10 List (in note form) three reasons why buyers seek the best value,
according to the author.

11 List five methods of offering a discount that have resulted from the
ending of retail price maintenance, with brief notes on each.

12 The register of this passage indicates that the original article was
written for a popular magazine rather than for the journal of a learned
society devoted to sociology. Pick ten words from the article which
illustrate this.

13 As the first sentence of this extract indicates, the original article went
on to deal with who now does the buying (is it still the woman of the
household?) and where buyers prefer to make their purchases (chain
store? city-centre shop? local corner shop? supermarket?).

EITHER (a) Write an article of about 250 words on the subject *Who buys
where?*

OR   (b) Discuss these points in class.

Passage 8

Psychologists are interested in the meaning of symbols, specifically as triggers of behaviour. In this context we may distinguish between two kinds of meaning, 'denotative' and 'connotative'. Denotative symbols refer to specific objects or directions, and the things that they symbolise can be 'pointed to'. The meaning of such   5
a symbol will be the same to all who comprehend it. Most symbols in practice, however, carry both denotative and connotative meaning. Connotative meanings are essentially subjective, often rather emotional, and they evaluate. Thus the symbol 'black-legging' does more than describe a certain kind of behaviour. It   10
evaluates and condemns such behaviour.

The American psychologist, Osgood, established three main dimensions of connotative meaning – an evaluative dimension (good – bad, clean – dirty), a strength dimension (strong – weak, large – small), and an activity dimension (fast – slow, active –   15
passive), the evaluative dimension carrying most weight. A phrase like 'planned redundancy' will carry many connotations, which are likely to vary considerably with the organisational status of the person hearing the phrase.

Communication occurs in the context of a whole range of   20
organisational behaviour. When we receive a message from someone, our understanding may be affected by his dress, his accent, and so forth. His role in the organisation may be equally important. The same words may be interpreted differently if they are uttered by the managing director on the one hand or a shop   25
steward on the other, for the 'who' is an important non-verbal symbol in the message.

When we examine a sample of industrial behaviour which involves communication, we are confronted with evidence of all kinds of organisational characteristics, such as power, authority,   30
conflict, leadership, control. When an executive communicates an order to his subordinate, their relationship might be complicated by the subordinate's experience of the executive's indifferent leadership, or by his resentment of what he thinks is a petty-minded control system, or by his own inability to make a certain type of   35
decision. This incapacity itself might be a product of the particular

organisational structure of the firm. The American Lyman Bryson, having defined executives as 'all members of an organisation who have access to the chief executive for purposes of policy discussion', points to some of the structural problems to which we refer. Where there is a choice between different courses of action, all executives are likely to be quite heavily committed to a point of view. In most cases they will express their honest conviction, but they are equally likely to have something in mind beyond the intrinsic worth of these opinions. They will be concerned for example with their own prestige, and they will want to make sure that they will be allowed to help in further decisions. 'In policy discussions,' says Bryson, 'it is a man and not an opinion who wins. Every member of staff wants to be that man, or associated with him.'

N. C. Bowker and M. F. Hall in *The Manager*, November 1963

1 Express in other words: *specifically as triggers of behaviour* (ll. 1–2).
2 Distinguish between *denotative* and *connotative* meanings (cf. *objective* and *subjective*, page 76).
3 To illustrate each of the three 'dimensions' of connotative meaning supply two pairs of antonyms other than those used in the article (ll. 12–16).
4 What connotations would you expect *planned redundancy* to carry for (*a*) the works manager, (*b*) a shop steward, (*c*) a newly appointed machine operator?
5 Consider the sentence *When ... so forth* (ll. 21–23). What further examples may be added in place of the words *and so forth*?
6 How satisfactory do you consider Lyman Bryson's definition of *executives* (ll. 38–9)?
7 What meaning did you assign to *cases* in line 43 when you read the passage? Can you now see a possible different meaning for this word in this context? Is the author's use of *cases* here justified?
8 Make a précis of the passage in not more than 150 words (one-third), and supply a title.

Passage 9

This flood of paper which now threatens to submerge the world is something peculiar to this century. The Hellenistic scribes who wrote on papyrus, the Chinese bureaucrats who exercised their penmanship on silk, and even the eighteenth century clerks who inscribed their civilities on rag paper with a quill pen, were guiltless of anything that could be called mass production. It is our own age that has developed the swiftness of communication, the abundance of paper, the multiplication of copies and the widespread semi-literacy which are the immediate causes of the paper flood. Ease of communication has also made practicable such a degree of centralised control as was never known before. Until a century ago every large-scale and scattered organisation or empire was engaged in a ceaseless struggle to make its distant units conform with central policy. For reference to headquarters there was neither the inclination nor the time. Those in positions of theoretical responsibility read with helpless dismay of provinces annexed, officials sacked, branches opened and ships sold, their bleating protests coming perpetually too late. With the laying of trans-oceanic cables they felt for the first time that they had their agents on the leash. From about 1875 began, therefore, that tightening of the chain that has finally destroyed the effectiveness of (among other things) colonialism and diplomacy. The professional bargaining of plenipotentiaries has given place to the bickering of impotent office boys, each tied to the apron-strings of a government which has never even heard the persuasions of the other side. Diplomatically, administratively, commercially, the process of centralisation has been carried to its logical conclusion with all authority vested too often in a single man; and he, from overwork, quite obviously off his head.

It was inevitable that the central administration would make full use of the tools that had suddenly become available. After centuries of frustration those in authority could at last impose their policy upon the whole organisation, not merely from day to day but from hour to hour. They could exact the fullest information, collate the most detailed returns, draw up the most voluminous directives and issue the most peremptory commands. Of these opportunities they have made the fullest use. But for all this they have had to pay the price. The penalty has been that correspondence pours on them in the present flood. Surrounding themselves with executives, they battle with a rising tide of paper. Ordinarily waist-deep in letters and memoranda, a week's illness will bring the high-water mark up to their chin. Rather than drown, the key man prefers to suppress his symptoms and stay at his desk; often with the worst results for all concerned.

C. Northcote Parkinson, In-laws and Outlaws, 1962

1 What is the connection between the references in the second sentence of this passage to *papyrus, silk, rag paper, quill pen*, and the first sentence?

2 *(a)* Re-express 'inscribed their civilities' (l. 5) in simpler language.

   (b) What loss does the passage suffer if your words are substituted for the author's?

3 *(a)* In what way is 'semi-literacy' a cause of the 'paper flood' (ll. 6–9)?

   (b) Is 'semi-literacy' here contrasted with literacy or with illiteracy?

   (c) Is this normal usage?

4 *(a)* Why are the positions of those who 'read with helpless dismay' (l.16) described as 'of theoretical responsibility'?

   (b) Why are their protests described as 'bleating'?

5 What is the essential antithesis between *plenipotentiaries* and *impotent office boys* (ll. 23, 24)?

6 While retaining the full meaning, re-express the following so that none of the author's original words are used:

> They could exact the fullest information, collate the most detailed returns, draw up most voluminous directives and issue the most peremptory commands (ll. 34–36).

7 The syntax of the penultimate sentence of this passage is open to two criticisms. What are they?

8 Make a précis of the passage in not more than 150 words (one-third) taking particular care to avoid all figurative language, and supply a title.

Passage 10

It is not sufficient to develop a sales strategy based on the premise that the attributes of your product will sell it for you: purchases based purely on comparative technical specifications are common to very few sections of modern society. Intuitively, this action would only apply to physical scientists (engineers, etc) in the   5
context of their work. An engineer, in the scientific community, has been trained in, and values, 'objectivity' and performance; therefore these are the criteria by which he will gauge product against product, and the characteristics which selling companies will employ in promoting their goods to him. This is what Olmosk   10
calls 'the Academic Strategy' where diligent sifting of fact against fact can lead to a significant change in attitude. People adopting such a strategy are seen as rational, analytical, and detached; and positive influence resides in presenting enough standardised information. In the case of marketing to engineers and scientists the   15

adoption of such a stratagem is more often accidental than deliberate, as it is usual that technologists market to other technologists and therefore the two parties speak the same language.

It would be fallacious to suggest that the scientific community is   20
characterised by total objectivity: as, although it may be difficult to differentiate products on purely technical specifications, even attributes such as price, after-sales service, delivery time, etc, cannot be separated from the personal value system of the buyer. This is essentially a solipsistic view of the individual; no aspect of   25
the product being free of his interpretation and perceptions. Using such a personalist framework one may postulate that a person will only buy that which he perceives to be a useful and meaningful extension of his *self*, defined as being the individual as he/she sees him/herself. According to Mead and other social psychologists, the   30
self is a product of social interaction and develops gradually. This picture of himself as he thinks he is, or wants to be, helps the individual organise his needs and goals. The defence of one's *self*, or more usually the individual's desire to experience his or her own identity, motivates people to actions; one of which may be the   35
incident of purchase.

When the marketing strategist begins to analyse the act of selling to the general public, the ascertaining of: (1) what constitutes the major selling points of a product, and (2) how to package those points in language most easily comprehensible to the population   40
chosen, is a taxing and difficult exercise. Of these, the moot point is that of gauging the advertising importance of the various facets of the product (comprehension being a necessary, if not in itself sufficient, condition conducive to sale), as it is here that the facilitating component which realises potential custom is found.   45
What is the nature of the relationship between this facilitating content of a product's presentation and the buyer's *self*?

G. W. Smith in European Journal of Marketing, 1975

1 What is the meaning of the following words and expressions as used in the passage: *fallacious* (l. 20) *attributes* (l. 23) *postulate* (l. 27) *the incident of purchase* (l. 35) *taxing* (l. 41) *facets* (l. 42) *conducive to sale* (l. 44).

2 *(a)* What do you understand the author to mean by *a sales strategy* (l. 1)?

(b) How does *strategy* differ from *tactics*?

(c) What does Olmosk refer to as 'The Academic Strategy'?

(d) Why are these words capitalised and enclosed between inverted commas?

3 *(a)* What is meant by a *premise* (l. 1) as used in the passage?

(b) What alternative spelling is there for this word?

(c) What is the name of the system of argument that bases each conclusion upon a pair of premises?

(d) The word *premises* has at least one area of meaning other than that in which it is used in the preceding question. What is this area of meaning? Can the alternative spelling referred to in 3 *(b)* be used for this area of meaning?

4 Rewrite, in your own words, the second half of the first sentence of the passage to show you understand its meaning.

5 What effect does the first word of the second sentence have on the total meaning of the sentence?

6 *(a)* What does *objectivity* mean as used in line 7?

(b) Why is it enclosed between inverted commas?

7 Do you consider *significant* in line 12 to mean

(i)   important

(ii) appreciable

(iii) something a little different from both of these?

If (iii) try to define the difference.

8 Describe, entirely in your own words, how – according to the author – people who employ 'the Academic Strategy' are seen by others.

9 *(a)* What does the author mean by *a solipsistic view of the individual* (l. 25)?

(b) What part does *essentially* play in the sentence in which these words appear?

10 In what specialised sense does the author use *population* in line 40?

11 *(a)* What is a *moot* point (l. 41)?

(b) A number of towns still have a Moot Hall. What was this originally?

12 *(a)* What does the author mean by *the facilitating component which realises potential custom* (l. 45)?

(b) Where does he say this is found?

13 Write a brief statement (not to exceed one hundred words) of what you have learned from this passage about the concept of *self* and its relationship to selling.

Passage 11

The importance of speech as an indicator of social class is not likely to be underestimated by anyone who has lived in England. Our reactions to speech are in any case fundamentally important for certain sounds, certain words, certain rhythms carry for most of us a very deep change of feeling and memory. The feeling that we should speak as other members of our group speak is also very strong. Indeed it is in just this imitative desire and capacity that the possibility of language, with its vital communication of our humanity, is centred. At the same time, this imitative process is dynamic, for no living language is ever fixed. There are variations of speech habit within the simplest group, and the complication of experience and of contacts with other groups is constantly modifying the very thing that we are imitating. Since it is both a confirmation and a discovery of our changing experience of reality, language must change if it is to live. Yet within any human lifetime, and within any society, our attachment to known ways will remain significant, and our important sense of belonging, to a family, to a group, to a people, will be vitally interwoven with the making and hearing of certain sounds – the making and hearing being a very large part of our social sense.

There is then a necessary tension in language, between powerful impulses to imitation and to change. This tension is part of our basic processes of growth and learning. In the general history of language, we can see two quite opposite tendencies: an extraordinary evolution of separate languages, and a remarkable growth, in certain conditions, of common languages. Almost all modern European languages, from Welsh and English to Italian and Russian, together with such Asian languages as Hindustani and Persian, have developed and separated, through history, from a common root. And still, in simple societies, there is an almost incredible variation, within tiny regions, so that villages six or eight miles apart can often hardly understand one another, or on an island of 100 000 people there can be as many as forty dialects, often mutually incomprehensible. As a group develops its own way of life, which may extend over a few miles or over half a continent, it will, as part of this development, create its own forms of language. The very factor which gives the group its social cohesion can become the factor cutting it off, to an important extent, from similar groups elsewhere. But on the other hand, and especially now as

communities become larger and develop greatly improved   40
communication systems, certain languages (of which English is
notably one) expand and flourish, serving as a common basis for
many different groups. Even within these common languages,
however, and alongside the powerful tendencies to expanded
community of speech, the processes of growth and variation will   45
continue, in different ways in different groups speaking the
common tongue. The variations may be of a regional or of a class
kind, and the case of class speech is particularly important, for here
the tension between community and variation may be seen at its
most sensitive.   50

A class is a group within a geographical community, and not a
community in its own right. In certain extreme cases, a class will so
emphasise its distinction from the community of which it is a part
that it will in fact use a separate language: either one of the various
hieratic languages, such as Sanskrit, or, as in nineteenth-century   55
Russia, a foreign language, French, which is thought of as a mark of
cultural superiority. More usually, however, class speech will be a
form of the ordinary speech of the region, and the relations between
the class dialect and the ordinary speech of the region (which will
usually itself be further sub-regionally varied) form a complex of   60
great importance in the development of a language. In the case of
English, the sensitivity of this complex is very high: a very large
number of Englishmen have become tense and anxious about the
way in which they speak their own language. This problem has a
deep bearing on the development of English society, but it is still   65
not very clearly understood. There is commonly a lack of historical
perspective, and there are also many prejudices, both theoretic and
practical.

Raymond Williams, *The Long Revolution*, 1961

1 What is the meaning of the following words as used in the passage:
reactions (l. 3) *dynamic* (l. 10) *significant* (l. 17) *tension* (l. 22 and l. 49)
evolution (l. 25) *mutually* (l. 34) *hieratic* (l. 55)?
2 What is the difference between the use of *complex* in ll. 60 and 62 and
the use of it in line 13 of Passage 4?
3 What is meant by:
social cohesion (l. 37)   *expanded community of speech* (ll. 44–5)
a mark of cultural superiority (ll. 56–7)
further sub-regionally varied (l. 60)   *historical perspective* (ll. 66–7)?

4 Do you agree with the first sentence of this passage? Give reasons for your answer.

5 Why must language *change if it is to live* (l. 15)?

6 The author refers in the compass of a few lines (ll. 24–31) to *extraordinary* evolution, *remarkable* growth, *almost incredible* variation. What does the passage gain by these adjectives?

7 What is the force of *notably* in the parenthesis *of which English is notably one* (ll. 41–2)?

8 Is the author's use of *case* in line 48 justifiable? Are the further uses at line 52 and line 61 equally justifiable? What about the use in l. 3?

9 Distinguish *theoretic* from *practical* prejudices in English speech (l. 67). What examples of prejudices of either kind can you think of?

10 Make a précis of the passage in not more than 190 words (one-quarter), and supply a title.

Passage 12

In order that speech might be evolved, the nervous system had to become capable of the complicated arrangements which underlie its anatomy and physiology, though, of course, speech could have developed only in a creature which possessed a suitable anatomical structure in the mouth, lips, tongue, palate, and larynx. The chimpanzee certainly possesses the necessary organs of articulation. Its inability to speak must therefore be due to lack of the appropriate neural organisation.

One of the most puzzling questions in the neurology of speech is the connexion between speech and handedness. Why is it that the majority of people are right-handed, and in almost all of those the nervous activities underlying speech are localized in the left cerebral hemisphere? And which came first, speech or handedness? We speak of the left cerebral hemisphere in right-handed people as the dominant hemisphere, or is it dominant because they are right-handed and is that why the speech centres are localised in it? Incidentally the opposite is not always true, for, although it had generally been believed that in left-handed people the speech centres are situated in the right cerebral hemisphere, recent work suggests that in at least some left-handed people speech may be represented in both hemispheres.

These questions are by no means easy to answer. One thing which is clear, however, is that the acquisition of speech was not the cause of handedness, for many animals, including chimpanzees, exhibit a preference for one hand or the other, and it is said that among chimpanzees right-handers and left-handers are almost equally distributed. There are obvious advantages in the location of the neurological arrangements underlying speech in one cerebral hemisphere rather than in both, since it would seem that coordination and control can best be exercised from one centre, and it is perhaps natural that if the speech centres are to be localised in one cerebral hemisphere, it should be the dominant hemisphere in relation to handedness, for in a right-handed individual the right hand would be used for gesticulation, for the manipulation of objects and for the exercise of skills, all activities which become closely linked with speech. So it would seem that handedness came first, and determined the dominant hemisphere with which speech became associated, and we are left with the question, why in the majority of human beings, the left cerebral hemisphere should be the dominant one? There seems no doubt that cerebral dominance is inherited, and we can only conclude that some evolutionary advantage has tended to favour right-handed people as opposed to left-handed, or at least to bring about a state of affairs in which right-handedness is dominant in the Mendelian as well as in the cerebral sense.

Failure to develop a dominant hemisphere is often linked with disorder of speech. Stuttering has some association with left-handedness in the patient or his family, and may be precipitated by compelling a naturally left-handed person to write with the right hand. And certain types of backwardness in speech, reading, writing, and spelling may be associated with lack of hemisphere dominance. If it is of clinical importance to know which is the dominant hemisphere this can now be discovered by observing the effect upon speech of injecting a barbiturate into either internal carotid artery. On the side on which the speech centres are situated it produces temporary aphasia.

Sir Russell Brain,

Some Reflections on Genius and other Essays, 1960

1 What is meant by the following expressions as used in the passage:
   its anatomy and physiology (l. 3)

lack of the appropriate neural organisation (ll. 7–8)
dominant in the Mendelian as well as in the cerebral sense (ll. 44–5)
of clinical importance (l. 52)

2 If *carotoid* (l. 55) and *aphasia* (l. 56) are new words to you, deduce their meaning from their contexts.

3 What answer does the author give to the question he asks in ll. 10–13?

4 Is it always true (a) that speech is located exclusively in the left cerebral hemisphere for right-handed people? (b) that speech is located exclusively in the right cerebral hemisphere for left-handed people?

5 (a) Why is it advantageous to have the neurological arrangement underlying speech in one cerebral hemisphere only?

   (b) Why is it natural that this should be the hemisphere dominant in relation to handedness?

6 Arrange in logical order the sequence of arguments that would show why it is that the majority of people have the neurological arrangement underlying speech in the left cerebral hemisphere.

7 Make a précis of the passage in approximately 150 words (one-quarter), and supply a title.

Passage 13

What is the present state of explicit conceptual knowledge about administration in general? There is no general theory, and a great paucity of concepts and hypotheses about managerial processes. The meaning of many of the words which we use in discussing our problems has no established or widely accepted content. No words   5
exist at all for many ideas and situations which occur daily in the lives of managers. Such ideas can only be discussed in terms of lengthy and often inconsistent description. Many of the words which are used with great frequency, such as 'manager', 'supervisor', 'specialist', 'policy', 'subordinate', 'authority', have   10
no generally accepted and precise meaning. How then can we use them in discussing industrial problems? In fact, we spend most of our time arguing about the meaning of the words we are using, instead of discussing the problems themselves. In the absence of a language, such as, for instance, the physicist has had to evolve, it is   15
extremely difficult to start substituting intuition by explicit knowledge.

The universities realise the need to equip graduates with as much knowledge as possible about management. They have been under

pressure from various quarters in industry, and from the British 20
Institute of Management, to set up Chairs of Administration.
There is, however, *no body of knowledge* available of the appropriate
level of abstraction on which a degree course could be founded.
There are as yet no 'laws of management'. The first concern of a
university department of management would be with research in 25
order that the required body of knowledge could then be
established.

Here again, however, difficulty arises. University departments
can function only in so far as they produce concepts having an
integral connection with the real industrial situation. This would 30
seem to involve much deeper relations with industry than at present
exist where administration is concerned. Is there as yet any real
acceptance in the universities of the need for deep and prolonged
study of this subject by the best brains available? Moreover, when
concepts emerge they will have to be tested in industrial situations. 35
If the engineering department of a university produces new ideas
on, say, some aspect of production technology and wish to have
these ideas tested by a particular company, they then would need to
make contact with that company's production engineers who are
responsible for advising its management on production techniques 40
and for implementing changes. But in the field which I am
discussing, no such specialist branch yet exists. Great difficulty
would arise, therefore, in getting new notions tested.

A theory of industrial administration cannot be developed in
isolation within the laboratories of a university. Unlike the physical 45
sciences, it is not possible to import samples of the 'materials' which
interact in social processes or to build models of the processes
which require analysis. These things exist only in the work setting;
their transplantation to a laboratory disrupts their reality. Picture
what would happen if universities and other bodies were to turn 50
seriously to research in this field and industrial companies were to
set up groups of specialists responsible for implementing the
results. Interchange of ideas about principles and concepts between
research workers and industrial specialists would lead to the
emergence of ideas that were of general validity for industry as a 55
whole. It would gradually become possible to teach administration.
A manager's task would be greatly helped by the existence of
accepted laws of administration, for his field of choice in making
almost daily decisions would be narrowed by his knowledge of

principles. The engineer who knows his fundamentals can, by   60
reference to them, reject many choices which an untrained man,
dependent on his intuition alone, might accept – to his own and his
company's later discomfiture.

Wilfred Brown, *Exploration in Management*, 1960

1 What do you consider to be the exact meaning of the following
expressions:

    explicit conceptual knowledge (l. 1)
    a great paucity of concepts and hypotheses (ll. 2–3)
    no established or widely accepted content (l. 5)
    the appropriate level of abstraction (ll. 22–23)
    an integral connection with the real industrial situation (l. 30)

2 What do you consider to be the meaning of *manager*; *supervisor*;
specialist; *policy*; *subordinate*; *authority*? What different meanings can
you see others might give to these words?

3 Distinguish between *intuition* and *explicit knowledge* (ll. 16–17). Why
is exact language an essential for the latter?

4 Why, according to the author, is it not yet possible to found a degree
course in Administration? Do not use the expression *body of knowledge* in
your answer.

5 Why would a university department of administration find it difficult to
have new notions tested out in firms?

6 Why is it impossible to devise laboratories within a university where
theories of industrial administration could be developed?

7 From the point of view of the author of this article (*a*) what is the most
important similarity between the tasks of engineer and manager in
Industry (*b*) what is the most important difference?

8 Can you give any examples of ideas or situations which are part of the
lives of managers but for which no words exist (ll. 5–7)?

9 Make a précis of the passage in not more than 160 words (one-quarter),
and supply a title.

Appendix I

Punctuation

Punctuation is often blamed by bad communicators for their bad communication. It seems that people are not ashamed to admit they cannot punctuate, but are ashamed to admit they cannot construct a sentence or use words clearly.

Faulty punctuation always slows up reading, and may lead to misinterpretation of meaning. Sound punctuation helps the Rx to grasp the structure and logic of a sentence quickly. But punctuation cannot compensate for misuse of words or faulty sentence structure.

The notes that follow are not intended to be comprehensive. All that is attempted is (1) to list the most common applications of our punctuation marks, with examples, and (2) to draw attention to a few applications where there is widespread uncertainty or difference of opinion.

A *Full stops*

1 The full stop marks the end of a sentence. One of the most widespread misuses of punctuation in business writing is to substitute a comma:

NOT *These units may be installed with the minimum of trouble and expense, they are silent and odourless in operation.*

This is clearly two sentences and there must be a full stop after *expense*, or a conjunction to join the sentences.

The opposite fault is to open with a capital letter, and close with a full stop, a unit of language which is not a sentence:

NOT *Their easy-clean finish and attractive design are outstanding features. Harmonise with modern kitchen surrounds.*

Although there is a finite verb in the second part of this, there is no subject and it cannot stand as an independent sentence. A very common version of this error is to start a letter:

NOT *With reference to your order of 10th May.*

In literary writing there has been much experimentation over the last half century with fragmented sentences in which either the subject or the finite verb has been omitted; but where such 'sentences' occur in business writing other than advertising it is the result of carelessness or ignorance, not experimentation.

2 Full stops are also used to mark shortened forms of words. The current position about this is a little confusing as more than one system is in use. The two most widely supported are as follows.

SYSTEM ONE All shortened forms marked by full stops – thus *Oct. Mr. B.B.C.*

SYSTEM TWO Abbreviations marked with a full stop (*Oct.*). Contractions (*viz* when middle of word is left out) – no full stop (*Mr*). Initials, at least of well known institutions etc – no full stop (*BBC*). This is the system used in this book.

Scientific and technical symbols should never be followed by full stops (*m A kW* etc).

Many firms, especially those with important technological divisions, seem to be moving towards abandoning the use of full stops to indicate abbreviations (*Oct Mr BBC*).[1]

Very frequently used abbreviations are commonly shown without full stops even by those using Systems One or Two (*lab ref enc*).

B *Commas*

Commas are essentially separators. (*Comma* is derived from a Greek word that means 'that which is cut off'.)

1 Single commas separate words, phrases, or clauses, in series:

   (a) *In this shop he bought newspapers, magazines, cigarettes, and matches.*
   (b) *He ran down the stairs, along the corridor, through the doorway, and down the road.*
   (c) *He dug the garden, planted some seedlings, and then went for a drink.*

Many writers systematically omit the comma before the *and* that links on the last item of a series. This is a matter about which the student must make up his own mind and then be consistent. The argument in favour of retaining this comma is that it allows the writer to differentiate between two items joined by *and* simply because they are the last two of a series (*cigarettes, and matches*) and two items joined by *and* because they are thought of as belonging together (*fish and chips*).

[1] The decision by the Royal Society of Arts in 1977 to recognise only this method or System One in its typewriting examinations will presumably result in reduced use of System Two.

As commas are separators we expect to find one comma fewer than there are items to separate:

(d) *You will find this a clean, silent, and odourless appliance.*

NOTE: No comma after *odourless*.

Where only two adjectives precede the noun, no comma is used, except where there is some disparity between the two adjectives. Thus *his short satisfactory reply* but *his immediate, inadequate reply*. It will be found that where the sense can be improved by inserting an *and* between the two adjectives, a similar effect is produced by inserting a comma.

The commas separating more than two adjectives preceding a noun are nowadays usually omitted also, unless it is felt that the adjectives build up in importance (as in example *(d)* above).

(e) *Tomkinsons, Allpress Ltd, and Bowlings have submitted their tenders.*

NOTE: Some writers would put a comma after *Bowlings*. This seems undesirable by the argument of 'one comma fewer', and it also introduces a comma between subject and verb.

Since some writers would not use the comma after *Allpress Ltd* (because in front of *and*), there are four 'correct' punctuations possible, for this short sentence; nevertheless the punctuation above is strongly recommended.

2 An introductory word or phrase is nowadays marked off from the main body of the sentence only where failure to do so would produce initial doubt how to read the sentence:

(a) *However we look at this matter we can see no excuse for him.*

(b) *However, we look at this matter in a rather different light.*

(c) *In spite of this improvement we are unable to increase the dividend.*

(d) *In spite of this, improvement has been steady throughout the year.*

NOTE: The modern tendency is towards reduction of commas and those marking off brief introductory matter are rapidly disappearing. Until quite recently it would have been considered obligatory to place commas after *matter* in *(a)* above and *improvement* in *(c)*.

3 Two commas are used to mark off:

(a) words in apposition

(b) the person/s addressed

(c) a parenthesis

(d) a participial phrase

(e) the non-defining relative clause.

NOTE: Where the item to be marked off starts the sentence, only one comma is needed (at the end of the item) and similarly where it ends the sentence (one comma at the start of the item).

EXAMPLES:

Of *(a) Our regional manager, Mr J. F. Jones, will deal with this matter.*

Of *(b) It is our opinion, gentlemen, that these figures compare favourably with any that could be supplied by any other company in the kingdom.*

Of *(c) These units, silent and odourless in operation, offer the minimum inconvenience in the kitchen.*

Of *(d) Referring to your letter, I find you quote the 1976 figures.*

Of *(e) Commas, which are frequently omitted, are probably the most useful punctuation marks.*

BUT NOTE: *Commas which are frequently omitted are those indicating a parenthesis.* Here *which are frequently omitted* is a defining relative clause – it defines which type of comma is referred to – and therefore must not be enclosed between commas. On the other hand, omission of the commas round *which are frequently omitted* in example *(e)* would make nonsense of the sentence – the most useful punctuation marks would seem to be omitted commas.

It will be observed that it is a characteristic of material enclosed between a pair of commas that it can be omitted without complete loss of sense.

C *Semicolons*

The semicolon is a heavier stop than a comma but less heavy than a full stop. In certain circumstances it can be used as a superior substitute for either.

1 Where two or more sentences are felt to be more closely connected in meaning than others in the paragraph, this connection can be indicated by linking the sentences together by means of semicolons:

> *The situation since he has taken over the area can hardly be described as satisfactory; sales have dropped by nearly half, and complaints about service have trebled.*

Of course, such sentences can be linked by other devices, such as conjunctions. There is, however, a crispness about this sentence that would be lost if, for example, the conjunction *for* were substituted for the semicolon. On other occasions the semicolon is too dramatic, too staccato, for the effect required.

2 Since semicolons are to some extent alternatives to conjunctions, it might be thought that the two would never be used together. This is true of the subordinating conjunctions (*because*, *as*, *since*, *if* etc) but a semicolon can be used immediately before the coordinating conjunctions (*and*, *but*, *or*, *yet* etc) where the effect of the more usual comma at that point would be reduced because the sentence already includes several commas.

3 To separate phrases or clauses in series, semicolons may be preferred to commas where the phrases or clauses are rather long and include commas of their own. However, the type of long literary sentence for which such punctuation is necessary is inappropriate to business communication.

4 Items in a list, especially if these include their own commas, are often more clearly separated by semicolons than by commas (see also first example under *Colons* below).

D *Colons*

In business writing the colon can be said to have only one function – 'that of delivering the goods that have been invoiced in the preceding words' (Fowler).

In other words it separates a clause introducing a list, quotation, or summary, from that which it introduces.

> (a) *Accessories available through your local distributor include: wing mirrors; seat belts; roof racks; auxiliary lamps; anti-mist panels; hand-tools; exhaust trims.*
>
> (b) *This then is the present position: he has caused a reduction in sales, alienated several old customers, and substantially damaged the firm's reputation for rapid and efficient servicing.*

NOTE: In *(a)* above an alternative punctuation would be no colon after *include*, and commas to separate items. The decision which to use is based upon the length and complexity of the list. Where a list is punctuated with semicolons it is usual not to add an *and* before the last item.

Where the material that follows starts on a fresh line the introductory colon is replaced by some writers (and most typists) by colon-and-dash (:—). This is quite unnecessary.

E *Dashes*

1 The habit of allowing dashes to usurp the roles of the four punctuation

points already dealt with has nothing to commend it; but this is not to say that dashes have no functions of their own in punctuation.

2 Their most valuable use is a pair to mark a parenthesis where commas would be inadequate either because there are other commas present that disguise the bracketing effect required, or because the material in parenthesis is rather abruptly inserted into the sentence (or both):

> *The rubber-insulated subframes, front and rear, serve to reduce road noise and in conjunction with other sound-insulating devices – the use of emulsion felt, for example – help to combat driving fatigue on long runs.*

3 Single dashes may be used:
   (a) to gather together the various elements of a compound subject, or list of items or series of clauses, preceding it:

> *The suspension, the steering, the transmission, the method of mounting the engine – all these incorporate new design principles.*

   (b) to attach a comment or afterthought to a sentence:

> *They are prepared to offer £5000 – more than I had expected.*

   (c) to indicate a surprising ending to the sentence, for the purpose of 'pointing' humour or drama.

> *They are prepared to offer £5000 – in cash.*

This last application *(c)* should be very sparingly employed. Since it signals so clearly to the Rx, 'This is going to be a shock or a joke', the expectation aroused has to be fully satisfied or the Rx feels frustrated.

F *Brackets*

Where heavier insulation of a parenthesis is required than even dashes provide, brackets are used. References and glosses (or other types of brief explanation or expansion) are the most usual material thus marked off. The previous sentence provides an example of this use of brackets, and many others will be found in this appendix.

Such bracketed material is inserted into the sentence without alteration of the punctuation that would have been correct before its insertion. Occasionally a complete sentence is inserted in brackets at the end of a complete sentence. In such a case the preceding sentence takes its full stop and the material in brackets has its own capital letter and full stop. The first sentences of Section B of this appendix provide an example.

G *Question marks*

Question marks are added to every direct question. This ruling includes commands couched in the form of a question:

Will you send me a copy of your current price list?

They must not be used after indirect questions:

NOT *He asked me why our tender was late?*

Direct questions use the actual questioning words, not a reported form of them.

H *Exclamation marks*

Since these should be reserved for genuine interjections and exclamations it is unlikely they will be employed in any form of business communication except advertising (where, in some of its manifestations, *Hurrah! Wham! New!* etc are only too plentiful).

I *Apostrophes*

1 Apostrophes are used to indicate missing letters as in *one o'clock*, for *one of the clock*, and the colloquial *can't, they're* etc.

2 To show that nouns are possessive, we have a choice between *of* and *'s*. There is a marked tendency to prefer the *of* form for the inanimate nouns and *'s* for the animate. Thus although *the river's bank* is sometimes written, *the bank of the river* sounds more natural; *the hat of John* is only theoretically possible – *John's hat* is what we really say. The *'s* should be used only to show possession; it is an unexpectedly common practice to place an apostrophe either before or after the 's' that ends most plural nouns, whether possessive or not.

The rule is that possession may be shown by adding *'s* – except with plural nouns ending in 's', when only the apostrophe is added.

Thus *one boy's cap*, but *ten boys' caps* and NOTE *ten children's caps*.

Singular nouns ending in 's' normally take the full *'s* ending. The most usual examples are personal names:

Keats's poems   *Delius's music*   *St James's Park*

Appendix II

Direct and Reported Speech

A When we wish to record what people have said (or reproduce what they once wrote) we can either quote their actual words (direct speech) or employ our own words to give the gist of what they said (indirect or 'reported' speech).

B Direct quotation is normally indicated by enclosing the quoted words between single or double inverted commas (which, is a matter of taste). Quotations within a quotation are indicated by the use of single inverted commas where double are the standard choice, or vice versa. Only the actual words of the speaker may be enclosed between inverted commas, never an indirect version.

In factual material of the kind dealt with in this book the words that indicate who is the speaker invariably precede the words spoken, and are linked to them by a comma:

> *Immediately after the breakdown Tomkins said, 'I am to blame. I have not been carrying out the monthly maintenance.'*

A colon may replace this comma for quotations from written material or when the introduction is more elaborate than a plain verb of saying.

Writers of fiction, who make extensive use of direct speech, introduce variety by such devices as indicating the speaker at the end of what is said or in the middle. During the last half century an increasing number of novelists have experimented with such devices as omitting the inverted commas, usually (but not always) using italic type to mark out the words purporting to be quoted, or omitting the linking comma. Such variants are not recommended for business use.

When it is necessary to record a number of short verbatim statements by various speakers, or a discussion, it is convenient to use the playwright's method – the name of the speaker (usually in capitals) followed by a colon directly introducing what is said with no inverted commas:

TOMKINS : *I am to blame etc.*

C The following are the principal ways in which a reported speech version differs from the words originally spoken.

1 First and second person pronouns are replaced by third person equivalents.

2 If the leading verb (i.e. the verb of saying introducing the reported speech) is past tense, all finite verbs change as follows:

Present becomes past (*he is* becomes *he was*)

Past becomes pluperfect (*he was* becomes *he had been*)

Future becomes secondary future – equivalent in form to the conditional (*he will* becomes *he would*)

3 *(a)* Adjectives and adverbs of place become more remote in place (*here* becomes *there*)

   (b) Adjectives and adverbs of time become more remote in time (*now* becomes *then*).

The following sentence illustrates these differences:

Direct speech: *The speaker said, 'Ladies and gentlemen, I[1] am[2] very happy to be here[3a] today[3b]*

Reported speech: *The speaker said he[1] was[2] very happy to be there[3a] that day.[3b]*

NOTES

1 Expressions such as *Ladies and gentlemen* which are characteristic of direct speech and make no contribution to meaning are ignored.

2 Some writers add a *that* after the leading verb – this sometimes aids clarity, but often serves no purpose.

3 It is often preferable to substitute a more specific word for the general one called for by the 'rules'. Thus a person's name may be substituted for *he*, a place name for *there*, a date for *that day*.

4 When the leading verb is in the present tense, the verbs of reported speech retain the tenses of the original.

Since a report of what has been said (or written) always follows the saying or writing, it might be expected that all reference to what was said would be past tense, but in fact leading verbs in the present tense are not uncommon:

Have you heard? Tomkins says he is to blame.

The Prime Minister says there is no cause for alarm.

Shakespeare tells us that it is Time's glory to stamp the seal of time on aged things. (Samuel Butler)

It would seem that we feel justified in using the present tense where the original Tx has said something and *continues to 'say' it*. Thus Tomkins and the Prime Minister have not changed their stories – as far as we know, if asked they would say the same thing again. As for Shakespeare – every time his works are read he speaks again. This justification of the present tense can always be made for written material. Spoken material – except of the kind represented by the statements of Tomkins and the Prime Minister above – does seem to belong more clearly to the past, and is best introduced by a past tense leading verb.

5 First person pronouns are retained in reported speech when the person making the report is either the original Tx or the original Rx.

Thus one of the speaker's audience may report:

The speaker told us he was very happy to be there that day.

Tomkins, reporting his own outburst, at the inquiry might say:

I said I was to blame. I had not been carrying out the monthly maintenance.

D Although reported speech is usually preferred to direct speech for reports (presumably because of its freedom from inverted commas) it has two disadvantages which should be borne in mind when deciding which to use.

1 Reported speech with its pile-up of third person pronouns tends to ambiguity, necessitating clumsy repetitions if the sentence is to be clear:

The sales manager reminded the area representative that he (the representative) had suggested an autumn selling campaign and the sales manager had expressed doubts as to its advisability.

2 Word-for-word transcriptions of direct speech into reported speech often sound rather unnatural; but freer versions introduce an element of distortion.

Thus a straightforward reported speech version of Tomkins's statement would be:

Immediately after the breakdown Tomkins said he was to blame and that he had not been carrying out the monthly maintenance.

A more polished version would be:

Immediately after the breakdown Tomkins admitted responsibility, revealing that he had not been carrying out the monthly maintenance.

If this version is now compared with the direct speech version on page 338 it will be seen to be subtly more damaging to Tomkins. Slight distortions and shifts of emphasis are very likely in reported speech as additional stages of decoding and coding are inserted into the communication process (see Figure 19).

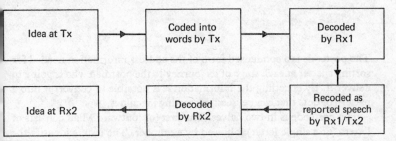

Figure 19 Reported speech flow diagram

Where circumstances demand extremely accurate reporting of what a man said (if his words are to be used as evidence, for example) only direct speech is satisfactory. With written material too, verbatim quotation is often the only fair representation of the original writer's meaning.

Appendix III

Postal Coding

The postcode is a condensed form of the address information needed for sorting a letter at each stage of its journey to the postman who is going to deliver it. By encoding the information it is possible to convert it into a pattern of dots that can be 'read' by sorting machines.

The postcode is in two halves. The first (or 'outward') half consists of letters (or a single letter) followed by a number. The letters identify the 'post town'; the number may indicate a smaller town within the area of the post town, or a district of the post town. The second (or 'inward') half of the postcode consists of a figure from 0 to 9 followed by two letters. This may identify a street, part of a street, even an individual address if it is one where more than twenty letters are normally received by the first delivery.

In the example CF6 2PR, *CF6* is the outward half, *2PR* the inward half. *CF* identifies the post town (Cardiff), *6* a small town (Barry), *2PR* a specific very small area of Barry, where the letter is to be delivered.

For efficient working of automatic sorting, and to avoid delay in delivery of letters, it is necessary to show postcodes as part of the address on envelopes. To ensure that letters sent to them are correctly postcoded, firms and local and central government departments have to incorporate their postcodes into their letter headings. Similarly people writing from private addresses have to remember to include their postcodes with their addresses. It is also necessary to include the postcode with the inside address of a business letter.

For all these applications the following rules, based on Post Office suggestions, should be observed:

1 Make the postcode the last item of the address. Preferably it should be on a separate line; if it has to share a line with other information it should be separated from this by at least the width of two characters in handwriting or two spaces on a typewriter.

2 If you consider that placing the postcode on a line by itself will make the address take up too much space, put the county on the same line as the post town.

3 Separate the two halves of the postcode by a space the width of one character in handwriting or one space on a typewriter.
4 In handwriting, use block capitals for the letters of the postcode. On a typewriter use upper case.
5 Do not join the characters of the postcode in any way.
6 Do not use full stops or other punctuation marks with the postcode.
7 Do not underline the postcode.

Appendix IV

Note-making

A The ability to write a short clear note will stand the apprentice businessman in good stead in a surprisingly wide range of situations. Here are a dozen practical applications:

1 Recording the material of lectures, courses etc he attends
2 Recording the material in articles, reports, legal documents referred to, books studied etc
3 Recording information received by telephone
4 Passing on to others information received by telephone
5 Recording oral instructions from his superior
6 Recording orders, requests, complaints etc from customers/clients
7 Entering appointments, conference commitments etc in his desk diary
8 Making out a list of items for action/a programme/an inventory
9 Leaving concise details for somebody who is taking over from him on an unfinished job
10 Preparing an outline of what he wants to say to somebody he is meeting, or telephoning
11 Planning a piece of writing
12 Planning a speech or oral report.

B Note-making is essentially a matter of producing a highly concentrated version of material heard or read that can be kept for future reference. It is thus fundamentally an Rx skill – but the same techniques are used in one's Tx capacity when preparing an outline for a speech or piece of writing. The degree of concentration depends upon circumstances. During an investigation, for example, which may result in legal action copious and detailed notes have to be taken which will be capable of supplying on subsequent expansion a reasonably accurate version of the words originally used by those giving evidence. On the other hand notes made during a lecture or after a telephone conversation or following a complaint by a customer can sometimes be very brief – just a few words to refresh the memory. Excessively short notes, especially one-word memory-joggers, are to be avoided. You can stare and stare at the one word, but memory remains unjogged. Thus for even a quite simple matter it is better to write down something like *Customer complained that stationery packaging burst* rather than just *Packaging!* on your note-pad. (You would have to include the date and the customer's name and address, of course.)

C To keep the note to the minimum length we:

1 Select points carefully, retaining only those that seem likely to have future reference.
2 Write in 'note form', i.e. omitting the little words such as *the, a, of*. (Notes do not have to be written in sentences, and verbs are frequently omitted to save time and space.)
3 Use abbreviations (These can be private ones if the notes are only for you, but must be standard ones if the notes are to go to anybody else.)

D Vital details (such as personal names, trading names of firms, addresses, dates, product names, titles of books, journals etc) should be written down accurately, in full. It is advisable to use block capitals.

E Notes of lengthy material will require organisation. The principles of analysis and classification detailed on pages 19–21 should be observed and a logical scheme evolved for arranging the notes under headings and subheadings. Full use should be made of numbering and lettering devices, underlining, and block capitals, to make it easy to find your way through the notes at a later date.

F Examples of the sort of organisation necessary will be found at pages 23–4 and 161 and an example of note-making on page 105. Practice work is provided by Exercise K on page 149 and in the exercises associated with Passages 3, 4, and 7 of Chapter 16.